Defensive Database Programming with SQL Server

By Alex Kuznetsov

Technical Review by Hugo Kornelis

First published by Simple Talk Publishing 2010

Technical Review by Hugo Kornelis

Technical edit by Tony Davis

Cover Photography by Paul Vlaar & Photodynamic

Typeset & Designed by Matthew Tye & Gower Associates

Table of Contents

Introduction...15

    What this book covers 16

    What this book does not cover..21

    Code examples 21

Chapter 1: Basic Defensive Database Programming Techniques............23

    Programming Defensively to Reduce Code Vulnerability...........................24

        Define your assumptions 24

        Rigorous testing...25

    Defending Against Cases of Unintended Use 26

    Defending Against Changes in SQL Server Settings.................................33

        How SET ROWCOUNT can break a trigger..34

        How SET LANGUAGE can break a query...42

    Defensive Data Modification 47

        Updating more rows than intended...47

        The problem of ambiguous updates..49

        How to avoid ambiguous updates 53

    Summary 59

Chapter 2: Code Vulnerabilities Due to SQL Server Misconceptions............61

Conditions in a WHERE clause can evaluate in any order 61

SET, SELECT, and the dreaded infinite loop...68

Specify ORDER BY if you need ordered data 76

Summary 78

Chapter 3: Surviving Changes to Database Objects............................81

Surviving Changes to the Definition of a Primary or Unique Key.............82

Using unit tests to document and test assumptions......................................86

Using @@ROWCOUNT to verify assumptions..89

Using SET instead of SELECT when assigning variables..............................90

Surviving Changes to the Signature of a Stored Procedure.........................92

Surviving Changes to Columns 95

Qualifying column names... 95

Handling changes in nullability: NOT IN versus NOT EXISTS 99

Handling changes to data types and sizes... 104

Summary 107

Chapter 4: When Upgrading Breaks Code 109

Understanding Snapshot Isolation 110

When Snapshot Isolation Breaks Code 114

Trigger behavior in normal READ COMMITTED mode 117

Trigger behavior in SNAPSHOT mode 122

Building more robust triggers? 126

Understanding MERGE 127

Issues When Triggers Using @@ROWCOUNT are Fired by MERGE 129

Summary 134

Chapter 5: Reusing T-SQL Code 135

The Dangers of Copy-and-Paste 136

How Reusing Code Improves its Robustness 141

Wrapping SELECTs in Views 145

Reusing Parameterized Queries: Stored Procedures versus Inline UDFs 145

Scalar UDFs and Performance 151

Multi-statement Table-valued UDFs 155

Reusing Business Logic: Stored Procedure, Trigger, Constraint or Index? 156

Use constraints where possible 156

Turn to triggers when constraints are not practical 158

Unique filtered indexes (SQL Server 2008 only) 164

Summary 164

Chapter 6: Common Problems with Data Integrity 167

Enforcing Data Integrity in the Application Layer 167

Enforcing Data Integrity in Constraints 170

Handling nulls in CHECK constraints 172

Foreign key constraints and NULLs 175

Understanding disabled, enabled, and trusted constraints 177

Problems with UDFs wrapped in CHECK constraints 184

Enforcing Data Integrity Using Triggers 196

Summary 211

Chapter 7: Advanced Use of Constraints 213

The Ticket-Tracking System 214

Enforcing business rules using constraints only 215

Removing the performance hit of ON UPDATE CASCADE 225

Constraints and Rock-Solid Inventory Systems 231

Adding new rows to the end of the inventory trail 241

Updating existing rows 249

Adding rows out of date order 253

Summary 258

Chapter 8: Defensive Error Handling..259

Prepare for Unanticipated Failure...259

Using Transactions for Data Modifications..261

Using Transactions and XACT_ABORT to Handle Errors 266

Using TRY...CATCH blocks to Handle Errors 270

A TRY...CATCH example: retrying after deadlocks 271

TRY...CATCH Gotchas 277

Re-throwing errors 277

TRY...CATCH blocks cannot catch all errors 282

Client-side Error Handling 289

Summary 294

Chapter 9: Concurrent Queries and Transaction Isolation Levels 297

A Brief Review of Traditional Isolation Levels.. 297

READ COMMITTED 299

REPEATABLE READ.. 302

SERIALIZABLE 303

When Queries Intermittently Return Incorrect Results.. 304

READ COMMITTED 304

REPEATABLE READ.. 312

SERIALIZABLE 316

SNAPSHOT 317

Choosing the right isolation level 318

Querying Multiple Tables that are being Simultaneously Modified 319

Behavior in READ COMMITTED mode 321

Behavior in SNAPSHOT mode 328

SNAPSHOT versus READ_COMMITTED_SNAPSHOT 330

Minimizing Deadlocks 332

Conclusion 336

Chapter 10: Developing Modifications that Survive Concurrency 337

Understanding Lost Modifications 338

Non-Overlapping Modifications 339

Only updating changed columns 342

Using concurrency control logic 343

Optimistic concurrency control to detect and prevent lost updates 344

Pessimistic Concurrency Control to Prevent Lost Updates 355

Serializing updates with UPDLOCK hint 355

Using sp_getapplock to prevent collisions 357

T-SQL Patterns that Fail High Concurrency Stress Tests 360

Problems with IF EXISTS(...) THEN 361

UPDATE ... IF (@@ROWCOUNT = 0) BEGIN 369

Stress Testing the MERGE Command.. 370

Creating New Objects May Hurt Concurrency 372

Conclusion 374

About the Author

Alex Kuznetsov has been working with object-oriented languages and databases for more than a decade. He has worked with Sybase, SQL Server, Oracle and DB2.

He currently works with DRW Trading Group in Chicago, where he leads a team of developers, practicing agile development, defensive programming, and database unit testing every day.

Alex contributes regularly to the SQL Server community. He blogs regularly on sqlblog.com, has written numerous articles on simple-talk.com and devx.com, contributed a chapter to the "MVP Deep Dives" book, and speaks at various community events, such as SQL Saturday.

In his leisure time, Alex prepares for, and runs, ultra-marathons.

Author Acknowledgements

First of all, let me thank Tony Davis, the editor of this book, who patiently helped me transform what was essentially a loose collection of blog posts into a coherent book. Tony, I greatly appreciate the time and experience you devoted to this book, your abundant helpful advice, and your patience.

Many thanks also to Hugo Kornelis, who agreed to review the book, and went very much beyond just reviewing. Hugo, you have come up with many highly useful suggestions which were incorporated in this book, and they made quite a difference! I hope you will agree to be a co-author in the next edition, and enrich the book with your contributions.

Finally, I would like to thank Aaron Bertrand, Adam Machanic, and Plamen Ratchev for interesting discussions and encouragement.

About the Technical Reviewer

Hugo Kornelis is co-founder and R&D lead of perFact BV, a Dutch company that strives to improve analysis methods, and to develop computer-aided tools that will generate completely functional applications from the analysis deliverable. The chosen platform for this development is SQL Server.

In his spare time, Hugo likes to share and enhance his knowledge of SQL Server by frequenting newsgroups and forums, reading and writing books and blogs, and attending and speaking at conferences.

Introduction

Resilient T-SQL code is code that is designed to last, and to be safely reused by others. The goal of defensive database programming, and of this book, is to help you to produce resilient T-SQL code that robustly and gracefully handles cases of unintended use, and is resilient to common changes to the database environment.

Too often, as developers, we stop work as soon as our code passes a few basic tests to confirm that it produces the "right result" in a given use case. We do not stop to consider the other possible ways in which the code might be used in the future, or how our code will respond to common changes to the database environment, such as a change in the database language setting, or a change to the nullability of a table column, and so on.

In the short-term, this approach is attractive; we get things done faster. However, if our code is designed to be used for more than just a few months, then it is very likely that such changes can and will occur, and the inevitable result is broken code or, even worse, code that silently starts to behave differently, or produce different results. When this happens, the integrity of our data is threatened, as is the validity of the reports on which critical business decisions are often based. At this point, months or years later, and long after the original developer has left, begins the painstaking process of troubleshooting and fixing the problem.

Would it not be easier to prevent all this troubleshooting from happening? Would it not be better to spend a little more time and effort during original development, to save considerably more time on troubleshooting, bug fixing, retesting, and redeploying? After all, many of the problems that cause our code to break are very common; they repeat over and over again in different teams and on different projects.

This is what defensive programming is all about: we learn what can go wrong with our code, and we proactively apply this knowledge during development. This book is filled with practical, realistic examples of the sorts of problems that beset database programs, including:

- changes in database objects, such as tables, constraints, columns, and stored procedures
- changes to concurrency and isolation levels

15

- upgrades to new versions of SQL Server

- changes in requirements

- code reuse

- problems causing loss of data integrity

- problems with error handling in T-SQL.

In each case, the book demonstrates approaches that will help you to understand and enforce (or eliminate) the assumptions on which your solution is based, and to improve its robustness.

What this book covers

This book describes a lot of specific problems, and typical approaches that will lead to more robust code, However, my main goal is more general: it is to demonstrate how to *think* defensively, and how to proactively identify and eliminate potential vulnerabilities in T-SQL code during development rather than after the event when the problems have already occurred.

The book breaks down into ten chapters, as described below. Eight of these chapters are available in this free eBook version; the final two chapters are included in paid versions only.

Ch. 01: Basic Defensive Database Programming Techniques

A high level view of the key elements of defensive database programming, illustrated via some simple examples of common T-SQL code vulnerabilities:

- unreliable search patterns

- reliance on specific SQL Server environment settings

- mistakes and ambiguity during data modifications.

Ch. 02: Code Vulnerabilities Due to SQL Server Misconceptions

Certain vulnerabilities occur due to a basic misunderstanding of how the SQL Server engine, or the SQL language, work. This chapter considers three common misconceptions:

- the **WHERE clause conditions will always be evaluated in the same order;** a common cause of intermittent query failure

- **SET and SELECT always change the values of variables**; a false assumption can lead to the dreaded infinite loop

- **data will be returned in some "natural order"** – another common cause of intermittent query failure.

Ch. 03: Surviving Changes to Database Objects

Perfectly-functioning SQL code can sometimes be broken by a simple change to the underlying database schema, or to other objects that are used in the code. This chapter examines several examples of how changes to database objects can cause unpredictable behavior in code that accesses them, and discusses how to develop code that will not break or behave unpredictably as a result of such changes. Specific examples include how to survive:

- **changes to the primary or unique keys**, and how to test and validate assumptions regarding the "uniqueness" of column data

- **changes to stored procedure signatures**, and the importance of using explicitly named parameters

- **changes to columns**, such as adding columns as well as modifying an existing column's nullability, size or data type.

Ch. 04: When Upgrading Breaks Code

Some potential changes cannot be foreseen and so we cannot "weatherproof" our code against them; we cannot know in advance, for example, how the use of a new feature might impact our existing code when we do not know what these new features are and how they behave. What a defensive programmer can and must do, however, is analyze fully how new features work with existing code, before using these new features in production. Specific examples demonstrate that:

- code that works perfectly when using `READ COMMITTED` isolation level, may fail to correctly enforce business rules under `SNAPSHOT` or `READ_COMMITTED_SNAPSHOT` isolation

- code that uses `@@ROWCOUNT` may behave incorrectly when used after a `MERGE` statement.

Ch. 05: Reusing T-SQL Code

A copy-and-paste approach to code reuse will lead to multiple, inconsistent versions of the same logic being scattered throughout your code base, and a maintenance nightmare. This chapter demonstrates how common logic can be refactored into a single reusable code unit, in the form of a constraint, stored procedure, trigger, UDF, or index. This careful reuse of code will reduce the possibility of bugs and greatly improve the robustness of our code. Specific examples covered include the following defensive programming techniques:

- using views to encapsulate simple queries

- using UDFs to encapsulate parameterized queries, and why UDFs may sometimes be preferable to stored procedures for this requirement

- how to avoid potential performance issues with UDFs

- using constraints, triggers and filtered indexes to implement business logic in one place.

Ch. 06: Common Problems with Data Integrity

Data integrity logic in the application layer is too easily bypassed, so SQL Server constraints and triggers are valuable weapons for the defensive programmer in the fight to safeguard the integrity of data. The only completely robust way to ensure data integrity is to use a trusted constraint. UDFs and triggers are dramatically more flexible than constraints, but we need to be very careful when we use them, as the latter, especially, are difficult to code correctly and, unless great care is taken, are vulnerable to failure during multi-row modifications, or to being bypassed altogether.

Specific examples demonstrate the following defensive programming lessons:

- when testing CHECK constraints, always include rows with NULLs in your test cases

- don't make assumptions about the data, based on the presence of FOREIGN KEY or CHECK constraints, unless they are all trusted

- UDFs wrapped in CHECK constraints are sometimes unreliable as a means to enforce data integrity rules; filtered indexes or indexed views are safer alternatives

- triggers require exceptional care and testing during development, and may still fail in certain cases (for example, when using Snapshot isolation).

Ch. 07: Advanced Use of Constraints

Received wisdom suggests that constraints can enforce only a very limited set of simple rules. In fact, in many cases, developers give up on constraints much too easily; they allow us to solve far more complex problems than many people realize. This chapter takes two common business systems, a ticket tracking system and an inventory system, and demonstrates how constraints can be used, exclusively, to guarantee the integrity of the data in these systems.

Constraint-only solutions, as you will see, are pretty complex too, but they have the advantage that, if you get them right, they will be completely robust under all conditions.

Ch. 08: Defensive Error Handling

The ability to handle errors is essential in any programming language and, naturally, we have to implement safe error handling in our T-SQL if we want to build solid SQL Server code. However, the TRY...CATCH error handling in SQL Server has certain limitations and inconsistencies that will trap the unwary developer, used to the more robust error handling of client-side languages such as C# and Java. The chapter includes specific advice to the defensive programmer in how best to handle errors, including:

- if you already use a modern language such as C# in your system, then it makes sense to utilize it to do complex handling of errors related to the database

- if handling errors on SQL Server, keep it simple where possible; set `XACT_ABORT` to ON and use transactions in order to roll back and raise an error

- if you wish to use `TRY...CATCH`, learn it thoroughly, and watch out for problems such as errors that cannot be caught, doomed transactions, the need to change the error number when raising errors, and so on.

Ch. 09: Concurrent Queries and Transaction Isolation Levels

A query that works splendidly in isolation can often fail miserably when put to work in a live OLTP system, with real life concurrency. To make a bad situation worse, in many cases such errors are subtle and intermittent, and therefore very difficult to reproduce and understand. This chapter considers the case of reporting queries running against tables that are being simultaneously modified, demonstrates how inconsistent results can be returned, assesses the impact of various isolation levels, and considers how best the defensive programmer can defend data integrity, while minimizing deadlocks.

Ch. 10: Developing Modifications that Survive Concurrency

Just like queries, modifications that work perfectly well in the isolated world of the test database, can suddenly start misbehaving intermittently when run in a production environment under conditions of concurrent access. The chapter covers some of the problems that might occur when "competing" connections try to simultaneously update the same data, and how to avoid them:

- **lost modifications, a.k.a. lost updates** – such problems occur when modifications performed by one connection are overwritten by another; they typically occur silently, and no errors are raised.

- **resource contention errors** – such as deadlocks and lock timeouts

- **primary key and unique constraint violations** – such problems occur when different modifications attempt to insert one and the same row.

What this book does not cover

Throughout the book I stress the importance of creating testable and fully-tested code modules. However, the focus of this book is on writing resilient T-SQL code, not on the implementation of unit tests. In some cases, I will describe which unit tests are required, and which checks must be wrapped as unit tests and must run automatically. However, I will not provide any specific details about writing unit tests.

When many people think of defensive programming, they tend to think in terms of vulnerabilities that can leave their code susceptible to "attack." A classic example is the SQL Injection attack, and the coding techniques that reduce the likelihood of a successful SQL Injection attack are excellent examples of defensive database programming. However, there already are lots of very useful articles on this subject, most notably an excellent article by Erland Sommerskog, THE CURSE AND BLESSINGS OF DYNAMIC SQL. The focus of this book is on very common, though much less publicized vulnerabilities that can affect the resilience and reliability of your code.

Due to the firm focus on defensive coding techniques, there is also no coverage in this book of what might be termed the "documentation" aspects of defensive programming, which would include such topics as documenting requirements, establishing code contracts, source control, versioning, and so on.

Finally, in this book I stay focused on practical examples. While some background material is occasionally required, I've strenuously tried to avoid rehashing MSDN. If you are not familiar with the syntax of some command that is used in the book, or you are unfamiliar with some terminology, MSDN is the source to which you should refer.

Code examples

Throughout this book are code examples demonstrating various defensive programming techniques. All examples should run on all versions of SQL Server from SQL Server 2005 upwards, unless specified otherwise. To download all the code samples presented in this book, visit the following URL:

HTTP://WWW.SIMPLE-TALK.COM/REDGATEBOOKS/ALEXKUZNETSOV/DEFENSIVE_CODE.ZIP

Chapter 1: Basic Defensive Database Programming Techniques

The goal of defensive database programming is to produce resilient database code; in other words, code that does not contain bugs and is not susceptible to being broken by unexpected use cases, small modifications to the underlying database schema, changes in SQL Server settings, and so on.

If you fail to program defensively, then code that runs as expected on a given standalone server, with a specific configuration, may run very differently in a different environment, under different SQL Server settings, against different data, or under conditions of concurrent access. When this happens, you will be susceptible to erratic behavior in your applications, performance problems, data integrity issues, and unhappy users.

The process of reducing the number of vulnerabilities in your code, and so increasing its resilience, is one of constantly questioning the assumptions on which your implementation depends, ensuring they are always enforced if they are valid, and removing them if not. It is a process of constantly testing your code, breaking it, and then refining it based on what you have learned.

The best way to get a feel for this process, and for how to expose vulnerabilities in your code and fix them using defensive programming techniques, is to take a look at a few common areas where I see that code is routinely broken by unintended use cases or erroneous assumptions:

- unreliable search patterns
- reliance on specific SQL Server environment settings
- mistakes and ambiguity during data modifications.

In each case, we'll identify the assumptions that lead to code vulnerability, and show how to fix them. All the examples in this chapter are as simple as possible, in that there is no concurrency, and the underlying database schema is fixed.

In subsequent chapters, we'll introduce the additional dangers that can arise when exposing the code to changes in the database schema and running it under high concurrency.

Programming Defensively to Reduce Code Vulnerability

There are four key elements to defensive database programming that, when applied, will allow you to eliminate bugs and make your code less vulnerable to be being subsequently broken by cases of unintended use.

1. Define and understand your assumptions.

2. Test as many use cases as possible.

3. Lay out your code in short, fully testable, and fully tested modules.

4. Reuse your code whenever feasible, although we must be very careful when we reuse T-SQL code, as described in Chapter 5.

As noted in the introduction to this book, while I will occasionally discuss the sort of checks and tests that ought to be included in your unit tests (Steps 2 and 3), this book is focused on defensive programming, and so, on the rigorous application of the first two principles.

Define your assumptions

One of the most damaging mistakes made during the development of SQL and any other code, is a failure to explicitly define the assumptions that have been made regarding how the code should operate, and how it should respond to various inputs. Specifically, we must:

- explicitly list the assumptions that have been made

- ensure that the these assumptions always hold

- systematically remove assumptions that are not essential, or are incorrect.

When identifying these assumptions, there can be one of three possible outcomes. Firstly, if an assumption is deemed essential, it must be documented, and then tested rigorously to ensure it always holds; I prefer to use unit tests to document such assumptions (more on this in Chapter 3). Failure to do so will mean that when the code makes it into production it will inevitably be broken as a result of usage that conflicts with the assumption.

Secondly, if the assumption is deemed non-essential, it should, if possible, be removed. Finally, in the worst case, the code may contain assumptions that are simply wrong, and can threaten the integrity of any data that the code modifies. Such assumptions must be eliminated from the code.

Rigorous testing

As we develop code, we must use all our imagination to come up with cases of unintended use, trying to break our modules. We should incorporate these cases into our testing suites.

As we test, we will find out how different changes affect code execution and learn how to develop code that does not break when "something," for example, a language setting or the value of ROWCOUNT, changes.

Having identified a setting that breaks one of our code modules, we should fix it and then identify and fix all other similar problems in our code. We should not stop at that. The defensive programmer must investigate all other database settings that may affect the way the code runs, and then review and amend the code again and again, fixing potential problems before they occur. This process usually takes a lot of iterations, but we end up with better, more robust code every time, and we will save a lot of potential wasted time in troubleshooting problems, as well as expensive retesting and redeployment, when the code is deployed to production.

Throughout the rest of this chapter, we'll discuss how this basic defensive coding philosophy is applied in practice, by way of some simple practical examples.

Defending Against Cases of Unintended Use

All too often, we consider our code to be finished as soon as it passes a few simple tests. We do not take enough time to identify and test all possible, reasonable use cases for our code. When the inevitable happens, and our code is used in a way we failed to consider, it does not work as expected.

To demonstrate these points, we'll consider an example that shows how (and how not) to use string patterns in searching. We'll analyze a seemingly working stored procedure that searches a `Messages` table, construct cases of unintended use, and identify an implicit assumption on which the implementation of this procedure relies. We will then need to decide whether to eliminate the assumption or to guarantee that it always holds. Either way, we will end up with a more robust procedure.

Listing 1-1 contains the code needed to create a sample `Messages` table, which holds the subject and body of various text messages, and load it with two sample messages. It then creates the stored procedure, `SelectMessagesBySubjectBeginning`, which will search the messages, using a search pattern based on the `LIKE` keyword. The stored procedure takes one parameter, `SubjectBeginning`, and is supposed to return every message whose subject starts with the specified text.

```
CREATE TABLE dbo.Messages
    (
        MessageID INT IDENTITY(1,1) NOT NULL
                                    PRIMARY KEY,
        Subject VARCHAR(30) NOT NULL ,
        Body VARCHAR(100) NOT NULL
    ) ;
GO

INSERT  INTO dbo.Messages
        ( Subject ,
          Body
        )
        SELECT  'Next release delayed' ,
                'Still fixing bugs'
        UNION ALL
```

```
        SELECT  'New printer arrived' ,
                'By the kitchen area' ;
GO

CREATE PROCEDURE dbo.SelectMessagesBySubjectBeginning
    @SubjectBeginning VARCHAR(30)
AS
    SET NOCOUNT ON ;
    SELECT  Subject ,
            Body
    FROM    dbo.Messages
    WHERE   Subject LIKE @SubjectBeginning + '%' ;
```

Listing 1-1: **Creating and populating the Messages table along with the stored procedure to search the messages.**

Some preliminary testing against this small set of test data, as shown in Listing 1-2, does not reveal any problems.

```
-- must return one row
EXEC dbo.SelectMessagesBySubjectBeginning
  @SubjectBeginning='Next';

Subject                              Body
------------------------------------ --------------------
Next release delayed                 Still fixing bugs

-- must return one row
EXEC dbo.SelectMessagesBySubjectBeginning
  @SubjectBeginning='New';

Subject                              Body
------------------------------------ --------------------
New printer arrived                  By the kitchen area

-- must return two rows
EXEC dbo.SelectMessagesBySubjectBeginning
```

```
    @SubjectBeginning='Ne';

Subject                         Body
-----------------------------   --------------------
Next release delayed            Still fixing bugs
New printer arrived             By the kitchen area

-- must return nothing
EXEC dbo.SelectMessagesBySubjectBeginning
    @SubjectBeginning='No Such Subject';

Subject                         Body
-----------------------------   --------------------
```

Listing 1-2:   A few simple tests against the provided test data demonstrate that
               results match expectations.

Handling special characters in searching

In defensive database programming, it is essential to construct cases of unintended use
with which to break our code. The test data in Listing 1-1 and the stored procedure calls
in Listing 1-2 demonstrate the cases of **intended** use, and clearly the procedure works,
when it is used as intended.

However, have we considered all the possible cases? Will the procedure continue to work
as expected in cases of **unintended** use? Can we find any hidden bugs in this procedure?
In fact, it is embarrassingly easy to break this stored procedure, simply by adding a few
"off-topic" messages to our table, as shown in Listing 1-3.

```
INSERT   INTO dbo.Messages
         ( Subject ,
           Body
         )
         SELECT   '[OT] Great vacation in Norway!' ,
                  'Pictures already uploaded'
         UNION ALL
         SELECT   '[OT] Great new camera' ,
```

28

```
                    'Used it on my vacation' ;
GO
-- must return two rows
EXEC dbo.SelectMessagesBySubjectBeginning
    @SubjectBeginning = '[OT]' ;


Subject                              Body
----------------------------------   --------------------
```

Listing 1-3: Our procedure fails to return "off-topic" messages.

Our procedure fails to return the expected messages. In fact, by loading one more message, as shown in Listing 1-4, we can demonstrate that this procedure can also return
incorrect data.

```
INSERT   INTO dbo.Messages
         ( Subject ,
           Body
         )
         SELECT  'Ordered new water cooler' ,
                 'Ordered new water cooler' ;
EXEC dbo.SelectMessagesBySubjectBeginning
    @SubjectBeginning = '[OT]' ;


Subject                              Body
----------------------------------   --------------------
Ordered new water cooler             Ordered new water cooler
```

Listing 1-4: Our procedure returns the wrong messages when the search pattern
contains [OT].

When using the LIKE keyword, square brackets ("[" and "]"), are treated as wildcard
characters, denoting a single character within a given range or set. As a result, while the
search was intended to be one for off-topic posts, it in fact searched for *"any messages
whose subject starts with O or T."* Therefore Listing 1-3 returns no rows, since no such
messages existed at that point, whereas Listing 1-4 "unexpectedly" returns the message
starting with "O," rather than the off-topic messages.

29

In a similar vein, we can also prove that the procedure fails for messages with the % sign in subject lines, as shown in Listing 1-5.

```
INSERT   INTO dbo.Messages
         ( Subject ,
           Body
         )
         SELECT  '50% bugs fixed for V2' ,
                 'Congrats to the developers!'
         UNION ALL
         SELECT  '500 new customers in Q1' ,
                 'Congrats to all sales!' ;
GO

EXEC dbo.SelectMessagesBySubjectBeginning
     @SubjectBeginning = '50%' ;

Subject                               Body
----------------------------------    ------------------
50% bugs fixed for V2                 Congrats to the developers!
500 new customers in Q1               Congrats to all sales!
```

Listing 1-5:   **Our stored procedure returns the wrong messages, along with the correct ones, if the pattern contains %.**

The problem is basically the same: the % sign is a wildcard character denoting "any string of zero or more characters." Therefore, the search returns the *"500 new customers..."* row in addition to the desired *"50% bugs fixed..."* row.

Our testing has revealed an implicit assumption that underpins the implementation of the SelectMessagesBySubjectBeginning stored procedure: the author of this stored procedure did not anticipate or expect that message subject lines could contain special characters, such as square brackets and percent signs. As a result, the search only works if the specified SubjectBeginning does not contain special characters.

Having identified this assumption, we have a choice: we can either change our stored procedure so that it does not rely on this assumption, or we can enforce it.

Enforcing or eliminating the special characters assumption

Our first option is to fix our data by enforcing the assumption that messages will not contain special characters in their subject line. We can delete all the rows with special characters in their subject line, and then add a CHECK constraint that forbids their future use, as shown in Listing 1-6. The patterns used in the DELETE command and in the CHECK constraint are advanced, and need some explanation. The first pattern, %[[]%, means the following:

- both percent signs denote "any string of zero or more characters"

- [[] in this case denotes "opening square bracket, ["

- the whole pattern means "any string of zero or more characters, followed by an opening square bracket, followed by another string of zero or more characters," which is equivalent to "any string containing at least one opening square bracket."

Similarly, the second pattern, %[%]%, means "any string containing at least one percent sign."

```
BEGIN TRAN ;
DELETE   FROM dbo.Messages
WHERE    Subject LIKE '%[[]%'
         OR Subject LIKE '%[%]%' ;

ALTER TABLE dbo.Messages
ADD CONSTRAINT Messages_NoSpecialsInSubject
    CHECK(Subject NOT LIKE '%[[]%'
       AND Subject NOT LIKE '%[%]%') ;

ROLLBACK TRAN ;
```

Listing 1-6: Enforcing the "no special characters" assumption.

Although enforcing the assumption is easy, does it make practical sense? It depends. I would say that, under most circumstances, special characters in subject lines should be allowed, so let's consider a second, better option – eliminating the assumption. Note that Listing 1-6 rolls back the transaction, so that our changes are not persisted in the database.

Listing 1-7 shows how to alter the stored procedure so that it can handle special characters. To better demonstrate how the procedure escapes special characters, I included some debugging output. Always remember to remove such debugging code before handing over the code for QA and deployment!

```
ALTER PROCEDURE dbo.SelectMessagesBySubjectBeginning
    @SubjectBeginning VARCHAR(50)
AS
    SET NOCOUNT ON ;
    DECLARE @ModifiedSubjectBeginning VARCHAR(150) ;
    SET @ModifiedSubjectBeginning =
            REPLACE(REPLACE(@SubjectBeginning,
                        '[',
                        '[[]'),
                '%',
                '[%]') ;
    SELECT  @SubjectBeginning AS [@SubjectBeginning] ,
            @ModifiedSubjectBeginning AS
                        [@ModifiedSubjectBeginning] ;
    SELECT  Subject ,
            Body
    FROM    dbo.Messages
    WHERE   Subject LIKE @ModifiedSubjectBeginning + '%' ;
GO
```

Listing 1-7:   Eliminating the "no special characters" assumption.

Listing 1-8 demonstrates that our stored procedure now correctly handles special characters. Of course, in a real world situation, all previous test cases have to be rerun, to check that we didn't break them in the process of fixing the bug.

```
-- must return two rows
EXEC dbo.SelectMessagesBySubjectBeginning
    @SubjectBeginning = '[OT]' ;
```

```
@SubjectBeginning                      @ModifiedSubjectBeginning
---------------------------------------------------------------
[OT]                                   [[]OT]


Subject                                Body
----------------------------------     ----------------------------
[OT] Great vacation in Norway!         Pictures already uploaded
[OT] Great new camera                  Used it on my vacation

-- must return one row
EXEC dbo.SelectMessagesBySubjectBeginning
   @SubjectBeginning='50%';

@SubjectBeginning                      @ModifiedSubjectBeginning
---------------------------------------------------------------
50%                                    50[%]


Subject                                Body
----------------------------------     ----------------------
50% bugs fixed for V2                  Congrats to the developers!
```

Listing 1-8: **Our search now correctly handles [ ] and %.**

Whether we ultimately decide to enforce or eliminate the assumption, we have created a more robust search procedure as a result.

Defending Against Changes in SQL Server Settings

A common mistake made by developers is to develop SQL code on a given SQL Server, with a defined set of properties and settings, and then fail to consider how their code will respond when executed on instances with different settings, or when users change settings at the session level.

For example, Chapters 4 and 9 of this book discuss transaction isolation levels, and explain how code may run differently under different isolation levels, and how to improve code so that it is resilient to changes in the isolation level.

However, in this chapter, let's examine a few simple cases of how hidden assumptions with regard to server settings can result in vulnerable code.

How SET ROWCOUNT can break a trigger

Traditionally, developers have relied on the SET ROWCOUNT command to limit the number of rows returned to a client for a given query, or to limit the number of rows on which a data modification statement (UPDATE, DELETE, MERGE or INSERT) acts. In either case, SET ROWCOUNT works by instructing SQL Server to stop processing after a specified number of rows.

However, the use of SET ROWCOUNT can have some unexpected consequences for the unwary developer. Consider a very simple table, Objects, which stores basic size and weight information about objects, as shown in Listing 1-9.

```
CREATE TABLE dbo.Objects
    (
        ObjectID INT NOT NULL PRIMARY KEY ,
        SizeInInches FLOAT NOT NULL ,
        WeightInPounds FLOAT NOT NULL
    ) ;
GO
INSERT  INTO dbo.Objects
        ( ObjectID ,
          SizeInInches ,
          WeightInPounds
        )
        SELECT  1 ,
                10 ,
                10
        UNION ALL
        SELECT  2 ,
```

```
                    12 ,
                    12
        UNION ALL
        SELECT  3 ,
                    20 ,
                    22 ;
GO
```

Listing 1-9: Creating and populating the Objects table.

We are required to start logging all updates of existing rows in this table, so we create a second table, ObjectsChangeLog, in which to record the changes made, and a trigger that will fire whenever data in the Objects table is updated, record details of the changes made, and insert them into ObjectsChangeLog.

```
CREATE TABLE dbo.ObjectsChangeLog
  (
    ObjectsChangeLogID INT NOT NULL
                            IDENTITY ,
    ObjectID INT NOT NULL ,
    ChangedColumnName VARCHAR(20) NOT NULL ,
    ChangedAt DATETIME NOT NULL ,
    OldValue FLOAT NOT NULL ,
    CONSTRAINT PK_ObjectsChangeLog PRIMARY KEY
                            ( ObjectsChangeLogID )
  ) ;
 GO

CREATE TRIGGER Objects_UpdTrigger ON dbo.Objects
  FOR UPDATE
AS
  BEGIN;
    INSERT  INTO dbo.ObjectsChangeLog
            ( ObjectID ,
              ChangedColumnName ,
              ChangedAt ,
              OldValue
```

```
            )
            SELECT    i.ObjectID ,
                      'SizeInInches' ,
                      CURRENT_TIMESTAMP ,
                      d.SizeInInches
            FROM      inserted AS i
                      INNER JOIN deleted AS d ON
                          i.ObjectID = d.ObjectID
            WHERE     i.SizeInInches <> d.SizeInInches
            UNION ALL
            SELECT    i.ObjectID ,
                      'WeightInPounds' ,
                      CURRENT_TIMESTAMP ,
                      d.WeightInPounds
            FROM      inserted AS i
                      INNER JOIN deleted AS d ON
                          i.ObjectID = d.ObjectID
            WHERE i.WeightInPounds <> d.WeightInPounds ;
    END ;
```

Listing 1-10: Logging updates to the Objects table.

Please note that my approach to all examples in this book is to keep them as simple as they can be, while still providing a realistic demonstration of the point, which here is the effect of SET ROWCOUNT. So, in this case, I have omitted:

- a "real" key on the ObjectsChangeLog table, enforced by a UNIQUE constraint (ObjectID, ChangedColumnName, ChangedAt), in addition to the surrogate key on ObjectsChangeLogID

- the equivalent insert and delete triggers to log INSERT and DELETE modifications, as well as UPDATEs.

Likewise, there are several ways of logging changes, and the one I chose here may not be the best approach; again, my goal was to keep the example focused and simple. Listing 1-11 shows the code that tests how our trigger logs changes against the Objects table.

```
BEGIN TRAN ;

-- TRUNCATE TABLE can also be used here
DELETE   FROM dbo.ObjectsChangeLog ;

UPDATE   dbo.Objects
SET      SizeInInches = 12 ,
         WeightInPounds = 14
WHERE    ObjectID = 1 ;

-- we are selecting just enough columns
-- to demonstrate that the trigger works

SELECT   ObjectID ,
         ChangedColumnName ,
         OldValue
FROM     dbo.ObjectsChangeLog ;

-- we do not want to change the data,
-- only to demonstrate how the trigger works
ROLLBACK ;
-- the data has not been modified by this script

ObjectID    ChangedColumnName    OldValue
----------- -------------------- ------
1           SizeInInches         10
1           WeightInPounds       10
```

Listing 1-11: Testing the trigger.

Apparently, our trigger works as expected! However, with a little further testing, we can prove that the trigger will sometimes fail to log UPDATEs made to the Objects table, due to an underlying assumption in the trigger code, of which the developer may not even have been aware!

37

The ROWCOUNT assumption

Let's consider what might happen if, within a given session, a user changed the default value for ROWCOUNT and then updated the Objects table, without resetting ROWCOUNT, as shown in Listing 1-12.

```
DELETE   FROM dbo.ObjectsChangeLog ;

SET ROWCOUNT 1 ;
-- do some other operation(s)
-- for which we needed to set rowcount to 1
-- do not restore ROWCOUNT setting
-- to its default value
BEGIN TRAN ;

UPDATE   dbo.Objects
SET      SizeInInches = 12 ,
         WeightInPounds = 14
WHERE    ObjectID = 1 ;

-- make sure to restore ROWCOUNT setting
-- to its default value so that it does not affect the
-- following SELECT

SET ROWCOUNT 0 ;

SELECT   ObjectID ,
         ChangedColumnName ,
         OldValue
FROM     dbo.ObjectsChangeLog ;

ROLLBACK ;
```

```
ObjectID      ChangedColumnName      OldValue
-----------   --------------------   ---------
1             SizeInInches           10
```

Listing 1-12: Breaking the trigger by changing the value of ROWCOUNT.

As a result of the change to the ROWCOUNT value, our trigger processes the query
that logs changes to the SizeInInches column, returns one row, and then ceases
processing. This means that it fails to log the change to the WeightInPounds
column. Of course, there is no guarantee that the trigger will log the change to the
SizeInInches column. On your server, the trigger may log only the change of
WeightInPounds but fail to log the change in SizeInInches. Which column will be
logged depends on the execution plan chosen by the optimizer, and we cannot assume
that the optimizer will always choose one and the same plan for a query.

Although the developer of the trigger may not have realized it, the implied assumption
regarding its implementation is that ROWCOUNT is set to its default value. Listing 1-12
proves that that, when this assumption is not true, the trigger will not work as expected.

Enforcing and eliminating the ROWCOUNT assumption

Once we understand the problem, we can fix the trigger very easily, by resetting
ROWCOUNT to its default value at the very beginning of the body of the trigger, as
shown in Listing 1-13.

```
ALTER TRIGGER dbo.Objects_UpdTrigger ON dbo.Objects
    FOR UPDATE
AS
    BEGIN;
-- the scope of this setting is the body of the trigger
        SET ROWCOUNT 0 ;
        INSERT  INTO dbo.ObjectsChangeLog
                ( ObjectID ,
                  ChangedColumnName ,
                  ChangedAt ,
                  OldValue
                )
```

```
                    SELECT   i.ObjectID ,
                             'SizeInInches' ,
                             CURRENT_TIMESTAMP ,
                             d.SizeInInches
                    FROM     inserted AS i
                             INNER JOIN deleted AS d ON
                                 i.ObjectID = d.ObjectID
                    WHERE    i.SizeInInches <> d.SizeInInches
                    UNION ALL
                    SELECT   i.ObjectID ,
                             'WeightInPounds' ,
                             CURRENT_TIMESTAMP ,
                             d.WeightInPounds
                    FROM     inserted AS i
                             INNER JOIN deleted AS d ON
                                 i.ObjectID = d.ObjectID
                    WHERE    i.WeightInPounds <>
                                 d.WeightInPounds ;
        END ;
-- after the body of the trigger completes,
-- the original value of ROWCOUNT is restored
-- by the database engine
```

Listing 1-13: Resetting ROWCOUNT at the start of the trigger.

We can rerun the test from Listing 1-12, and this time the trigger will work as required, logging both changes. Note that the scope of our SET ROWCOUNT is the trigger, so our change will not affect the setting valid at the time when the trigger was fired.

SET ROWCOUNT *is deprecated in SQL Server 2008...*

...and eventually, in some future version, will have no effect on INSERT, UPDATE or DELETE statements. Microsoft advises rewriting any such statements that rely on ROWCOUNT to use TOP instead. As such, this example may be somewhat less relevant for future versions of SQL Server; the trigger might be less vulnerable to being broken, although still not immune. However, at the time of writing, this example is very relevant.

In this case, one simple step both enforces the underlying assumption, by ensuring that it is always valid, and eliminates it, by ensuring that the code continues to work in cases where ROWCOUNT is not at its default value.

Proactively fixing SET ROWCOUNT vulnerabilities

We have fixed the ROWCOUNT vulnerability in our trigger, but our job is not done. What about other modules in our system? Might they not have the same vulnerability?

Having learned of the potential side effects of SET ROWCOUNT, we can now analyze all the other modules in our system, determine if they have the same problem, and fix them if they do. For example, our stored procedure, SelectMessagesBySubjectBeginning (Listing 1-1) has the same vulnerability, as demonstrated by the test in Listing 1-14.

```
SET ROWCOUNT 1 ;
-- must return two rows
EXEC dbo.SelectMessagesBySubjectBeginning
    @SubjectBeginning = 'Ne' ;

...(Snip)...

Subject                              Body
------------------------------       --------------------
Next release delayed                 Still fixing bugs
```

Listing 1-14: SET ROWCOUNT can break a stored procedure just as easily as it can break a trigger.

We can apply the same fix, adding SET ROWCOUNT 0; to the very beginning of this stored procedure. Similarly, we should apply this fix to all other modules that need it.

If your code is supposed to exist for a considerable time, then it makes perfect sense to fix problems proactively. It is usually faster and easier to do so than to wait until the problem occurs, spend considerable time troubleshooting, and then eventually implement the same fix.

41

How SET LANGUAGE can break a query

Just as the value of ROWCOUNT can be changed at the session level, so can other settings, such as the default language. Many developers test their code only under the default language setting of their server, and do not test how their code will respond if executed on a server with a different language setting, or if there is a change in the setting at the session level.

This practice is perfectly correct, as long as our code always runs under the same settings as those under which we develop and test it. However, if or when the code runs under different settings, this practice will often result in code that is vulnerable to errors, especially when dealing with dates.

Consider the case of a stored procedure that is supposed to retrieve from our ObjectsChangeLog table (Listing 1-10) a listing of all changes made to the Objects table over a given date range. According to the requirements, only the beginning of the range is required; the end of the range is an optional parameter. If an upper bound for the date range is not provided, we are required to use a date far in the future, December 31, 2099, as the end of our range.

```
CREATE PROCEDURE dbo.SelectObjectsChangeLogForDateRange
    @DateFrom DATETIME ,
    @DateTo DATETIME = NULL
AS
    SET ROWCOUNT 0 ;
    SELECT  ObjectID ,
            ChangedColumnName ,
            ChangedAt ,
            OldValue
    FROM    dbo.ObjectsChangeLog
    WHERE ChangedAt BETWEEN @DateFrom
            AND  COALESCE(@DateTo, '12/31/2099') ;
GO
```

Listing 1-15: Creating the SelectObjectsChangeLogForDateRange stored procedure.

42

Note that this stored procedure uses a string literal, 12/31/2099, to denote December 31, 2099. Although 12/31/2099 does represent December 31, 2099 in many languages, such as US English, in many other cultures, such as Norwegian, this string does not represent a valid date. This means that the author of this stored procedure has made an implicit assumption: the code will always run under language settings where 12/31/2099 represents December 31, 2099.

When we convert string literals to DATETIME values, we do not have to make assumptions about language settings. Instead, we can explicitly specify the DATETIME format from which we are converting.

The following scripts demonstrate both the safe way to convert character strings to DATETIME values, and the vulnerability of our stored procedure to changes in language settings. The script shown in Listing 1-18 populates the ObjectsChangeLog table and calls the SelectObjectsChangeLogForDateRange stored procedure under two different language settings, US English and Norwegian.

```
-- we can populate this table via our trigger, but
-- I used INSERTs,to keep the example simple
INSERT   INTO dbo.ObjectsChangeLog
        ( ObjectID ,
          ChangedColumnName ,
          ChangedAt ,
          OldValue
        )
        SELECT  1 ,
                'SizeInInches' ,
-- the safe way to provide July 7th, 2009
                '20090707',
                12.34 ;
  GO


SET LANGUAGE 'us_english' ;
-- this conversion always works in the same way,
-- regardless of the language settings,
-- because the format is explicitly specified
EXEC dbo.SelectObjectsChangeLogForDateRange
```

```
        @DateFrom = '20090101';

SET LANGUAGE 'Norsk' ;

EXEC dbo.SelectObjectsChangeLogForDateRange
        @DateFrom = '20090101';

-- your actual error message may be different from mine,
-- depending on the version of SQL Server

Changed language setting to us_english.
(successful output skipped)

Changed language setting to Norsk.
ObjectID    ChangedColumnName    ChangedAt      OldValue
----------- -------------------- -------------- --------------
Msg 242, Level 16, State 3, Procedure SelectObjectsChangeLogF
orDateRange, Line 6
The conversion of a char data type to a datetime data type
resulted in an out-of-range datetime value.
```

Listing 1-16: Our stored procedure breaks under Norwegian language settings.

Under the Norwegian language settings we receive an error at the point where it attempts to convert 12/31/2099 into a DATETIME string.

Note that we are, in fact, quite fortunate to receive an error message right away. Should we, in some other script or procedure, convert '10/12/2008' to DATETIME, SQL Server would silently convert this constant to a wrong value and we'd get incorrect results.

Listing 1-17 shows how our stored procedure can return unexpected results without raising errors; such silent bugs may be very different to troubleshoot.

```
INSERT  INTO dbo.ObjectsChangeLog
        ( ObjectID ,
          ChangedColumnName ,
          ChangedAt ,
```

```
            OldValue
        )
        SELECT  1 ,
                'SizeInInches' ,
                 -- this means June 15th, 2009
                '20090615',
                12.3
        UNION ALL
        SELECT  1 ,
                'SizeInInches' ,
                -- this means September 15th, 2009
                '20090915',
                12.5

SET LANGUAGE 'us_english' ;

-- this call returns rows from Jul 6th to Sep 10th, 2009
-- one log entry meets the criteria
EXEC SelectObjectsChangeLogForDateRange
  @DateFrom = '07/06/2009',
  @DateTo = '09/10/2009' ;

SET LANGUAGE 'Norsk' ;

-- this call returns rows from Jun 7th to Oct 9th, 2009
-- three log entries meet the criteria
EXEC SelectObjectsChangeLogForDateRange
  @DateFrom = '07/06/2009',
  @DateTo = '09/10/2009' ;

Changed language setting to us_english.
ObjectID    ChangedColumnName    ChangedAt        OldValue
----------- -------------------- ---------------- -------------------
1           SizeInInches         2009-07-07       12.34

-- because the stored procedure does not have an ORDER BY
-- clause, your results may show up in a different
-- order
```

```
Changed language setting to Norsk.

ObjectID      ChangedColumnName      ChangedAt               OldValue
-----------   --------------------   ---------------------   ------------
1             SizeInInches           2009-07-07              12.34
1             SizeInInches           2009-06-15              12.3
1             SizeInInches           2009-09-15              12.5
```

**Listing 1-17: Our stored procedure call returns different results, depending on
language settings.**

To fix the stored procedure, as shown in Listing 1-18, we need to explicitly specify the
format from which we convert the VARCHAR values provided when the stored procedure
is executed.

```
ALTER PROCEDURE dbo.SelectObjectsChangeLogForDateRange
    @DateFrom DATETIME ,
    @DateTo DATETIME = NULL
AS
    SET ROWCOUNT 0 ;
    SELECT   ObjectID ,
             ChangedColumnName ,
             ChangedAt ,
             OldValue
    FROM     dbo.ObjectsChangeLog
    WHERE    ChangedAt BETWEEN @DateFrom
                      AND      COALESCE(@DateTo,
                               '20991231') ;
```

Listing 1-18: Fixing the stored procedure.

The stored procedure will now run correctly, regardless of the language settings. In this
case, we chose to fix the problem by eliminating the assumption. Alternatively, in some
cases, we might choose to enforce it by setting the language at the beginning of the
stored procedure, just as we did with the ROWCOUNT setting.

Of course, there are situations when our code will always run under one and the same settings, in which case there is no need to do anything. For example, if a module implements business rules specific to the state of Minnesota, it is reasonable to assume that it will always run under the same language settings.

Defensive Data Modification

Data modification is, in general, an area in which I see developers getting into trouble time and again. We'll start with a case that demonstrates how data can be erroneously updated as a result of a false assumption in the stored procedure that modifies it. It is a simple example, but the underlying problem is a very common one: using search criteria that affect more rows than intended.

We'll then discuss a second, somewhat more complex case, where an UPDATE can go wrong because it fails to unambiguously identify the row(s) to be modified, perhaps falsely assuming that the underlying data structures will ensure that no such ambiguity exists.

Updating more rows than intended

Listing 1-19 creates a simple Employee table, and a SetEmployeeManager stored procedure that assigns a manager to a given employee.

```
CREATE TABLE dbo.Employee
  (
    EmployeeID INT NOT NULL ,
    ManagerID INT NULL ,
    FirstName VARCHAR(50) NULL ,
    LastName VARCHAR(50) NULL ,
    CONSTRAINT PK_Employee_EmployeeID
        PRIMARY KEY CLUSTERED ( EmployeeID ASC ) ,
    CONSTRAINT FK_Employee_EmployeeID_ManagerID
        FOREIGN KEY ( ManagerID )
            REFERENCES dbo.Employee ( EmployeeID )
  ) ;
```

```
GO

CREATE PROCEDURE dbo.SetEmployeeManager
  @FirstName VARCHAR(50) ,
  @LastName VARCHAR(50) ,
  @ManagerID INT
AS
  SET NOCOUNT ON ;
  UPDATE  dbo.Employee
  SET     ManagerID = @ManagerID
  WHERE   FirstName = @FirstName
          AND LastName = @LastName ;
```

Listing 1-19: The Employee **table and** SetEmployeeManager **stored procedure.**

Clearly, the person who developed the stored procedure assumed that, at most, one employee may have the provided first and last name. If there happen to be two people in the organization with the same name, then this stored procedure will assign them both to the same manager.

Again, having uncovered the assumption, we need to decide whether to enforce it or eliminate it. We could enforce it by simply placing a UNIQUE constraint on the FirstName and LastName columns. However, in this case, it seems much more reasonable to assume that there may well be more than one employee with the same first and last name, and that these namesake employees may report to different managers. We therefore need to eliminate the incorrect assumption.

There are many ways to do this, the simplest being to ensure that the parameter supplied to the stored procedure, and used in the search criteria, identifies a unique row, as shown in Listing 1-20.

```
ALTER PROCEDURE dbo.SetEmployeeManager
    @EmployeeID INT ,
    @ManagerID INT
AS
    SET NOCOUNT ON ;
    UPDATE  dbo.Employee
```

```
SET      ManagerID = @ManagerID
WHERE    EmployeeID = @EmployeeID ;
```

Listing 1-20: Using unambiguous search criteria.

As long as EmployeeID is the primary key on the dbo.Employee table, this procedure will work correctly.

The problem of ambiguous updates

The results of data modifications may be unpredictable in the hands of the careless programmer. Let's consider a very common requirement: populating a permanent table from a staging table. First of all, let's create our permanent table, Codes, and a staging table, CodesStaging, as shown in Listing 1-21. Note that CodesStaging does not have a primary key. This is very common for staging tables, because data is often loaded into such tables before detecting duplicates and other data integrity violations.

```
CREATE TABLE dbo.Codes
    (
        Code VARCHAR(5) NOT NULL ,
        Description VARCHAR(40) NOT NULL ,
        CONSTRAINT PK_Codes PRIMARY KEY ( Code )
    ) ;
GO



CREATE TABLE dbo.CodesStaging
    (
        Code VARCHAR(10) NOT NULL ,
        Description VARCHAR(40) NOT NULL
    ) ;
GO
```

Listing 1-21: Creating the Codes and CodesStaging tables.

49

Now, let's populate each table with some sample data, as shown in Listing 1-22.

```
DELETE   FROM dbo.Codes ;
INSERT   INTO dbo.Codes
         ( Code ,
           Description
         )
         SELECT  'AR' ,
                 'Old description for Arkansas'
         UNION ALL
         SELECT  'IN' ,
                 'Old description for Indiana' ;

DELETE   FROM dbo.CodesStaging ;
INSERT   INTO dbo.CodesStaging
         ( Code ,
           Description
         )
         SELECT  'AR' ,
                 'description for Argentina'
         UNION ALL
         SELECT  'AR' ,
                 'new description for Arkansas'
         UNION ALL
         SELECT  'IN' ,
                 'new description for Indiana ' ;
```

Listing 1-22: Populating the Codes and CodesStaging tables.

Now, we'll examine two different ways of updating data in the permanent table, based on data in the staging table, both of which are subject to ambiguities if care is not taken.

1. Using UPDATE...FROM.

2. Updating an inline view.

We'll then discuss strategies for avoiding such ambiguities.

Using UPDATE...FROM

Notice, in Listing 1-22, that the incoming data in our staging table has a duplicate: the code AR occurs twice, with different descriptions. Suppose that we have not detected or resolved this duplicate, and that we are updating our Codes table from the staging table.

```
UPDATE    dbo.Codes


SET Description = s.Description
FROM      dbo.Codes AS c INNER JOIN dbo.CodesStaging AS s
             ON c.Code = s.Code ;

SELECT    Code ,
          Description
FROM      dbo.Codes ;

Code          Description
----------    ------------------------------------------
AR            description for Argentina
IN            new description for Indiana

(2 row(s) affected)
```

Listing 1-23: An ambiguous UPDATE...FROM, when loading data from a staging table (CodesStaging) into a target table (Codes).

Although two descriptions were provided for the AR code, the UPDATE...FROM command did not raise an error; it just silently updated the corresponding row in the Codes table with one of the two provided values. In this case, the 'old description for Arkansas' has been overwritten with the 'description for Argentina.'

Updating inline views

When we update inline views, we may encounter exactly the same problem. First, repopulate each of the tables with the original data, using the code from Listing 1-22. Next, create an inline view, and then use it to implement exactly the same functionality as the previous UPDATE...FROM commands, as shown in Listing 1-24.

```
WITH    c AS ( SELECT    c.Code ,
                         c.Description ,
                         s.Description AS NewDescription
               FROM      dbo.Codes AS c
                         INNER JOIN dbo.CodesStaging AS s
                              ON c.Code = s.Code
             )
     UPDATE   c
     SET      Description = NewDescription ;

SELECT   Code ,
         Description
FROM     dbo.Codes ;

Code        Description
---------   ----------------------------------------
AR          description for Argentina
IN          new description for Indiana
```

Listing 1-24: An ambiguous update of an inline view.

Note that, neither in this example nor in the previous UPDATE...FROM example, can we predict which of these two values will end up in the target table – that, as usual, depends on the execution plan and, as such, is completely unpredictable. It is by pure chance that, in my examples, Argentina was chosen over Arkansas in both cases. I was able to get different results, with the description of Arkansas rather than Argentina inserted into Codes, just by changing the order in which the rows are inserted into CodesStaging. However, again, there is no guarantee that you will get the same results on your box. Also, bear in mind that, if we ever did add an index to the staging table, this would almost certainly affect the result as well.

How to avoid ambiguous updates

In both previous examples, the developer has written the UPDATE command apparently under the assumption that there can be no duplicate data in the CodesStaging – which cannot be guaranteed in the absence of a UNIQUE or PRIMARY KEY constraint no the Code column – or that any duplicate data should have been removed before updating the permanent table.

Generally, performing this sort of ambiguous update is unacceptable. In some cases, we might want to refine the query to make sure it never yields ambiguous results. Typically, however, we want either to raise an error when an ambiguity is detected, or to update only what is unambiguous.

In SQL Server 2008, we can circumvent such problems with UPDATE...FROM or CTE-based updates, by use of the MERGE command. However, prior to SQL Server 2008, we have to detect these ambiguities.

Using MERGE to detect ambiguity (SQL Server 2008 only)

If you are working with SQL Server 2008, then easily the best option is to use the MERGE command (covered in further detail in Chapter 4, *When Upgrading Breaks Code*). In Listing 1-25, we use the MERGE command to update our primary table from our staging table and immediately encounter the expected error.

```
MERGE INTO dbo.Codes AS c
    USING dbo.CodesStaging AS s
    ON c.Code = s.Code
    WHEN MATCHED
        THEN UPDATE
            SET       c.Description = s.Description ;
```

```
Msg 8672, Level 16, State 1, Line 1
The MERGE statement attempted to UPDATE or DELETE the same
row more than once. This happens when a target row matches
more than one source row. A MERGE statement cannot UPDATE/
DELETE the same row of the target table multiple times.
Refine the ON clause to ensure a target row matches at most
one source row, or use the GROUP BY clause to group the
source rows.
```

Listing 1-25: MERGE detects an ambiguity in incoming data.

An ANSI-standard method

Pre-SQL Server 2008, we are forced to seek alternative ways to raise an error whenever
there is an ambiguity. The code in Listing 1-26 is ANSI-standard SQL and accomplishes
that goal.

```
-- rerun the code from Listing 1-22
-- before executing this code
UPDATE    dbo.Codes
SET       Description =
                ( SELECT   Description
                  FROM     dbo.CodesStaging
                  WHERE    Codes.Code = CodesStaging.Code
                )
WHERE     EXISTS ( SELECT *
                   FROM    dbo.CodesStaging AS s
                   WHERE   Codes.Code = s.Code
                 ) ;
Msg 512, Level 16, State 1, Line 3
Subquery returned more than 1 value. This is not permitted
when the subquery follows =, !=, <, <= , >, >= or when the
subquery is used as an expression.
The statement has been terminated.
```

Listing 1-26: An ANSI-standard UPDATE command, which raises an error when
there is an ambiguity.

Note that, in order to update just one column, we had to use two almost identical subqueries in this command. This is definitely not a good practice. Should we need to update ten columns, we would have to repeat almost the same code eleven times! If, at some later time, we need to modify the subquery, we will have to make one and the same change in eleven places, which is very prone to errors.

Defensive inline view updates

Fortunately, there are several ways to improve the robustness of inline view updates, as well as UPDATE...FROM updates (covered in the next section), which work with SQL 2005.

In the previous two examples, an error was raised when ambiguity was detected. This is usually preferable but, if your business rules allow you to ignore ambiguities and only update that which is unambiguous, then the solution shown in Listing 1-27 will work.

```
-- rerun the code from Listing 1-22
-- before executing this code
BEGIN TRAN ;

WITH   c AS ( SELECT  c.Code ,
                      c.Description ,
                      s.Description AS NewDescription
             FROM    dbo.Codes AS c
                     INNER JOIN dbo.CodesStaging AS s
                         ON c.Code = s.Code
                             AND ( SELECT COUNT(*)
                             FROM   dbo.CodesStaging AS s1
                             WHERE c.Code = s1.Code
                                 ) = 1
             )
   UPDATE  c
   SET     Description = NewDescription ;

ROLLBACK ;
```

Listing 1-27: Using a subquery to ignore ambiguities when updating an inline view.

This time, only the description of Indiana is updated. In a similar fashion, we could filter out (i.e. ignore) ambiguities with the help of an analytical function, as shown in Listing 1-28.

```
-- rerun the code from Listing 1-22
-- before executing this code
BEGIN TRAN ;

WITH c AS ( SELECT c.Code ,
                   c.Description ,
                   s.Description AS NewDescription ,
                   COUNT(*) OVER ( PARTITION BY s.Code )
                                           AS NumVersions
            FROM    dbo.Codes AS c
                    INNER JOIN dbo.CodesStaging AS s
                      ON c.Code = s.Code
          )
  UPDATE  c
  SET     Description = NewDescription
  WHERE   NumVersions = 1 ;

ROLLBACK ;
```

Listing 1-28: Using PARTITION BY to ignore ambiguities when updating an inline view.

In some cases, the approach of only performing unambiguous updates, and silently ignoring ambiguous ones, is unacceptable. In the absence of built-in methods, we can use tricky workarounds to reuse the code as much as possible and still raise an error if there is an ambiguity. Consider the example shown in Listing 1-29, in which a divide by zero occurs if there is an ambiguity.

```
-- rerun the code from Listing 1-22
-- before executing this code
DECLARE @ambiguityDetector INT ;
WITH c AS ( SELECT c.Code ,
                   c.Description ,
```

```
                        s.Description AS NewDescription ,
                COUNT(*) OVER ( PARTITION BY s.Code )
                                        AS NumVersions
            FROM     dbo.Codes AS c
                     INNER JOIN dbo.CodesStaging AS s
                        ON c.Code = s.Code
            )
  UPDATE    c
  SET       Description = NewDescription ,
            @ambiguityDetector = CASE WHEN NumVersions = 1
                                    THEN 1
-- if we have ambiguities, the following branch executes
-- and raises the following error:
-- Divide by zero error encountered.
                                    ELSE 1 / 0
                        END ;

Msg 8134, Level 16, State 1, Line 4
Divide by zero error encountered.
The statement has been terminated.
```

Listing 1-29: An UPDATE command using an inline view and raising a divide by zero error when there is an ambiguity.

Of course, the error message raised by this code (divide by zero) is misleading, so we should only use this approach when none of the previous options are viable.

Defensive UPDATE...FROM

Some of the approaches just outlined for improving the robustness of inline view updates, apply equally as well to improving the UPDATE...FROM command. For example, we can use a subquery to ignore ambiguities, as shown in Listing 1-30.

```
-- rerun the code from Listing 1-22
-- before executing this code
BEGIN TRAN ;
UPDATE    dbo.Codes
```

```
SET      Description = 'Old Description' ;

UPDATE   dbo.Codes
SET      Description = s.Description
FROM     dbo.Codes AS c
         INNER JOIN dbo.CodesStaging AS s
             ON c.Code = s.Code
                AND ( SELECT COUNT(*)
                      FROM    dbo.CodesStaging AS s1
                      WHERE   s.Code = s1.Code
                    ) = 1 ;
SELECT   Code ,
         Description
FROM     dbo.Codes ;
ROLLBACK ;
```

Listing 1-30: Using a subquery to ignore ambiguities when using UPDATE...FROM.

Likewise, we can use an analytical function for detecting and ignoring ambiguities, as shown in Listing 1-31.

```
-- rerun the code from Listing 1-22
-- before executing this code
BEGIN TRAN ;
UPDATE   dbo.Codes
SET      Description = 'Old Description' ;

UPDATE dbo.Codes
SET    Description = s.Description
FROM   dbo.Codes AS c
       INNER JOIN ( SELECT Code ,
                           Description ,
                           COUNT(*) OVER ( PARTITION BY Code )
                                         AS NumValues
                    FROM    dbo.CodesStaging
                  ) AS s
                      ON c.Code = s.Code
```

58

```
                        AND NumValues = 1 ;
SELECT    Code ,
          Description
FROM      dbo.Codes ;
ROLLBACK ;
```

Listing 1-31: Using an analytical function to detect and ignore ambiguities when using UPDATE...FROM.

Summary

The goal of this chapter was to introduce, by way of some simple examples, some of the basic ideas that underpin defensive database programming. It is vital that you understand and document the assumptions that underpin your implementation, test them to ensure their validity, and eliminate them if they are not. It is also vital that you consider as many use cases as possible for your code, and ensure it behaves consistently in each case. Where inconsistencies or incorrect behavior are found, the defensive programmer will not only fix the offending module, but also test all other modules that might suffer from a similar problem and proactively safeguard against it.

Along the way, I hope you've learned the following specific lessons in defensive programming:

- how to use complex patterns to improve the robustness of LIKE searches

- how to avoid potential difficulties with SET ROWCOUNT

- the importance of safe date formats and of explicitly specifying the required format when converting dates

- how to avoid dangerous ambiguity when performing updates by, for example:

  - using MERGE, in SQL Server 2008

  - using subqueries, pre-SQL Server 2008.

- how to use subqueries or the COUNT(*) OVER analytic function to improve the robustness of modifications when using UPDATE...FROM, or updating inline views, so that ambiguous updates are ignored.

59

Chapter 2: Code Vulnerabilities Due to SQL Server Misconceptions

In Chapter 1, we discussed several examples where we could choose whether to ensure that an assumption that underpinned our code implementation was always true, or to eliminate that assumption, if possible. However, certain vulnerabilities occur due to a basic misunderstanding of how the SQL Server engine, or the SQL language, work. Such vulnerabilities should always be eliminated, or they will ultimately lead to code failure.

This chapter will discuss the following three very common misconceptions:

- **WHERE clause conditions will always be evaluated in the same order** – a common cause of intermittent query failure

- **SET and SELECT always change the values of variables** – this false assumption can lead to the dreaded infinite loop

- **Data will be returned in some "natural order"** – another common cause of intermittent query failure.

In each case we'll examine how, with simple defensive coding techniques, we can improve the quality and resilience of our database code.

Conditions in a WHERE clause can evaluate in any order

Quite a few languages explicitly guarantee that logical expressions will evaluate in a certain order, from left to right. SQL is not one of them. Never assume that the conditions in your WHERE clause will evaluate in the left-to-right order in which you list them. If your code relies on the WHERE clause conditions being evaluated in a given order, then the resulting query is unsafe.

Consider, for example, the query shown in Listing 2-1. At first glance, it seems straightforward enough: we check that a provided expression is a valid date and, if so, CAST it to a specific date format; in many client-side languages this approach would always work.

```
-- this is example syntax only. The code will not run
-- as the EmailMesssages table does not exist
SELECT   Subject ,
         Body
FROM     dbo.EmailMessages
WHERE    ISDATE(VarcharColumn) = 1
         AND CAST(VarcharColumn AS DATETIME) = '20090707';
```

Listing 2-1: A potentially unsafe query.

This query might work for some data, but it can blow up at any time, and the reason is simple: the conditions in the WHERE clause can evaluate in any order, and the order can change from one execution of the query to the next. If the CAST is evaluated before the ISDATE validity check, and if the string is not a valid date, than the query will fail.

I would like to demonstrate how brittle this sort of code can be, and how little it may take to break such code. I will provide a script in which a query originally succeeds, but fails after I have added an index. Usually, such problems occur intermittently, but this example has been devised in such a way that it behaves consistently on different servers, running different versions of SQL Server (though, even having done this, there is no guarantee that it will run in your environment exactly like it does in mine).

Listing 2-2 shows how to create a helper table, Numbers, with over a million integer numbers.

Helper tables

Helper tables such as Numbers are probably familiar to most SQL programmers and have a variety of uses. If you don't already have one, it's worth creating the one in Listing 2-2, and keeping it around for future use.

It also creates a **Messages** table and populates it with test data (if you already have a table with this name, from running examples in Chapter 1, you will need to drop it). To make sure that the example consistently executes in the same way on different servers, I had to populate the table with a large number of wide rows; this is why we need to insert one million rows, and that every row has a **CHAR(200)** column. As a result, the code may take some time to complete. Note also that only one row out of one million has a valid date in the **MessageDateAsVarcharColumn** column.

```
-- helper table
CREATE TABLE dbo.Numbers
    (
        n INT NOT NULL
                PRIMARY KEY
    ) ;
GO

DECLARE @i INT ;
SET @i = 1 ;
INSERT   INTO dbo.Numbers
         ( n )
         SELECT  1 ;
WHILE @i < 1000000
    BEGIN;
        INSERT   INTO dbo.Numbers
                 ( n )
                 SELECT   n + @i
                 FROM     dbo.Numbers ;
        SET @i = @i * 2 ;
    END ;
GO

CREATE TABLE dbo.Messages
    (
        MessageID INT NOT NULL
                      PRIMARY KEY ,
-- in real life the following two columns
-- would have foreign key constraints;
```

```
-- they are skipped to keep the example short
     SenderID INT NOT NULL ,
     ReceiverID INT NOT NULL ,
     MessageDateAsVarcharColumn VARCHAR(30) NULL ,
     SomeMoreData CHAR(200) NULL
   ) ;
GO

INSERT   INTO dbo.Messages
         ( MessageID ,
           SenderID ,
           ReceiverID ,
           MessageDateAsVarcharColumn ,
           SomeMoreData
         )
         SELECT   n ,
                  n % 1000 ,
                  n / 1000 ,
                  'Wrong Date' ,
                  'SomeMoreData'
         FROM     dbo.Numbers ;
GO
-- after the insert all the messages have wrong dates

UPDATE   dbo.Messages
SET      MessageDateAsVarcharColumn = '20090707'
WHERE    SenderID = 123
         AND ReceiverID = 456 ;
-- after the update exactly one message has a valid date
```

Listing 2-2: Creating the helper Numbers table and Messages table.

Given that almost all the rows in this table have invalid DATETIME values, attempting to convert such invalid values to DATETIME leads to conversion errors, such as shown in Listing 2-3.

```
SELECT    MessageID ,
          SenderID ,
          ReceiverID ,
          MessageDateAsVarcharColumn ,
          SomeMoreData
FROM      dbo.Messages
WHERE     CAST(MessageDateAsVarcharColumn AS DATETIME) =
              '20090707';


-- your actual error message may be different
-- depending on the version of SQL Server

Msg 241, Level 16, State 1, Line 1
Conversion failed when converting datetime from character
string.
```

Listing 2-3:   A simple query against the Messages table fails with a conversion error.

Clearly, we need to filter out invalid values before converting to DATETIME. The naïve query shown in Listing 2-4 may or may not work on your server.

```
SELECT    MessageID ,
          SenderID ,
          ReceiverID ,
          MessageDateAsVarcharColumn ,
          SomeMoreData
FROM      dbo.Messages
WHERE     ISDATE(MessageDateAsVarcharColumn) = 1
          AND CAST(MessageDateAsVarcharColumn AS DATETIME)
              = '20090707' ;
```

Listing 2-4:   An unsafe way to filter out invalid DATETIME values.

There is no way to predict whether or not this query will work for you; the database engine will evaluate the WHERE conditions in any order it wishes. In fact, if it does work for you, you are unlucky. If it is going to break, as it inevitably will, it is best to know immediately rather than find out later, at some inconvenient moment.

The safe way to develop such queries is to use CASE expressions to explicitly specify the order in which our conditions must evaluate, as demonstrated in Listing 2-5.

```
SELECT   MessageID ,
         SenderID ,
         ReceiverID ,
         MessageDateAsVarcharColumn ,
         SomeMoreData
FROM     dbo.Messages
WHERE    CASE WHEN ISDATE(MessageDateAsVarcharColumn) = 1
              THEN CAST(MessageDateAsVarcharColumn
                                         AS DATETIME)
         END = '20090707' ;
```

Listing 2-5: CASE expressions ensure that only valid DATETIME values are converted

Before we move on, let's consider a variation of our previous unsafe date-filtering query, shown in Listing 2-6.

```
SELECT   MessageID ,
         SenderID ,
         ReceiverID ,
         MessageDateAsVarcharColumn ,
         SomeMoreData
FROM     dbo.Messages
WHERE    SenderID = 123
         AND ReceiverID = 456
         AND CAST(MessageDateAsVarcharColumn AS DATETIME)
                    = '20090707' ;
```

Listing 2-6: Attempting to select the only valid date.

This query attempts to select the only row that contains a valid date, and it succeeded on quite a few servers on which I have tried it out. I need to state clearly again, though, that **there is no guarantee that this query will succeed on your server.**

66

However, in this case and under these conditions, the optimizer was choosing to convert the MessageDate value to DATETIME only after both other conditions were evaluated, and it was doing so consistently on several servers running different versions of SQL Server. We can confirm this is the case by changing the order of conditions in our WHERE clause, as shown in Listing 2-7.

```
SELECT   MessageID ,
         SenderID ,
         ReceiverID ,
         MessageDateAsVarcharColumn ,
         SomeMoreData
FROM     dbo.Messages
WHERE    CAST(MessageDateAsVarcharColumn AS DATETIME) =
               '20090707'
         AND SenderID = 123
         AND ReceiverID = 456 ;
```

Listing 2-7: Even though CAST now appears first in the WHERE clause, it may (or may not) be evaluated last.

As we have discussed, the conditions in the WHERE clause are not evaluated in left-to-right order. More to the point, the next time this (or any other) query runs, the order in which the conditions are evaluated can change.

To demonstrate this, let's create an index on the SenderID column of the Messages table, as shown in Listing 2-8.

```
CREATE INDEX Messages_SenderID_MessageDate
ON dbo.Messages(SenderID, MessageDateAsVarcharColumn) ;
```

Listing 2-8: Creating an index on the Messages table.

Now, when I rerun the query in Listing 2-6, the query blows up, presenting the same conversion error as shown in Listing 2-3. Clearly, in the presence of this index, my server converts to DATETIME *before* evaluating both other conditions. Here is one possible explanation: without the index, the optimizer chooses to scan the whole table (basically

67

there are no other possible plans). As the table is scanned, the conditions on integer columns are evaluated first because integer comparisons are cheaper than `DATETIME` conversions.

In any event, after creating the new index, the optimizer has decided that the new index `Messages_SenderID_MessageDate` is selective enough to be used in our query. So the database engine begins a range scan of the index `Messages_SenderID_MessageDate` on the condition `SenderID=123`. For each index entry that satisfies this condition, it also evaluates the condition `CAST(MessageDateAsVarcharColumn AS DATETIME)='20090707'` to narrow down the search, because the column `MessageDateAsVarcharColumn` is also stored in the same index entry.

Let me repeat my disclaimer: there is no guarantee that this query will succeed or fail on your server the way it does on mine. We cannot assume that conditions in the `WHERE` clause execute in any particular order. We have learned that the safe way to guarantee the order in which conditions evaluate is to use `CASE` expressions.

SET, SELECT, and the dreaded infinite loop

We cannot assume that `SET` and `SELECT` always change the values of variables. If we rely on that incorrect assumption, our code may not work as expected, so we need to eliminate it. Listing 2-9 demonstrates a case where `SELECT` leaves the value of a variable unchanged, if the result set is empty.

```
SET NOCOUNT ON ;

DECLARE @i INT ;
SELECT  @i = -1 ;

SELECT  @i AS [@i before the assignment] ;
SELECT  @i = 1
WHERE   1 = 2 ;
SELECT  @i AS [@i after the assignment] ;
```

```
@i before the assignment
------------------------
-1

@i after the assignment
------------------------
-1
```

Listing 2-9: SELECT **may leave a variable unchanged if the result set is empty.**

Listing 2-10 shows that that, in the same case, SET changes the values of variables even if the result set is empty.

```
SET NOCOUNT ON ;
DECLARE @i INT ;
SELECT  @i = -1 ;

SELECT  @i AS [@i before the assignment] ;
SET @i = ( SELECT    1
            WHERE     1 = 2
        ) ;
SELECT  @i AS [@i after the assignment] ;

@i before the assignment
------------------------
-1

@i after the assignment
------------------------
NULL
```

Listing 2-10: SET **will change the value of the variable.**

If SET raises an error, the value of the variable is also unchanged.

```
SET NOCOUNT ON ;
DECLARE @i INT ;
```

```
SELECT   @i = -1 ;

SELECT   @i AS [@i before the assignment] ;
SET @i = ( SELECT    1
            UNION ALL
            SELECT    2
        ) ;
SELECT   @i AS [@i after the assignment] ;



@i before the assignment
------------------------
-1

Msg 512, Level 16, State 1, Line 6
Subquery returned more than 1 value. This is not permitted
when the subquery follows =, !=, <, <= , >, >= or when the
subquery is used as an expression.
@i after the assignment
------------------------
-1
```

Listing 2-11: SET may leave a variable unchanged if it raises an error.

Similarly, if SELECT raises an error, the value of the variable can also be left unchanged.
Run Listing 2-12 and you will get the same output as in Listing 2-11.

```
SET NOCOUNT ON ;
DECLARE @i INT ;
SELECT   @i = -1 ;

SELECT   @i AS [@i before the assignment] ;
SELECT   @i = 1
WHERE    ( SELECT    1 AS n
            UNION ALL
            SELECT    2
        ) = 1 ;
```

```
SELECT  @i AS [@i after the assignment] ;
```

Listing 2-12: SELECT may leave a variable unchanged if it raises an error.

Understanding how SET and SELECT behave is very important. In particular, the behavior of SELECT demonstrated in Listing 2-9, whereby it leaves a variable unchanged if the selected result set is empty, can lead to the dreaded infinite loop.

Use set-based solutions where possible

Of course, wherever possible we should avoid procedural, row-by-row processing in our T-SQL code, in favor of proper set-based aggregation. However, sometimes loops are unavoidable.

In order to demonstrate the infinite loop problem, create the Orders table shown in Listing 2-13 and populate it with sample data.

```
CREATE TABLE dbo.Orders
    (
       OrderID INT NOT NULL ,
       OrderDate DATETIME NOT NULL ,
       IsProcessed CHAR(1) NOT NULL ,
       CONSTRAINT PK_Orders PRIMARY KEY ( OrderID ) ,
       CONSTRAINT CHK_Orders_IsProcessed
          CHECK ( IsProcessed IN ( 'Y', 'N' ) )
    ) ;
GO


INSERT   dbo.Orders
         ( OrderID ,
           OrderDate ,
           IsProcessed
         )
         SELECT  1 ,
                 '20090420' ,
                 'N'
         UNION ALL
```

```
     SELECT   2 ,
                '20090421' ,
                'N'
     UNION ALL
     SELECT   3 ,
                '20090422' ,
                'N' ;
```

Listing 2-13: Creating and populating the Orders table.

When creating the stored procedure shown in Listing 2-14, the developer made the following assumption: the SELECT at the end of the loop will always change the value of the variable @ID. As we now know, this assumption is incorrect.

```
CREATE PROCEDURE dbo.ProcessBatchOfOrders
   @IDsIntervalSize INT
AS
     DECLARE @minID INT ,
         @ID INT ;

     SELECT   @minID = MIN(OrderID) ,
              @ID = MIN(OrderID)
     FROM     dbo.Orders ;

     WHILE @ID < ( @minID + @IDsIntervalSize )
         BEGIN;

                UPDATE   dbo.Orders
                SET      IsProcessed = 'Y'
                WHERE    OrderID = @ID ;

-- this SELECT may leave the value
-- of @ID unchanged
                SELECT TOP (1)
                        @ID = OrderID
                FROM    dbo.Orders
                WHERE   IsProcessed = 'N'
```

```
        ORDER BY OrderID ;

-- PRINT is needed for debugging purposes only
        PRINT @ID ;
    END ;
```

Listing 2-14: The loopy stored procedure.

As shown in Listing 2-15, if we do not request to process all the orders, then the stored procedure completes.

```
EXEC dbo.ProcessBatchOfOrders 2;
GO
-- restore the data to its original state
UPDATE [dbo].[Orders]
  SET IsProcessed='N';
```

Listing 2-15: The stored procedure completes as long as we don't try to process all the orders.

If, however, we attempt to process more orders than there are unprocessed orders in the table (in this case, more than three orders), then our stored procedure runs into an infinite loop. When the last order has been processed, the SELECT in the stored procedure leaves the value of @ID unchanged and so the code iterates again and again using the same unchanged value of @ID – here is the dreaded infinite loop.

```
-- this call processes 3 orders and then runs infinitely
-- cancel it
EXEC dbo.ProcessBatchOfOrders 10 ;
```

Listing 2-16: The execution of dbo.ProcessBatchOfOrders results in an infinite loop.

Clearly, we should not assume that our SELECT statements will always change the value of the variable used to terminate the loop. Yet, as soon as we know what is wrong, it is easy to fix the loop in order to make sure that the variable does always change. The first possible fix, shown in Listing 2-17, uses an unconditional assignment.

73

```
ALTER PROCEDURE dbo.ProcessBatchOfOrders @IDsIntervalSize INT
AS
    DECLARE @minID INT ,
        @ID INT ;

    SELECT  @minID = MIN(OrderID) ,
            @ID = MIN(OrderID)
    FROM    dbo.Orders ;

    WHILE @ID < ( @minID + @IDsIntervalSize )
        BEGIN;
            UPDATE  dbo.Orders
            SET     IsProcessed = 'Y'
            WHERE   OrderID = @ID ;
-- this unconditional assignment fixes the problem
            SET @ID = NULL ;

            SELECT TOP (1)
                    @ID = OrderID
            FROM    dbo.Orders
            WHERE   IsProcessed = 'N'
            ORDER BY OrderID ;
-- PRINT is needed for debugging purposes
            PRINT @ID ;
        END ;
```

Listing 2-17: Using an unconditional assignment to fix the problem.

Listing 2-18 demonstrates that the fixed stored procedure completes the call that the original one could not.

```
-- restoring the data to its original state
UPDATE  dbo.Orders
SET     IsProcessed = 'N' ;
GO
```

74

```
-- this call processes 3 orders and then completes
EXEC dbo.ProcessBatchOfOrders 10 ;
```

Listing 2-18: Invoking the fixed procedure.

Alternatively, we can fix this problem by replacing the SELECT with a SET assignment, as shown in Listing 2-19.

```
ALTER PROCEDURE dbo.ProcessBatchOfOrders @IDsIntervalSize INT
AS
    DECLARE @minID INT ,
        @ID INT ;

    SELECT   @minID = MIN(OrderID) ,
             @ID = MIN(OrderID)
    FROM     dbo.Orders ;

    WHILE @ID < ( @minID + @IDsIntervalSize )
        BEGIN;
            UPDATE   dbo.Orders
            SET      IsProcessed = 'Y'
            WHERE    OrderID = @ID ;

-- SELECT is replaced with SET
            SET @ID = ( SELECT TOP (1)
                               OrderID
                        FROM   dbo.Orders
                        WHERE  IsProcessed = 'N'
                        ORDER BY OrderID
                      ) ;
-- PRINT is needed for debugging purposes
            PRINT @ID ;
        END ;
```

Listing 2-19: Replacing the SELECT with a SET removes the infinite loop.

We can rerun Listing 2-18 to verify that the procedure works.

In Chapter 3, we will discuss the dangers of using SELECT, rather than SET, to assign a variable when multiple rows can be returned, and how use of the latter can make your code much more resilient to changes to the underlying schema objects.

Specify ORDER BY if you need ordered data

If your query does not have an ORDER BY clause, the data can be returned in any order. This may sound trivial, but all too many developers who are new to SQL assume that the data has some "natural" or "default" order. This is simply not true; there is no such thing as default or natural order.

To demonstrate this fact, I have chosen to use a really wide table; a table with just a few rows on every page.

```
CREATE TABLE dbo.WideTable
    (
        ID INT NOT NULL ,
        RandomInt INT NOT NULL ,
        CharFiller CHAR(1000) NULL ,
        CONSTRAINT PK_WideTable PRIMARY KEY ( ID )
    ) ;
```

Listing 2-20: Creating a wide table.

Also, let us make sure that the table is big enough (100K rows), so that it is stored on many pages. As such, the script in Listing 2-21 may take some time to run.

```
SET NOCOUNT ON ;

DECLARE @ID INT ;
SET NOCOUNT ON ;
SET @ID = 1 ;
WHILE @ID < 100000
    BEGIN ;
        INSERT  INTO dbo.WideTable
                ( ID, RandomInt, CharFiller )
```

```
              SELECT  @ID ,
                      RAND() * 1000000 ,
                      'asdf' ;

         SET @ID = @ID + 1 ;
      END ;
GO
```

Listing 2-21: Adding 100K rows to the wide table.

If we select the data from this table, without providing an ORDER BY clause, the data may be retrieved in the order in which it was inserted, as was the case when I ran the query shown in Listing 2-22 on my server.

```
SELECT TOP ( 1000 )
        ID
FROM    dbo.WideTable ;

ID
-----------
1
2
3
4
5
(snip)
```

Listing 2-22: Without an ORDER BY clause, the rows are returned in the order they were inserted.

However, there is no guarantee that this script will work on your server in exactly the same way that it did on mine. Many people assume that, in the absence of an ORDER BY clause, the data will be returned "in the order of the primary key," or "in the order of the clustering index," or "in the order it was inserted." None of these assumptions is correct. Listing 2-23 demonstrates that after we have added a non-clustered index, the result of our query is different.

```
CREATE  INDEX WideTable_RandomInt
    ON dbo.WideTable(RandomInt) ;
GO
SELECT TOP ( 1000 )
        ID
FROM    dbo.WideTable ;


ID
-----------
61345
78137
36333
76724
65341
(snip)
```

Listing 2-23: When an index is added the rows are returned in a different order.

In this example, I tried hard to ensure that the example works the same on your server as on mine: I made sure that the table was wide and the non-clustered index was narrow, so there is a very strong reason to prefer reading from a non-clustered index over reading from the clustered one. Nevertheless, there is no guarantee that this script will work on your server exactly as it did on mine.

Anyway, the lesson to learn is that, if we need the data returned in some particular order, we must explicitly provide an ORDER BY clause.

Summary

If you don't understand how SQL works, then your code will inevitably be plagued by intermittent failure, resulting in incorrect results, or worse. This chapter covered just three common examples of how misplaced assumptions about the way certain constructs behaved led to unreliable code, but the message is clear: such assumptions must always be eliminated from your code.

Along the way, I hope you've learned the following lessons in defensive programming:

- use CASE expressions instead of relying on WHERE clause conditions being evaluated in a specific order
- make sure variable assignments are unconditional, and use SET rather than SELECT to avoid infinite loops
- don't rely on data being returned in some default order. If order is required, use ORDER BY.

Chapter 3: Surviving Changes to Database Objects

It is quite common for perfectly-functioning SQL code to be knocked off its feet by a change to the underlying database schema, or to other objects that are used in the code. If we are "lucky," the code will suddenly start producing error messages; if not, it may just silently start producing different results. In either case, once the problem is discovered, the process of adjusting all of the application code can be long and painstaking.

Fortunately, there are a few simple defensive techniques that take little time to implement, but yet may significantly reduce the possibility of such errors. Once again, the relatively small extra effort up front will save a lot of maintenance toil later.

In this chapter, we'll examine several examples of how changes to database objects can cause unpredictable behavior in code that accesses them, and discuss how to develop code that will not break, or behave unpredictably, as a result of such changes. Specifically, we will cover:

- **changes to the primary or unique keys**, and how to test and validate assumptions regarding the "uniqueness" of column data

- **changes to stored procedure signatures**, and the importance of using explicitly named parameters

- **changes to columns**, such as adding columns as well as modifying an existing column's nullability, size or data type.

One of the main lessons to be learned is that if your implementation relies on a particular property of the underlying schema, such as the uniqueness of a given column, then you must document that assumption, preferably in your unit tests, and make sure it always holds true.

Surviving Changes to the Definition of a Primary or Unique Key

Changes to the keys in your tables should, hopefully, be rare, but they can cause trouble to the unwary when they happen. In a broader context, the defensive programmer should always fully document and test any assumptions about the underlying uniqueness of the column data, as we saw in the sections of Chapter 1 about ambiguous updates. The following examples demonstrate what can happen to perfectly correct code when changes are made to the underlying unique or primary keys, thus invalidating assumptions in the code regarding the uniqueness of the column data. We'll then discuss how a query against the system views, or use of @@ROWCOUNT, can detect if such assumptions are still true.

In Listing 3-1, we create a table, Customers, using a UNIQUE constraint to guarantee the uniqueness of phone numbers, and then populate it with some test data.

```
CREATE TABLE dbo.Customers
  (
    CustomerId INT NOT NULL ,
    FirstName VARCHAR(50) NOT NULL ,
    LastName VARCHAR(50) NOT NULL ,
    Status VARCHAR(50) NOT NULL ,
    PhoneNumber VARCHAR(50) NOT NULL ,
    CONSTRAINT PK_Customers PRIMARY KEY ( CustomerId ) ,
    CONSTRAINT UNQ_Customers UNIQUE ( PhoneNumber )
  ) ;
GO
INSERT   INTO dbo.Customers
         ( CustomerId ,
           FirstName ,
           LastName ,
           Status ,
           PhoneNumber
         )
         SELECT  1 ,
                 'Darrel' ,
                 'Ling' ,
```

```
                    'Regular' ,
                    '(123)456-7890'
        UNION ALL
        SELECT   2 ,
                    'Peter' ,
                    'Hansen' ,
                    'Regular' ,
                    '(234)123-4567' ;
```

Listing 3-1: Creating the `Customers` table, with a `UNIQUE` constraint on the `PhoneNumber` column.

We need to implement a simple stored procedure, shown in Listing 3-2, which will allow users to find a customer based on their phone number, and set their customer status (regular, preferred, or VIP). If no customer exists for a given phone number, we don't need to raise an exception; we simply do nothing.

```
CREATE PROCEDURE dbo.SetCustomerStatus
    @PhoneNumber VARCHAR(50) ,
    @Status VARCHAR(50)
AS
    BEGIN;
          UPDATE   dbo.Customers
          SET      Status = @Status
          WHERE    PhoneNumber = @PhoneNumber ;
    END ;
```

Listing 3-2: The `SetCustomerStatus` stored procedure, which finds a customer by phone number and sets their status.

This implementation assumes that at most one customer has any given phone number. Clearly, right now, this assumption is true as it is guaranteed by the UNQ_Customers constraint.

Suppose, however, that at some later time we need to store data about customers from different countries. At this point, the phone number alone no longer uniquely indentifies a customer, but the combination of country code and phone number does.

In order to accommodate this requirement, our `Customers` table is altered to add the new column, `CountryCode`, and our `UNQ_Customers` constraint is modified so that it enforces uniqueness based on a combination of the `CountryCode` and `PhoneNumber` columns. These alterations are shown in Listing 3-3.

```
ALTER TABLE dbo.Customers
   ADD CountryCode CHAR(2)  NOT NULL
      CONSTRAINT DF_Customers_CountryCode
         DEFAULT('US') ;
GO


ALTER TABLE dbo.Customers DROP CONSTRAINT UNQ_Customers;
GO


ALTER TABLE dbo.Customers
   ADD CONSTRAINT UNQ_Customers
      UNIQUE(PhoneNumber, CountryCode) ;
```

Listing 3-3: Adding a `CountryCode` column to the table and to the unique constraint.

Note that, in reality, we should have added a lookup table, `dbo.CountryCodes`, referred to by a `FOREIGN KEY` constraint. However, I've avoided a lookup table in this case, in favor of keeping the example simple.

At this point, our constraint is no longer enforcing the uniqueness of values in the `PhoneNumber` column, so we can insert a customer with an identical phone number to an existing customer, but with a different country code, as shown in Listing 3-4.

```
UPDATE   dbo.Customers
SET      Status = 'Regular' ;

INSERT   INTO dbo.Customers
         ( CustomerId ,
           FirstName ,
           LastName ,
           Status ,
```

```
        PhoneNumber ,
        CountryCode
    )
    SELECT  3 ,
            'Wayne' ,
            'Miller' ,
            'Regular' ,
            '(123)456-7890' ,
            'UK' ;
```

Listing 3-4: **Wayne Miller has the same phone number as Darrell Ling, but with a different country code.**

Our Stored procedure, however, is still working on the assumption that a customer can be *uniquely* identified by their phone number alone. Since this assumption is no longer valid, the stored procedure, in its current form, could erroneously update more than one row of data, as demonstrated in Listing 3-5.

```
-- at this moment all customers have Regular status
EXEC dbo.SetCustomerStatus
    @PhoneNumber = '(123)456-7890',
    @Status = 'Preferred' ;

-- the procedure has modified statuses of two customers
SELECT  CustomerId ,
        Status
FROM    dbo.Customers ;

CustomerId  Status
----------- -------------
1           Preferred
2           Regular
3           Preferred
```

Listing 3-5: **The unchanged stored procedure modifies two rows instead of one.**

As noted in Chapter 1, perhaps the most prevalent and damaging mistake made during the development of SQL code is a failure to define or recognize the assumptions on which the implementation relies. The result, as demonstrated here, is code that is brittle, and liable to behave unpredictably when these assumptions are invalidated by changes to the underlying database objects.

Of course, the most obvious lesson to be learned here is that whenever we change our unique and/or primary keys, we need to review all the procedures that depend on the modified tables. However, the manual process of reviewing the potentially affected code is, like all manual processes, slow and prone to error. It may be more efficient to automate the process of identifying the modules that rely on particular assumptions about the underlying schema. Unit tests allow us to accomplish exactly that; we can easily, for example, write a unit test that succeeds if there is a UNIQUE constraint on the PhoneNumber column alone, and fails when this is no longer the case.

Using unit tests to document and test assumptions

Let's translate the assumption that the PhoneNumber column uniquely identifies a customer into a query against the system views. The query is rather complex, so we'll develop it in several steps. First of all, we need to know if there are any constraints on the PhoneNumber column, as shown in Listing 3-6.

```
SELECT   COUNT(*)
FROM     INFORMATION_SCHEMA.CONSTRAINT_COLUMN_USAGE AS u
WHERE    u.TABLE_NAME = 'Customers'
         AND u.TABLE_SCHEMA = 'dbo'
         AND u.COLUMN_NAME = 'PhoneNumber' ;
```

Listing 3-6:   Step 1, a query to check for constraints on PhoneNumber.

This query returns 1, confirming that there is a constraint on that column. Next, we need to verify that the constraint is either a primary key or a unique constraint:

```
SELECT   COUNT(*)
FROM     INFORMATION_SCHEMA.CONSTRAINT_COLUMN_USAGE AS u
         JOIN INFORMATION_SCHEMA.TABLE_CONSTRAINTS AS c
             ON c.TABLE_NAME = u.TABLE_NAME
             AND c.TABLE_SCHEMA = u.TABLE_SCHEMA
             AND c.CONSTRAINT_NAME = u.CONSTRAINT_NAME
WHERE    u.TABLE_NAME = 'Customers'
         AND u.TABLE_SCHEMA = 'dbo'
         AND u.COLUMN_NAME = 'PhoneNumber'
         AND c.CONSTRAINT_TYPE
             IN ( 'PRIMARY KEY', 'UNIQUE' ) ;
```

Listing 3-7: **Step 2 determines if the constraint on column PhoneNumber is a primary key or unique.**

Finally, we need to make sure that no other columns are included in that UNIQUE or PRIMARY KEY constraint, as follows:

```
SELECT   COUNT(*)
FROM     INFORMATION_SCHEMA.CONSTRAINT_COLUMN_USAGE AS u
         JOIN INFORMATION_SCHEMA.TABLE_CONSTRAINTS AS c
             ON c.TABLE_NAME = u.TABLE_NAME
             AND c.TABLE_SCHEMA = u.TABLE_SCHEMA
             AND c.CONSTRAINT_NAME = u.CONSTRAINT_NAME
WHERE    u.TABLE_NAME = 'Customers'
         AND u.TABLE_SCHEMA = 'dbo'
         AND u.COLUMN_NAME = 'PhoneNumber'
         AND c.CONSTRAINT_TYPE
             IN ( 'PRIMARY KEY', 'UNIQUE' )
  -- this constraint involves only one column
         AND ( SELECT    COUNT(*)
           FROM INFORMATION_SCHEMA.CONSTRAINT_COLUMN_USAGE
                 AS u1
```

```
        WHERE       u1.TABLE_NAME = u.TABLE_NAME
                AND u1.TABLE_SCHEMA = u.TABLE_SCHEMA
                AND u1.CONSTRAINT_NAME =
                            u.CONSTRAINT_NAME
    ) = 1 ;
```

Listing 3-8: **Step 3, the final query determines whether there is a unique or primary key constraint that is built on only the** PhoneNumber **column.**

When we run this query against the original database schema, with a UNIQUE constraint on the PhoneNumber column, it returns a value of 1 indicating that there is indeed a constraint built only on the PhoneNumber column. However, when we run it after the column CountryCode has been added to the definition of the unique constraint, the second subquery returns the value 2, which means that the UNIQUE constraint UNQ_Customers is built on two columns, and so the outer query returns a value of 0.

In short, this query provides us with a means to verify the validity of the assumption that the PhoneNumber column uniquely identifies a customer. By incorporating this query into our **unit test harness**, we can accomplish two goals:

- **our assumption is documented** – the code in Listing 3-8 clearly documents the fact that the dbo.SetCustomerStatus stored procedure needs a unique or primary constraint on a single column, PhoneNumber

- **our assumption is tested** – if the required constraint is dropped, or includes more than one column, we shall get a clear warning, because the unit test will fail.

Of course, we should wrap this query in a stored procedure and reuse it, because there will surely be other cases when we rely on the uniqueness of a column used in our search condition.

We can use a similar technique to verify whether or not a combination of columns, considered together, are guaranteed to be unique. Implementing this query is left as an exercise to the reader.

Using @@ROWCOUNT to verify assumptions

Alternatively, instead of documenting our assumption as a unit test, we can have our stored procedure detect how many rows it modified, and roll back if it updated more than one row, as shown in Listing 3-9.

```
ALTER PROCEDURE dbo.SetCustomerStatus
    @PhoneNumber VARCHAR(50) ,
    @Status VARCHAR(50)
AS
    BEGIN ;
        BEGIN TRANSACTION ;

        UPDATE   dbo.Customers
        SET      Status = @Status
        WHERE    PhoneNumber = @PhoneNumber ;

        IF @@ROWCOUNT > 1
            BEGIN ;
                ROLLBACK ;
                RAISERROR('More than one row updated',
                           16, 1) ;
            END ;
        ELSE
            BEGIN ;
                COMMIT ;
            END ;
    END ;
```

Listing 3-9: A stored procedure that will not modify more than one row.

To see it in action, run Listing 3-10; the stored procedure raises an error and does not modify the data.

```
UPDATE    dbo.Customers
SET       Status = 'Regular' ;

EXEC dbo.SetCustomerStatus
    @PhoneNumber = '(123)456-7890',
    @Status = 'Preferred' ;

Msg 50000, Level 16, State 1, Procedure SetCustomerStatus,
Line 15
More than one row updated
-- verify if the procedure has modified any data
SELECT    CustomerId ,
          Status
FROM      dbo.Customers ;
```

Listing 3-10: Testing the altered stored procedure.

In general, this approach could be useful although, in this particular case, it is less preferable than a unit test. The reason is very simple: a unit test will alert us about a problem *before deployment*, allowing us fix the problem early, and to deploy without this particular bug. The altered stored procedure might not indicate a problem until the code has been deployed to production, which means troubleshooting a production system and redeploying a fix; a situation we usually want to avoid.

Using SET instead of SELECT when assigning variables

In the previous chapter, we discussed how important it is to understand the different behavior of SET and SELECT when assigning values to variables. That same knowledge will help you write application code that is resistant to changes to the underlying schema objects.

Let's consider a second example whereby a search condition contains an implied assumption regarding the uniqueness of the underlying data column. The search condition, and subsequent variable assignment, shown in Listing 3-11 assumes, again, that the PhoneNumber column can uniquely identify a customer.

```
DECLARE @CustomerId INT ;

SELECT   @CustomerId = CustomerId
FROM     dbo.Customers
WHERE    PhoneNumber = '(123)456-7890' ;

SELECT   @CustomerId AS CustomerId ;

-- Do something with CustomerId
```

Listing 3-11: **Unpredictable variable assignment, using SELECT.**

In our original database schema, before we added CountryCode column to the
Customers table, the result of this assignment was predictable. However, in our new
schema, the UNQ_Customers constraint only guarantees the uniqueness of the values
in the PhoneNumber and CountryCode columns, considered together. As a result,
we have two customers with this phone number and so the variable assignment is
unpredictable; we do not, and cannot, know which of the two CustomerId values,
1 or 3, will populate the variable.

In most cases, such ambiguity is not acceptable. The simplest fix is to use SET instead of
SELECT to populate the variable, as shown in Listing 3-12.

```
DECLARE @CustomerId INT ;

-- this assignment will succeed,
-- because in this case there is no ambiguity
SET @CustomerId = ( SELECT CustomerId
                    FROM    dbo.Customers
                    WHERE   PhoneNumber = '(234)123-4567'
                  ) ;

SELECT   @CustomerId AS CustomerId ;

CustomerId
-----------
2
```

```
-- this assignment will fail,
-- because there is ambiguity,
-- two customers have the same phone number
SET @CustomerId = ( SELECT CustomerId
                      FROM   dbo.Customers
                      WHERE  PhoneNumber = '(123)456-7890'
                    ) ;

Msg 512, Level 16, State 1, Line 16
Subquery returned more than 1 value. This is not permitted
when the subquery follows =, !=, <, <= , >, >= or when the
subquery is used as an expression.

-- the above error must be intercepted and handled
-- See Chapter 8
-- the variable is left unchanged
SELECT  @CustomerId AS CustomerId ;

CustomerId
-----------
2
```

Listing 3-12: Whereas SELECT ignores the ambiguity, SET detects it and raises an error.

Surviving Changes to the Signature of a Stored Procedure

Consider the stored procedure shown in Listing 3-13, SelectCustomersByName, which takes two optional search conditions, and selects data from the Customers table, as defined in Listing 3-1.

```
CREATE PROCEDURE dbo.SelectCustomersByName
   @LastName VARCHAR(50) = NULL ,
   @PhoneNumber VARCHAR(50) = NULL
```

```
AS
  BEGIN ;
    SELECT  CustomerId ,
            FirstName ,
            LastName ,
            PhoneNumber ,
            Status
    FROM    dbo.Customers
    WHERE   LastName = COALESCE(@LastName, LastName)
            AND PhoneNumber = COALESCE(@PhoneNumber,
                                         PhoneNumber) ;
  END ;
```

Listing 3-13: The SelectCustomersByName stored procedure.

When we invoke this stored procedure, we can explicitly name its parameters, and make the code more readable, but we are not forced to do so, as shown in Listing 3-14.

```
EXEC dbo.SelectCustomersByName
     'Hansen',              -- @LastName
     '(234)123-4567' ; -- @PhoneNumber

EXEC dbo.SelectCustomersByName
     @LastName = 'Hansen',
     @PhoneNumber = '(234)123-4567' ;
```

Listing 3-14: Two ways to invoke the SelectCustomersByName stored procedure.

At the moment, either way of invoking the stored procedure produces the same result. Suppose, however, that the signature of this stored procedure is subsequently modified to accept an optional @FirstName parameter, as described in Listing 3-15.

```
ALTER PROCEDURE dbo.SelectCustomersByName
   @FirstName VARCHAR(50) = NULL ,
   @LastName VARCHAR(50) = NULL ,
   @PhoneNumber VARCHAR(50) = NULL
```

```
AS
  BEGIN ;
    SELECT  CustomerId ,
      FirstName ,
      LastName ,
      PhoneNumber ,
      Status
    FROM    dbo.Customers
    WHERE   FirstName = COALESCE (@FirstName, FirstName)
            AND LastName = COALESCE (@LastName,LastName)
            AND PhoneNumber = COALESCE (@PhoneNumber,
                                          PhoneNumber) ;
  END ;
GO
```

Listing 3-15: **The modified** `SelectCustomersByName` **stored procedure includes an additional** `FirstName` **parameter.**

As a result of this modification, the two ways of invoking the stored procedure are no longer equivalent. Of course, we will not receive any error message; we will just silently start getting different results, as shown in Listing 3-16.

```
-- in the new context this call is interpreted
-- differently. It will return no rows
EXEC dbo.SelectCustomersByName
    'Hansen',           -- @FirstName
    '(234)123-4567' ; -- @LastName

-- this stored procedure call is equivalent
-- to the previous one
EXEC dbo.SelectCustomersByName
    @FirstName = 'Hansen',
    @LastName = '(234)123-4567' ;
```

```
-- this call returns the required row
EXEC dbo.SelectCustomersByName
    @LastName = 'Hansen',
    @PhoneNumber = '(234)123-4567' ;
```

Listing 3-16: The same stored procedure call is interpreted differently after the signature of that stored procedure has changed.

The lesson here is clear: stored procedure calls with explicitly named parameters are more robust; they continue to work correctly even when the signature of the stored procedure changes, or they give explicit errors instead of silently returning incorrect results.

Surviving Changes to Columns

One of the most common causes of brittle code is a failure to program defensively against subsequent changes to the columns of the underlying data tables. These changes can take the form of adding columns, or changing the definition of existing columns, for example, their data type or size.

Of course, some changes are so serious that our code cannot survive them. For example, if a column that is required in a query is removed, then that is a breaking change that we can do nothing to protect against. However, in many other cases, we can develop code that is resilient to changes to the underlying columns. In this section, we'll examine a few examples, explaining how to make our code more robust in each case.

Qualifying column names

It takes a few extra keystrokes to qualify column names when writing our queries, but these keystrokes pay healthy dividends in terms of the resilience of the resulting code. Consider the example tables created in Listing 3-17, `Shipments` and `ShipmentItems`, populated with sample data.

```
CREATE TABLE dbo.Shipments
    (
      Barcode VARCHAR(30) NOT NULL PRIMARY KEY,
      SomeOtherData VARCHAR(100) NULL
    ) ;
GO


INSERT   INTO dbo.Shipments
         ( Barcode ,
           SomeOtherData
         )
         SELECT  '123456' ,
                 '123456 data'
         UNION ALL
         SELECT  '123654' ,
                 '123654 data' ;
GO


CREATE TABLE dbo.ShipmentItems
    (
      ShipmentBarcode VARCHAR(30) NOT NULL,
      Description VARCHAR(100) NULL
    ) ;
GO


INSERT   INTO dbo.ShipmentItems
         ( ShipmentBarcode ,
           Description
         )
         SELECT  '123456' ,
                 'Some cool widget'
         UNION ALL
         SELECT  '123456' ,
                 'Some cool stuff for some gadget' ;
GO
```

Listing 3-17: The Shipments and ShipmentItems tables.

96

Against this schema, we develop the query shown in Listing 3-18, which, for every shipment, selects its `Barcode` and calculates the number of shipment items with a `ShipmentBarcode` matching the `Barcode` for that shipment.

```
SELECT   Barcode ,
         ( SELECT   COUNT(*)
           FROM     dbo.ShipmentItems
           WHERE    ShipmentBarcode = Barcode
         ) AS NumItems
FROM     dbo.Shipments ;


Barcode                               NumItems
------------------------------------------------
123456                                2
123654                                0
```

Listing 3-18: A correlated subquery that works correctly even though column names are not qualified.

The inner query is an example of a correlated subquery; it uses in its WHERE clause the `Barcode` column from the `Shipments` table in the outer query. Notice that the query works even though we failed to qualify the column names.

Yet the situation can change. Rather than just having a barcode to identify shipments, we start using barcodes to identify individual items in the shipment, so we need to add a `Barcode` column to the `ShipmentItems` table, as shown in Listing 3-19.

```
ALTER TABLE dbo.ShipmentItems
ADD Barcode VARCHAR(30) NULL ;
GO
SELECT   Barcode ,
         ( SELECT   COUNT(*)
           FROM     dbo.ShipmentItems
           WHERE    ShipmentBarcode = Barcode
         ) AS NumItems
FROM     dbo.Shipments ;
```

Barcode	NumItems
123456	0
123654	0

Listing 3-19: **The query works differently when a** Barcode **column is added to the** ShipmentItems **table.**

We do not get any error messages; our query continues to work but silently changes its behavior. With the addition of the Barcode column to the ShipmentItems table, our query is interpreted quite differently. Now, for every shipment, it selects its barcode followed by the number of ShipmentItems whose Barcode value matches their ShipmentBarcode value. In other words, the correlated subquery becomes uncorrelated; the WHERE clause of the inner query no longer uses a value from the outer query.

It takes just a few moments to properly qualify all the column names in our query, and the improved query will continue to work correctly even after the addition of the Barcode column to our ShipmentItems table, as shown in Listing 3-20.

```
SELECT   s.Barcode ,
         ( SELECT    COUNT(*)
           FROM      dbo.ShipmentItems AS i
           WHERE     i.ShipmentBarcode = s.Barcode
         ) AS NumItems
FROM     dbo.Shipments AS s ;
```

Barcode	NumItems
123456	2
123654	0

Listing 3-20: Qualified column names lead to more robust code.

As I hope this example proves, qualifying column names improves the robustness of our queries. The same technique also ensures that you get an error, instead of incorrect results, when a column is removed or when a column name is misspelled. For example, consider the case of an uncorrelated subquery that becomes correlated because a column from a table in the subquery is removed (or misspelled in the query), but happens to match a column in the outer query. Many developers forget that the parser will look in the outer query if it fails to find a match in the inner query.

Handling changes in nullability: NOT IN versus NOT EXISTS

Queries with NOT IN have a well known vulnerability. They do not work as an inexperienced database programmer might expect, if the subquery contained in the NOT IN clause returns at least one NULL. This is easy to demonstrate. In Listing 3-21, we recreate our ShipmentItems table with a Barcode column that does not accept NULLs, and then insert some fresh data. We then execute a query that uses the NOT IN clause.

```
DROP TABLE dbo.ShipmentItems ;
GO

CREATE TABLE dbo.ShipmentItems
    (
        ShipmentBarcode VARCHAR(30) NOT NULL ,
        Description VARCHAR(100) NULL ,
        Barcode VARCHAR(30) NOT NULL
    ) ;
GO


INSERT   INTO dbo.ShipmentItems
         ( ShipmentBarcode ,
           Barcode ,
           Description
         )
         SELECT   '123456' ,
                  '1010203' ,
                  'Some cool widget'
         UNION ALL
```

```
        SELECT  '123654' ,
                '1010203' ,
                'Some cool widget'
        UNION ALL
        SELECT  '123654' ,
                '1010204' ,
                'Some cool stuff for some gadget' ;
GO

-- retrieve all the items from shipment 123654
-- that are not shipped in shipment 123456
SELECT  Barcode
FROM    dbo.ShipmentItems
WHERE   ShipmentBarcode = '123654'
        AND Barcode NOT IN ( SELECT Barcode
                             FROM   dbo.ShipmentItems
                             WHERE  ShipmentBarcode =
                                        '123456' ) ;


Barcode
-------------------------------
1010204
```

Listing 3-21: Creating the new ShipmentItems table, populating it with some test
             data, and proving that the query using the NOT IN clause succeeds.

The query works as expected, and will continue to do so as long as the Barcode column
disallows NULLs. However, let's see what happens when we change the nullability of that
column, as shown in Listing 3-22.

```
ALTER TABLE dbo.ShipmentItems
ALTER COLUMN Barcode VARCHAR(30) NULL ;
INSERT  INTO dbo.ShipmentItems
        ( ShipmentBarcode ,
          Barcode ,
          Description
        )
```

```
        SELECT  '123456' ,
                NULL ,
                'Users manual for some gadget' ;
GO

SELECT  Barcode
FROM    dbo.ShipmentItems
WHERE   ShipmentBarcode = '123654'
        AND Barcode NOT IN ( SELECT Barcode
                             FROM   dbo.ShipmentItems
                             WHERE  ShipmentBarcode =
                                        '123456' ) ;

Barcode
-------------------------------

(0 row(s) affected)
```

Listing 3-22: Now that the Barcode column accepts NULL, our NOT IN query
no longer works as expected.

This can often seem like a very subtle bug; sometimes the query works as expected,
but sometimes it does not. In fact, the behavior is completely consistent. Every time
the subquery inside the NOT IN clause returns at least one NULL, then the query
returns nothing. Listing 3-23 shows a much simpler script that demonstrates this
behavior very clearly.

```
SELECT  CASE WHEN 1 NOT IN ( 2, 3 ) THEN 'True'
             ELSE 'Unknown or False'
        END ,
        CASE WHEN 1 NOT IN ( 2, 3, NULL ) THEN 'True'
             ELSE 'Unknown or False'
        END ;


----------------------
True       Unknown or False
```

Listing 3-23: NOT IN queries will work differently when there are NULLs
in the subquery.

This behavior may seem counterintuitive, but it actually makes perfect sense. Let me explain why, in just two simple steps. Listing 3-24 shows two queries. The first one uses an IN clause; the second is logically equivalent to the first, but the IN clause has been expressed using OR predicates.

```
-- A query using the IN clause:
SELECT  CASE WHEN 1 IN ( 1, 2, NULL ) THEN 'True'
             ELSE 'Unknown or False'
        END ;
-- its logical eqiuvalent using OR
SELECT  CASE WHEN ( 1 = 1 )
                  OR ( 1 = 2 )
                  OR ( 1 = NULL ) THEN 'True'
             ELSE 'Unknown or False'
        END ;
```

Listing 3-24: A query with an IN clause, and a logically equivalent query using OR.

In the second step, we must consider the NOT IN version of our query, convert it to use OR predicates, and then apply DeMorgan's law, which states that for the logical expressions P and Q:

```
NOT(P OR Q) = (NOT P) AND (NOT Q)
```

The result is shown in Listing 3-25.

```
-- A query using the NOT IN clause:
SELECT  CASE WHEN 1 NOT IN ( 1, 2, NULL ) THEN 'True'
             ELSE 'Unknown or False'
        END ;

-- its logical eqiuvalent using OR
SELECT  CASE WHEN NOT ( ( 1 = 1 )
                       OR ( 1 = 2 )
                       OR ( 1 = NULL )
                      ) THEN 'True'
             ELSE 'Unknown or False'
```

```
      END ;
-- applying DeMorgan's law, replacing every OR with AND,
-- and every = with <>
SELECT  CASE WHEN ( ( 1 <> 1 )
                  AND ( 1 <> 2 )
                  AND ( 1 <> NULL )
                ) THEN 'True'
            ELSE 'Unknown or False'
        END ;
```

Listing 3-25: Three equivalent queries, the first using NOT IN, the second using two OR predicates and the third one with two AND predicates.

Take note of the (1<>NULL) condition in the final query; by definition, the result of this condition is always unknown and, when joined with other conditions using AND, the result of the whole expression will always be false. This is why no row can ever qualify a NOT IN condition if the subquery inside that NOT IN returns at least one NULL.

Whenever we write a query using the NOT`IN clause, we implicitly assume that the subquery can never return a NULL. Usually, we do not need to rely on such assumptions, because it is very easy to develop correct queries without making them. For example, Listing 3-26 shows how to remove this assumption from our original SELECT query.

```
SELECT  Barcode
FROM    dbo.ShipmentItems
WHERE   ShipmentBarcode = '123654'
  AND Barcode NOT IN ( SELECT Barcode
                       FROM    dbo.ShipmentItems
                       WHERE   ShipmentBarcode = '123456'
                         AND Barcode IS NOT NULL ) ;
```

Listing 3-26: A query with a subquery that never returns any NULLs.

By adding just one short and simple line to our query, we have improved its robustness. Alternatively, we can develop a query that does not assume anything about the nullability of any columns, as shown in Listing 3-27.

```
-- retrieve all the items from shipment 123654
-- that are not shipped in shipment 123456
SELECT   i.Barcode
FROM     dbo.ShipmentItems AS i
WHERE    i.ShipmentBarcode = '123654'
  AND NOT EXISTS ( SELECT *
                   FROM    dbo.ShipmentItems AS i1
                   WHERE   i1.ShipmentBarcode = '123456'
                     AND i1.Barcode = i.Barcode ) ;
```

Listing 3-27: An equivalent query with NOT EXISTS.

This query will work in the same way, regardless of whether or not the Barcode column is nullable.

Handling changes to data types and sizes

We frequently develop stored procedures with parameters, the types and lengths of which must match the types and lengths of some underlying columns. By way of an example, Listing 3-28 creates a Codes table, and populates it with test data. It then to creates a SelectCode stored procedure with one parameter, @Code, the type and length of which must match the type and length of the Code column in Codes table.

```
DROP TABLE dbo.Codes -- created in previous Chapters
GO

CREATE TABLE dbo.Codes
    (
      Code VARCHAR(5) NOT NULL ,
      Description VARCHAR(40) NOT NULL ,
      CONSTRAINT PK_Codes PRIMARY KEY ( Code )
    ) ;
GO
```

```
INSERT   INTO dbo.Codes
         ( Code ,
           Description
         )
VALUES   ( '12345' ,
           'Description for 12345'
         ) ;
INSERT   INTO dbo.Codes
         ( Code ,
           Description
         )
VALUES   ( '34567' ,
           'Description for 34567'
         ) ;
GO


CREATE PROCEDURE dbo.SelectCode
-- clearly the type and length of this parameter
-- must match  the type and length of Code column
-- in dbo.Codes table
    @Code VARCHAR( 5 )
AS
    SELECT   Code ,
             Description
    FROM     dbo.Codes
    WHERE    Code = @Code ;
GO
```

Listing 3-28: The Codes table and SelectCode stored procedure.

When we execute the stored procedure, supplying an appropriate value for the @Code parameter, the result is as expected, and is shown in Listing 3-29.

```
EXEC dbo.SelectCode @Code = '12345' ;

Code          Description
----------    ----------------------------------------
12345         Description for 12345
```

Listing 3-29: The SelectCode stored procedure works as expected.

Suppose, however, that we have to change the length of the Code column to accept longer values, as shown in Listing 3-30.

```
ALTER TABLE dbo.Codes DROP CONSTRAINT PK_Codes ;
GO

ALTER TABLE dbo.Codes
  ALTER COLUMN Code VARCHAR(10) NOT NULL ;
GO

ALTER TABLE dbo.Codes
ADD CONSTRAINT PK_Codes
PRIMARY KEY(Code) ;
GO

INSERT  INTO dbo.Codes
        ( Code ,
          Description
        )
VALUES  ( '1234567890' ,
          'Description for 1234567890'
        ) ;
```

Listing 3-30: Increasing the length of the Code column and adding a row with maximum Code length.

However, the unmodified stored procedure still expects a VARCHAR(5) parameter, and it silently truncates any longer value, as shown in Listing 3-31.

```
EXEC dbo.SelectCode @Code = '1234567890' ;

Code        Description
----------  ----------------------
12345       Description for 12345
```

Listing 3-31: The unchanged stored procedure retrieves the wrong row.

Such bugs are quite subtle, and may take considerable time to troubleshoot. How can we prevent such errors, except for manually referring to a data dictionary every time we change column types? The best way, in my opinion, is to document the requirement that the type and lengths of our stored procedure parameters must match the type and lengths of our columns and then incorporate this requirement into a boundary case unit test, to protect us from such errors.

Summary

In this chapter, we have seen how changes in database objects may break our code, and discussed several defensive techniques that improve the robustness of our code, so that it better survives changes in other database objects. Specifically, I hope you've learned the following lessons in defensive programming:

- how to test the continuing validity of your assumptions about the characteristics of the underlying primary and unique keys

- why using SET is generally safer than using SELECT when assigning values to variables

- the importance of explicitly named parameters in stored procedure calls

- the need to qualify column names in queries

- why NOT EXISTS leads to more resilient queries than NOT IN

- the importance of testing and validating even the "obvious" assumptions, such as the need for the types and length of parameters to match those of the underlying columns.

Chapter 4: When Upgrading Breaks Code

In previous chapters, we have discussed the sort of weaknesses that might exist in your code that, if left unchecked, will undermine its consistency and reliability, and make it vulnerable to breaking when, for example, environmental settings are changed, or objects in the underlying schema are modified. The goal of the defensive programmer is to root out as many of these weaknesses as possible and remove them, *before the potential problems even arise.*

However, there are times when potential changes cannot be foreseen and so we cannot "weatherproof" our code against them; we cannot know in advance, for example, how use of a new feature might affect our existing code when we do not know what these new features are, and how they behave.

A SQL Server upgrade is always a time of concern for the applications that use it, and for the developers of those applications. It's a time when the defensive programmer must proactively research how existing applications will behave when the new database settings or features are enabled, investigate how these features can be implemented in the most robust way possible, and then revisit and revise existing code as appropriate.

This chapter does not, and cannot, provide a complete list of new features in SQL Server 2005 and 2008 that could potentially break existing code. Instead, it is intended as an eye-opener, an encouragement to analyze fully how new features work with existing code, before using these new features in production. In order to demonstrate the difficulties that can arise, we'll discuss the following new features, both of which are highly useful, and so are very likely to be used, but yet may break existing code:

- snapshot isolation (new in 2005)
- MERGE statement (new in 2008).

Understanding Snapshot Isolation

The default transaction isolation level in SQL Server is READ COMMITTED, which prevents statements from reading data that has been modified by another transaction, but not committed. Most applications are developed to run in this mode. However, in order to enforce this mode, SQL Server has to use shared and exclusive locks in order to prevent data being read that is currently being modified by another connection, and to prevent other transactions modifying data that is currently being read. If a statement running under READ COMMITTED isolation level encounters data that is being modified by another transaction, it must wait until those changes are either committed or rolled back before proceeding. This can limit concurrency. Furthermore, as will be demonstrated in Chapters 9 and 10, under conditions of high concurrency, the READ COMMITTED mode can return inconsistent results.

SQL Server 2005 introduced the new snapshot isolation levels, with the goal of "enhancing concurrency for OLTP applications." It is well beyond the scope of this book to offer a full explanation of how the snapshot isolation levels work, and I refer you to Books Online for that. However, the essential difference is that under snapshot isolation, SQL Server maintains in tempdb a time-stamped "version store" of all data changes since the beginning of the oldest outstanding transaction. Instead of blocking when it encounters an exclusive lock, a reader transaction will simply "read around" the lock, retrieving from the version store the version of the row consistent with a certain point in time. Snapshot isolation introduces two new modes of operation:

- SNAPSHOT mode – queries running in this mode return committed data as of the beginning of the transaction

- READ_COMMITTED_SNAPSHOT mode – queries return committed data as of the beginning of the current statement.

To demonstrate how snapshot isolation works, it first has to be enabled, as shown in Listing 4-1. Note that it is enabled at the database level and, because we cannot use either of the types of snapshot isolation in tempdb, be sure to choose a database other than tempdb for these examples.

```
-- Replace Test with the name of your database
-- in both commands and make sure that no other
-- connections are accessing the database
```

```
-- as a result of this command,
-- READ_COMMITTED_SNAPSHOT becomes
-- the default isolation level.
ALTER DATABASE Test  SET READ_COMMITTED_SNAPSHOT ON ;
GO

-- as a result of this command,
-- we can explitly specify that SNAPSHOT is
-- the current isolation level,
-- but it does not affect the default behavior.
ALTER DATABASE Test  SET ALLOW_SNAPSHOT_ISOLATION ON ;
GO
```

Listing 4-1: Enabling snapshot isolation.

Next, create the TestTable table, for use in our example.

```
CREATE TABLE dbo.TestTable
    (
       ID INT NOT NULL
               PRIMARY KEY ,
       Comment VARCHAR(100) NOT NULL
    ) ;
GO
INSERT  INTO dbo.TestTable
        ( ID ,
          Comment
        )
VALUES  ( 1 ,
          'row committed before transaction began'
        ) ;
```

Listing 4-2: Creating and populating TestTable.

Open a tab in SSMS and start a transaction that inserts one more row into the table, and keep the transaction open.

```
BEGIN TRANSACTION ;
INSERT   INTO dbo.TestTable
         ( ID ,
           Comment
         )
VALUES   ( 2 ,
             'row committed after transaction began'
         ) ;

-- COMMIT ;
```

Listing 4-3: Tab 1, an open transaction that inserts a row into `TestTable`.

Without snapshot isolation, a query may be blocked if some of the data it needs to read is locked. To demonstrate this, open a second tab and run the code in Listing 4-4.

```
SET TRANSACTION ISOLATION LEVEL REPEATABLE READ ;

SELECT   ID ,
         Comment
FROM     dbo.TestTable ;
-- This statement hangs in lock-waiting state.
-- Cancel the query.
```

Listing 4-4: Tab 2, when not using snapshot isolation, a query is blocked by the outstanding transaction in Tab 1.

Cancel the query in Tab 2, and run it again under **SNAPSHOT** isolation level, as shown in Listing 4-5.

```
IF @@TRANCOUNT = 0
    BEGIN ;
        SET TRANSACTION ISOLATION LEVEL SNAPSHOT ;
        PRINT 'Beginning transaction' ;
        BEGIN TRANSACTION ;
    END ;
```

```
SELECT   ID ,
         Comment
FROM     dbo.TestTable ;
--COMMIT ;


Beginning transaction

ID               Comment
-----------      ----------------------------------------
1                Row committed before transaction began


(1 row(s) affected)
```

Listing 4-5: Tab 2, when using snapshot isolation, the same query completes.

The same query under READ_COMMITTED_SNAPSHOT also completes, and the output is exactly the same as in the previous listing. Open a new tab and run the script shown in Listing 4-6.

```
IF @@TRANCOUNT = 0
    BEGIN ;
-- this is actually READ_COMMITTED_SNAPSHOT because
-- we have already set READ_COMMITTED_SNAPSHOT to ON
        SET TRANSACTION ISOLATION LEVEL READ COMMITTED ;
        PRINT 'Beginning transaction' ;
        BEGIN TRANSACTION ;
    END ;

SELECT   ID ,
         Comment
FROM     dbo.TestTable ;

--COMMIT ;
```

Listing 4-6: Tab 3, when using READ_COMMITTED_SNAPSHOT isolation, the query also completes right away.

So far, the queries return exactly the same results under either SNAPSHOT or READ_COMMITTED_SNAPSHOT mode. To observe the difference between the two modes, return to Tab 1 (Listing 4-3) and commit the modification. Go to Tab 2 (Listing 4-5), which is running in SNAPSHOT mode, and rerun the query. Since we started the initial transaction before the addition of the second row was committed, only the row committed before the transaction began is returned. Now go to Tab 3 (Listing 4-6), which is running in SNAPSHOT_READ_COMMITTED mode, and rerun the query. Since the second row was committed before the statement was run, both rows will be returned.

As a final clean up, highlight and execute COMMIT in the tabs for Listings 4-5 and 4-6.

When Snapshot Isolation Breaks Code

Queries that may previously have been blocked, in lock-waiting state, under traditional isolation levels, can complete when running under the snapshot isolation levels. This feature is highly useful in many situations but, unfortunately, it may in some cases break existing code, such as triggers.

The following example demonstrates a typical scenario where triggers are used to enforce a business rule that involves rows in different tables. The triggers, previously working normally, begin to intermittently fail when they run under snapshot isolation. Note that, although I have chosen triggers to demonstrate the problem, I could just as easily provide similar examples using stored procedures. In other words, triggers are no more or less vulnerable to this issue than stored procedures.

Suppose that we need to implement two business rules, expressed as follows:

- developers cannot go on vacation if they have active tickets assigned to them

- inactive tickets cannot be changed to active status if they are assigned to developers who are on vacation.

We are going to use triggers to implement these business rules. As noted, this is not the only implementation option, but it is a very common approach. Listing 4-7 creates the Developers and Tickets tables that form the basis of our implementation. Let me repeat that these examples should be not be run in the tempdb database.

```
CREATE TABLE dbo.Developers
  (
     DeveloperID INT NOT NULL ,
     FirstName VARCHAR(30) NOT NULL ,
     Lastname VARCHAR(30) NOT NULL ,
     Status VARCHAR(10) NOT NULL ,
     CONSTRAINT PK_Developers PRIMARY KEY (DeveloperID) ,
     CONSTRAINT CHK_Developers_Status CHECK ( Status IN
                                              ( 'Active',
                                           'Vacation' ) )
  ) ;
GO
CREATE TABLE dbo.Tickets
  (
     TicketID INT NOT NULL ,
     AssignedToDeveloperID INT NULL ,
     Description VARCHAR(50) NOT NULL ,
     Status VARCHAR(10) NOT NULL ,
     CONSTRAINT PK_Tickets PRIMARY KEY ( TicketID ) ,
     CONSTRAINT FK_Tickets_Developers
       FOREIGN KEY ( AssignedToDeveloperID )
         REFERENCES dbo.Developers ( DeveloperID ) ,
     CONSTRAINT CHK_Tickets_Status
       CHECK ( Status IN ( 'Active', 'Closed' ) )
  ) ;
```

Listing 4-7: Creating the Developers and Tickets tables.

Note that, thanks to our **FOREIGN KEY** constraint, FK_Tickets_Developers, newly added developers cannot have tickets assigned to them. We only need to make sure our rules are enforced at the point when a developer's status is updated. Therefore, on the Developers table, we create an **AFTER UPDATE** trigger, as shown in Listing 4-8. It is designed to make sure that developers cannot go on vacation if they have active tickets assigned to them.

115

```
CREATE TRIGGER dbo.Developers_Upd ON dbo.Developers
    AFTER UPDATE
AS
    BEGIN ;
        IF EXISTS ( SELECT  *
                    FROM    inserted AS i
                            INNER JOIN dbo.Tickets AS t
                            ON i.DeveloperID =
                                t.AssignedToDeveloperID
                    WHERE   i.Status = 'Vacation'
                            AND t.Status = 'Active' )
            BEGIN ;

-- this string has been wrapped for readability here
-- it appears on a single line in the code download file
                RAISERROR ('Developers must assign their
                            active tickets to someone
                            else before going on
                            vacation', 16, 1 ) ;
                ROLLBACK ;
            END ;
    END ;
```

Listing 4-8: The `Developers_Upd` trigger.

Similarly, on the `Tickets` table, we create an **AFTER UPDATE** trigger, as shown in
Listing 4-9. It is designed to make sure that inactive tickets cannot be changed to active
status if they are assigned to developers who are on vacation. In a complete solution,
we would also need to create an **AFTER INSERT** trigger to ensure that it is impossible
to insert a new ticket with active status and assign it to a developer who is on vacation.
However, we will focus only on the **AFTER UPDATE** trigger here.

```
CREATE TRIGGER dbo.Tickets_Upd ON dbo.Tickets
    AFTER UPDATE
AS
    BEGIN ;
        IF EXISTS (SELECT *
```

```
                        FROM    inserted AS i
                                INNER JOIN dbo.Developers AS d
                                ON i.AssignedToDeveloperID =
                                                d.DeveloperID
                        WHERE   d.Status = 'Vacation'
                                AND i.Status = 'Active' )
                BEGIN ;
                    RAISERROR ( 'Cannot change status to
                            Active if the developer in
                            charge is on vacation',
                        16, 1 ) ;
                    ROLLBACK ;
                END ;
        END ;
```

Listing 4-9: The `Tickets_Upd` trigger.

Trigger behavior in normal READ COMMITTED mode

Let's test these triggers out under the default **READ COMMITTED** isolation level. First of all, we need to make sure that we are not running under **READ_COMMITTED_SNAPSHOT** isolation level, as shown in Listing 4-10.

```
-- Replace Test with the name of your database
-- it must not be tempdb

-- Before running this code, close or disconnect any
-- tabs conneted to the same database

ALTER DATABASE Test SET READ_COMMITTED_SNAPSHOT OFF ;
```

Listing 4-10: Make sure that `READ_COMMITTED_SNAPSHOT` is turned off.

Next, add some test data to our tables, as shown in Listing 4-11.

```
INSERT INTO dbo.Developers
        (
          DeveloperID,
          FirstName,
          Lastname,
          Status
        )
        SELECT  1,
                'Arnie',
                'Brown',
                'Active'
        UNION ALL
        SELECT  2,
                'Carol',
                'Dale',
                'Active' ;
GO
INSERT  INTO dbo.Tickets
        (
          TicketID,
          AssignedToDeveloperID,
          Description,
          Status
        )
        SELECT  1,
                1,
                'Order entry form blows up',
                'Active'
        UNION ALL
        SELECT  2,
                2,
                'Incorrect totals in monthly report',
                'Closed' ;
```

Listing 4-11: Adding test data to the Developers and Tickets tables.

Our test data includes one developer (Arnie) who is currently active and has one active ticket assigned to him, so we can test what happens if Arnie attempts to go on holiday without assigning his ticket to someone else. Apparently, under READ COMMITTED isolation level, our Developers_Upd trigger prevents violation of this business rule, as shown in Listing 4-12.

```
SET TRANSACTION ISOLATION LEVEL READ COMMITTED ;
UPDATE   dbo.Developers
SET      Status = 'Vacation'
WHERE    DeveloperID = 1 ;


Msg 50000, Level 16, State 1, Procedure Developers_Upd, Line
11
Developers must assign their active tickets to someone else
before going on vacation
Msg 3609, Level 16, State 1, Line 2
The transaction ended in the trigger. The batch has been
aborted.
```

Listing 4-12: Testing the Developers_Upd trigger.

Similarly, our dbo.Tickets_Upd trigger ensures that inactive tickets cannot be changed to active status if they are assigned to developers who are on vacation, as shown in Listing 4-13.

```
SET TRANSACTION ISOLATION LEVEL READ COMMITTED ;

-- make sure Carol's ticket is closed
UPDATE   dbo.Tickets
SET      Status = 'Closed'
WHERE    TicketID = 2 ;

-- Carol can now go on vacation
UPDATE   dbo.Developers
SET      Status = 'Vacation'
WHERE    DeveloperID = 2 ;
```

```
-- can we reopen Carol's ticket?
UPDATE    dbo.Tickets
SET       Status = 'Active'
WHERE     TicketID = 2 ;
(1 row(s) affected)


(1 row(s) affected)
Msg 50000, Level 16, State 1, Procedure Tickets_Upd, Line 10
Cannot change status to Active if the developer in charge is
on vacation
Msg 3609, Level 16, State 1, Line 10
The transaction ended in the trigger. The batch has been
aborted.
```

Listing 4-13: Testing out the Tickets_Upd trigger.

So, it looks like our triggers work and our two business rules are enforced. However, so far we have only tested them from a single connection. What happens when we have concurrent access, so our triggers are being fired from multiple connections?

To mimic real life concurrency, we'll begin two transactions in two tabs, but not commit them. That will ensure that two modifications are active at the same time. In one tab, run the script shown in Listing 4-14, which first resets the test data to ensure Arnie's ticket is closed, and then starts the test transaction, which will send him on vacation.

```
-- Tab 1
-- reset the test data; close Arnie's ticket
UPDATE    dbo.Tickets
SET       Status = 'Closed'
WHERE     TicketID = 1 ;

-- start the transaction that sends Arnie on vacation
SET TRANSACTION ISOLATION LEVEL READ COMMITTED ;
BEGIN TRANSACTION ;
```

```
UPDATE   dbo.Developers
SET      Status = 'Vacation'
WHERE    DeveloperID = 1 ;

-- COMMIT ;
```

Listing 4-14: Arnie is on vacation, but the change has not committed yet.

Note that, when this script has finished, the transaction opened by this connection is still outstanding, because we have neither committed it nor rolled it back. In a second tab, try to reopen the ticket assigned to Arnie, as shown in Listing 4-15.

```
-- Tab 2
SET TRANSACTION ISOLATION LEVEL READ COMMITTED ;
BEGIN TRANSACTION ;
UPDATE   dbo.Tickets
SET      Status = 'Active'
WHERE    TicketID = 1 ;

-- COMMIT ;
```

Listing 4-15: Attempting to reopen a ticket assigned to Arnie.

This script will not complete; it will stay in lock-waiting state, because the Tickets_Upd trigger needs to read the Developers table and find out whether Arnie is active or on vacation, and that row has been changed and is locked by the transaction in the first tab (Listing 4-14).

Go back to the first tab, and commit the outstanding transaction. The script in the second tab will immediately fail with the same error message as shown in Listing 4-13, which is the expected behavior.

Trigger behavior in SNAPSHOT mode

In fact, our triggers work in all the versions of SQL Server prior to SQL Server 2005. However, in SQL Server 2005, our triggers may fail when working in either READ_ COMMITTED_SNAPSHOT or SNAPSHOT isolation mode.

This is very easy to demonstrate, simply by rerunning the previous example in SNAPSHOT isolation mode. If you haven't done so already, then you'll first need to enable SNAPSHOT isolation by running the ALTER DATABASE Test SET ALLOW_SNAPSHOT_ ISOLATION ON command from Listing 4-1.

In one tab, run the script shown in Listing 4-16, which first resets the test data so that all tickets are closed, one developer (Arnie) is currently active, and the other (Carol) is on vacation. It then starts (but does not commit) a transaction that sets Arnie's status to Vacation.

```
-- Tab 1
SET TRANSACTION ISOLATION LEVEL SNAPSHOT ;

-- reset the  test data
UPDATE   dbo.Tickets
SET      Status = 'Closed'
WHERE    TicketID = 1 ;
UPDATE   dbo.Developers
SET      Status = 'Active'
WHERE    DeveloperID = 1 ;

-- begin the transaction
BEGIN TRANSACTION ;
UPDATE   dbo.Developers
SET      Status = 'Vacation'
WHERE    DeveloperID = 1 ;

-- COMMIT ;
```

Listing 4-16: The code in Tab 1 begins a transaction to set Arnie's status to Vacation.

In the second tab, reopen the closed ticket, as shown in Listing 4-17.

```
-- Tab 2
SET TRANSACTION ISOLATION LEVEL SNAPSHOT ;
BEGIN TRANSACTION ;
UPDATE    dbo.Tickets
SET       Status = 'Active'
WHERE     TicketID = 1 ;

-- COMMIT ;
```

Listing 4-17: The code in Tab 2 starts a transaction to reopen a ticket that is assigned to Arnie.

This time, under SNAPSHOT isolation level, this script also completes. The reason is simple: under SNAPSHOT isolation writers do not block readers; when the SELECT statement in the Tickets_Upd trigger executes, SQL Server detects that the required row is subject to pending changes and so retrieves from the "version store" the row as it existed at the time the transaction started.

In other words, from the perspective of Tickets_Upd trigger Arnie's status is still Active (I shall prove this shortly).

To complete the example, commit the transactions in both tabs and, as you can see in Listing 4-18, our data now violates our business rules.

```
SELECT    d.DeveloperID,
          d.Status AS DeveloperStatus,
          t.TicketID,
          t.Status AS TicketStatus
FROM      dbo.Developers AS d
          INNER JOIN dbo.Tickets AS t
              ON t.AssignedToDeveloperID = d.DeveloperID ;
```

DeveloperID	DeveloperStatus	TicketID	TicketStatus
1	Vacation	1	Active
2	Vacation	2	Closed

Listing 4-18: Data integrity is violated; we have an active ticket assigned to the developer who is on vacation.

To prove that the `Tickets_Upd` trigger does not see the uncommitted changes from another transaction, we can embed a query in the trigger's body that will show exactly what data our trigger sees. Of course, this embedded query is for troubleshooting only and should never be included in production code.

```
ALTER TRIGGER dbo.Tickets_Upd ON dbo.Tickets
    AFTER UPDATE
AS
    BEGIN ;
        SELECT  d.DeveloperID ,
                d.Status AS DeveloperStatus ,
                t.TicketID ,
                t.Status AS TicketStatus
        FROM    dbo.Developers AS d
                INNER JOIN inserted AS t
            ON t.AssignedToDeveloperID = d.DeveloperID ;

        IF EXISTS (SELECT *
                   FROM  inserted AS i
                         INNER JOIN dbo.Developers AS d
                         ON i.AssignedToDeveloperID =
                                        d.DeveloperID
                        WHERE   d.Status = 'Vacation'
                        AND i.Status = 'Active' )
                BEGIN ;
```

```
            RAISERROR ( 'Cannot change status to
                         Active if the developer in
                         charge is on vacation',
                    16, 1 ) ;
            ROLLBACK ;
        END ;
    END ;
```

Listing 4-19: Modifying the `Tickets_Upd` trigger so that it reports the data, as it sees it, in the `Developers` table.

Now, simply run through the example again, running Listing 4-16 in one tab, resetting the test data and then starting a transaction to set Arnie's status to "vacation," and Listing 4-20 in a second tab.

```
SET TRANSACTION ISOLATION LEVEL SNAPSHOT ;
BEGIN TRANSACTION ;
UPDATE    dbo.Tickets
SET       Status = 'Active'
WHERE     TicketID = 1 ;

-- COMMIT ;

DeveloperID DeveloperStatus TicketID     TicketStatus
----------- --------------- -----------  ------------
1           Active          1            Active
```

Listing 4-20: The `Tickets_Upd` trigger does not see the uncommitted changes from the other transaction.

Clearly the `Tickets_Upd` trigger is not blocked by the modification in the first tab; it just reads the corresponding row in the `Developers` table as it existed at the time the transaction began.

Before moving on, remember to commit (or roll back) both of the open transactions.

Building more robust triggers?

Our example has demonstrated that triggers that work perfectly well under traditional isolation levels can fail when using the new snapshot isolation level. Could we have developed more robust triggers; ones that continue to enforce our business rules under snapshot isolation? In this case, I do not think so. We might have been completely unaware of snapshot isolation at the time we were developing our triggers.

However, at the point that we plan to implement a new feature, such as snapshot isolation, we need to be fully aware of all the downstream ramifications of using it, and look for ways to either ensure our triggers function correctly, or find an alternative way to enforce our business rules. In this case, the fix takes the form of a very simple modification to our `Tickets_Upd` trigger, to add the `READCOMMITTEDLOCK` hint, as shown in Listing 4-21. Note that we also remove our previous "troubleshooting" query.

```
ALTER TRIGGER dbo.Tickets_Upd ON dbo.Tickets
    AFTER UPDATE
AS
    BEGIN ;
        IF EXISTS (SELECT *
                    FROM   inserted AS i
                           INNER JOIN dbo.Developers AS d
                           WITH ( READCOMMITTEDLOCK )
                           ON i.AssignedToDeveloperID =
                                            d.DeveloperID
                    WHERE   d.Status = 'Vacation'
                    AND i.Status = 'Active' )
            BEGIN ;
                RAISERROR ( 'Cannot change status to
                            Active if the developer in
                            charge is on vacation',
                        16, 1 ) ;
                ROLLBACK ;
            END ;
    END ;
```

Listing 4-21: Adding the `READCOMMITTEDLOCK` hint to the `Tickets_Upd` trigger.

The READCOMMITTEDLOCK hint in the body of our trigger ensures that the query to which it applies, against the Developers table, runs under the READ COMMITTED isolation level. If we rerun our tests, the Tickets_Upd trigger behaves under SNAPSHOT isolation level exactly as it does under READ COMMITTED isolation level.

Alternatively, presented in Chapter 7, *Advanced Use of Constraints*, is a rather advanced, non-trigger-based solution to this type of problem. It uses constraints and, at the time of writing, works consistently under all isolation levels.

Before moving on, commit or roll back any outstanding transactions and then re-establish READ COMMITTED as our default isolation level, by rerunning Listing 4-10.

Understanding MERGE

The MERGE statement was introduced in SQL Server 2008 as a way to allow us to both insert new rows and update or delete existing ones, in a single command. The following simple example should demonstrate how it works, for those unfamiliar with it. First, we need a table and some test data.

```
CREATE TABLE dbo.FrontPageArticles
    (
        ArticleID INT NOT NULL PRIMARY KEY ,
        Title VARCHAR(30) NOT NULL ,
        Author VARCHAR(30) NULL ,
        NumberOfViews INT NOT NULL
    ) ;
GO
INSERT  dbo.FrontPageArticles
        ( ArticleID ,
          Title ,
          Author ,
          NumberOfViews
        )
```

```
VALUES  ( 1 ,
            'Road Construction on Rt 59' ,
            'Lynn Lewis' ,
            0
        ) ;
```

Listing 4-22: The `FrontPageArticles` table, with test data.

The MERGE command shown in Listing 4-23 will update the existing article and insert a new one.

```
MERGE dbo.FrontPageArticles AS target
    USING
        ( SELECT  1 AS ArticleID ,
                    'Road Construction on Rt 53' AS Title
          UNION ALL
          SELECT  2 AS ArticleID ,
                    'Residents are reaching out' AS Title
        ) AS source ( ArticleID, Title )
    ON ( target.ArticleID = source.ArticleID )
    WHEN MATCHED
        THEN  UPDATE
          SET  Title = source.Title
    WHEN NOT MATCHED
        THEN INSERT
                    (
                    ArticleID ,
                    Title ,
                    NumberOfViews
                    )
            VALUES  ( source.ArticleID ,
                    source.Title ,
                    0
                    ) ;
SELECT  ArticleID ,
        Title ,
        NumberOfViews
```

```
FROM     dbo.FrontPageArticles ;

ArticleID   Title                               NumberOfViews
----------- ----------------------------------  --------------
1           Road Construction on Rt 53          0
2           Residents are reaching out          0
```

Listing 4-23: Demonstrating the MERGE command (SQL 2008 and upwards).

Issues When Triggers Using @@ROWCOUNT are Fired by MERGE

The MERGE statement is a powerful new feature but, again, we need to be mindful of its use alongside existing code. In this example, I will demonstrate how a previously working trigger may start to misbehave when called from a MERGE statement.

Consider the trigger shown in Listing 4-24, designed to prevent the deletion of more than one row at a time from the FrontPageArticles table.

```
CREATE TRIGGER CannotDeleteMoreThanOneArticle
  ON dbo.FrontPageArticles
    FOR DELETE
AS
    BEGIN ;
        IF @@ROWCOUNT > 1
            BEGIN ;
                RAISERROR ( 'Cannot Delete More Than One
                            Row', 16, 1 ) ;
            END ;
    END ;
```

Listing 4-24: Creating the CannotDeleteMoreThanOneRow trigger.

We can test out our trigger using the code shown in Listing 4-25.

```
-- this fails. We cannot delete more than one row:
BEGIN TRY ;
    BEGIN TRAN ;
    DELETE  FROM dbo.FrontPageArticles ;
    PRINT 'Previous command failed;this will not print';
    COMMIT ;
END TRY
BEGIN CATCH ;
    SELECT  ERROR_MESSAGE() ;
    ROLLBACK ;
END CATCH ;

-- this succeeds:
BEGIN TRY ;
    BEGIN TRAN ;
    DELETE  FROM dbo.FrontPageArticles
    WHERE   ArticleID = 1 ;
    PRINT 'The second DELETE completed' ;
-- we are rolling back the change, because
-- we still need the original data in the next listing
    ROLLBACK ;
END TRY
BEGIN CATCH ;
    SELECT  ERROR_MESSAGE() ;
    ROLLBACK ;
END CATCH ;
```

Listing 4-25: Our trigger allows us to delete one row, but prevents us from deleting two rows.

So, we have proven that the trigger works when it is fired by a DELETE command. Note that our trigger implicitly assumes that @@ROWCOUNT is equal to the number of rows being deleted. Prior to SQL Server 2008, issuing a DELETE command is the only way to fire an AFTER DELETE trigger, so this assumption is correct.

In SQL Server 2008, however, we can also fire this trigger by executing a MERGE command. After a MERGE command completes, @@ROWCOUNT is set to the total number of rows affected by it, including inserted, updated, and deleted rows. Therefore, our assumption is no longer correct and our trigger is broken, as is shown in the following example.

The intent of the MERGE command shown in Listing 4-26 is to modify one row and delete exactly one row, yet the trigger mistakenly interprets this command as an attempt to delete two rows, because @@ROWCOUNT is set to 2.

```
BEGIN TRY ;
    BEGIN TRAN ;

    MERGE dbo.FrontPageArticles AS target
        USING
            ( SELECT  2 AS ArticleID ,
                    'Residents are reaching out!' AS Title
            ) AS source ( ArticleID, Title )
        ON ( target.ArticleID = source.ArticleID )
        WHEN MATCHED
            THEN UPDATE
            SET Title = source.Title
        WHEN NOT MATCHED BY SOURCE
            THEN DELETE ;

    PRINT 'MERGE Completed' ;

    SELECT  ArticleID ,
            Title ,
            NumberOfViews
    FROM    dbo.FrontPageArticles ;

-- we are rolling back the change, because
-- we still need the original data in the next examples.
    ROLLBACK ;
END TRY
```

```
BEGIN CATCH ;
    SELECT  ERROR_MESSAGE() ;
    ROLLBACK ;
END CATCH ;


Cannot Delete More Than One Row
```

Listing 4-26: The MERGE command intends to delete only one row (and to modify another one) but falls foul of our trigger. These commands run only on SQL 2008 and upwards.

Let us drop the trigger altogether, as shown in Listing 4-27.

```
DROP TRIGGER dbo.CannotDeleteMoreThanOneArticle ;
```

Listing 4-27: Dropping the trigger before rerunning the MERGE command.

And now we can rerun the code from Listing 4-26 and see that this MERGE command modified one row and deleted only one row, so it should **not** have failed.

We have proved that, when we start using MERGE, some of our triggers may malfunction. Again, assuming this trigger was developed prior to SQL Server 2008, I would argue that there is little the developer could have done at the time to anticipate that it might no longer work in a later version. However, at the point where we upgrade to SQL Server 2008, the defensive programmer must get to work investigating how the use of MERGE might affect existing code, and fixing the issues that are found.

In this case, the fix is quite straightfoward, as shown in Listing 4-28. Rather than rely on @@ROWCOUNT, we simply query the deleted table to ensure that we are not deleting more than one row at a time.

```
CREATE TRIGGER CannotDeleteMoreThanOneArticle
  ON dbo.FrontPageArticles
    FOR DELETE
AS
    BEGIN ;
```

```
-- these two queries are provided for better
-- understanding of the contents of inserted and deleted
-- virtual tables.
-- They should be removed before deploying!
        SELECT  ArticleID ,
                Title
        FROM    inserted ;


        SELECT  ArticleID ,
                Title
        FROM    deleted ;


        IF ( SELECT COUNT(*)
             FROM    deleted
           ) > 1
           BEGIN ;
                RAISERROR ( 'Cannot Delete More Than One
                            Row', 16, 1 ) ;
           END ;
    END ;
```

Listing 4-28: The improved trigger.

To test this trigger, just rerun Listings 4-25 and 4-26; they both produce the expected results, proving that now the trigger works when it is fired by our MERGE command as well as when it is fired by DELETE.

Summary

Hopefully the examples in this chapter have clearly demonstrated that when we start using new features, we can break our existing code. When we upgrade our servers, it is important that the defensive programmer researches all of the downstream ramifications before deciding when and how to use the new features.

Specifically, I hope you've learned the following lessons in defensive programming:

- code that works perfectly when using READ COMMITTED isolation level, may fail to correctly enforce business rules under SNAPSHOT or READ_COMMITTED_SNAPSHOT isolation

- code that uses @@ROWCOUNT may behave incorrectly when used after a MERGE statement.

Chapter 5: Reusing T-SQL Code

Often, we have code that works perfectly well for a particular purpose, and then we find that we need to implement some very similar functionality in another database. It is all too tempting to just copy the code, adapt it to meet the new requirements, and then deploy this slightly modified code. However, every time we copy and paste code in this manner, we are exposed to the following risk: the requirements change, and we fail to change the code in both places.

Whenever evidence of repetition is found in the code base, a defensive programmer should seek to refactor, so that the code to tackle a given problem or enforce a given rule is implemented in one place only. In other words, common logic should be refactored into a single reusable code unit, in the form of a constraint, stored procedure, trigger, user-defined function (UDF), or index. Whichever approach we use in each particular case, this proper form of code reuse reduces the possibility of bugs and is a vitally important part of defensive programming.

Unfortunately, many developers find it difficult to choose the correct implementation for the given requirement; in this chapter I will offer some useful pointers as to the approach that will lead to the most defensive, and therefore robust, code. We must, as always, benchmark our solutions because the one that most conveniently promotes reuse is not necessarily the one that will perform the best.

Specifically, this chapter will cover:

- why copy-and-paste will get you into trouble

- how proper code reuse will help

- using views to encapsulate simple queries

- using UDFs to encapsulate parameterized queries; and why UDFs may sometimes be preferable to stored procedures for this requirement

- potential performance issues with UDFs

- using constraints, triggers and filtered indexes to implement business logic in one place.

The Dangers of Copy-and-Paste

The biggest problem with copy-and-paste as a means of solving a set of similar problems is that, of course, it leads to code duplication. In turn, this means that we need to maintain multiples copies of essentially the same code, but with each copy subtly modified to suit a particular need. The real danger arises when requirements change, and we need to make sure that this is reflected, not just in the original code, but in all the subsequent copies. We can easily demonstrate this risk with an example. Listing 5-1 creates the Sales table and loads it with some test data.

```
CREATE TABLE dbo.Sales
  (
    SalesID INT NOT NULL
                IDENTITY
                PRIMARY KEY ,
    StateCode CHAR(2) NOT NULL ,
    SaleDateTime DATETIME NOT NULL ,
    Amount DECIMAL(10, 2) NOT NULL
  ) ;
GO
SET NOCOUNT ON ;
DECLARE @d DATETIME ,
  @i INT ;
SET @d = '20091002' ;
SET @i = 0 ;
WHILE @i < 40
  BEGIN ;
    INSERT INTO dbo.Sales
            ( StateCode ,
              SaleDateTime ,
              Amount
            )
            SELECT 'CA' ,
                   @d ,
                   case WHEN @d <'20091001' THEN 5000000
                        ELSE 5000
                   END
```

```
          UNION ALL
          SELECT 'OR' ,
                  @d ,
                  case WHEN @d <'20091001' THEN 1000000
                       ELSE 1000
                    END ;
  SELECT  @d = DATEADD(day, -1, @d) ,
          @i = @i + 1 ;
  END ;
```

Listing 5-1: Creating the Sales table and populating it with test data.

Listing 5-2 shows the stored procedure, SelectTotalSalesPerStateForMonth, which returns the **total** sales per state for a given month.

```
CREATE PROCEDURE dbo.SelectTotalSalesPerStateForMonth
  @AsOfDate DATETIME
AS
  SELECT  SUM(Amount) AS SalesPerState ,
          StateCode
  FROM    dbo.Sales
-- month begins on the first calendar day of the month
  WHERE SaleDateTime >= DATEADD(month,
                                DATEDIFF(month, '19900101',
                                         @AsOfDate),
                          '19900101')
          AND SaleDateTime <= @AsOfDate
  GROUP BY StateCode ;
```

Listing 5-2: The SelectTotalSalesPerStateForMonth stored procedure.

At the time we developed this code, our understanding of a report "for a given month" is one that covers the period of time from the first calendar day of the month until the day we run the report. For this purpose, our stored procedure serves the customers' needs well, and we soon receive a request for a similar report, returning the **average** sales per state, for a given month. Note that our new report is required to use the same definition of "for a given month."

137

It is very tempting to just copy the existing `SelectTotalSalesPerStateForMonth`
procedure, and replace sum with avg to meet the new requirements, as shown in
Listing 5-3.

```
CREATE PROCEDURE dbo.SelectAverageSalesPerStateForMonth
    @AsOfDate DATETIME
AS
    SELECT  AVG(Amount) AS SalesPerState ,
            StateCode
    FROM    dbo.Sales
-- month begins on the first calendar day of the month
    WHERE   SaleDateTime >= DATEADD(month,
                                    DATEDIFF(month, '19900101',
                                                    @AsOfDate),
                                    '19900101')
            AND SaleDateTime <= @AsOfDate
    GROUP BY StateCode ;
```

Listing 5-3: **A simple adaptation of our "total sales" stored procedure allows us to
produce an "average sales" equivalent.**

In this way, we have completed the task in just a few seconds and, in the short term at
least, it will do the job.

Suppose, however, that at some later time the users request to change the definition of
"for a given month" to "thirty consecutive calendar days, ending on the day we run the
report." Unfortunately, the definition of "for a given month" is implemented twice, both
in `SelectTotalSalesPerStateForMonth` and in `SelectAverageSalesPer-`
`StateForMonth`. Even if one and the same person developed them both, it is possible
to forget it by the time we need to implement the change. Even if it is clearly documented that both procedures should use one and the same definition, it is still possible
that the developer implementing the change has failed to modify both stored procedures
in a consistent way.

Suppose, for example, that only the `SelectAverageSalesPerStateForMonth`
stored procedure was modified to meet this new requirement. Listing 5-4 shows how
it was changed.

138

```
ALTER PROCEDURE dbo.SelectAverageSalesPerStateForMonth
  @AsOfDate DATETIME
AS
  SELECT  AVG(Amount) AS SalesPerState ,
          StateCode
  FROM    dbo.Sales
-- month means 30 calendar days
  WHERE   SaleDateTime >= DATEADD(day, -29, @AsOfDate)
          AND SaleDateTime <= @AsOfDate
  GROUP BY StateCode ;
```

Listing 5-4: The modified SelectAverageSalesPerStateForMonth stored procedure, accomodating the new definition of "for a given month."

When we make such changes, it is very easy to forget that we have implemented the definition of "for a given month" in two places. If we update the definition in one place and not the other, we will get inconsistent results, as demonstrated by Listing 5-5.

```
PRINT 'Total Sales Per State For Month:' ;
EXEC dbo.SelectTotalSalesPerStateForMonth
  @AsOfDate = '20091005' ;

PRINT 'Average Sales Per State For Month:' ;
EXEC dbo.SelectAverageSalesPerStateForMonth
  @AsOfDate = '20091005' ;


Total Sales Per State For Month:
SalesPerState                              StateCode
---------------------------------------    ---------
10000.00                                   CA
2000.00                                    OR

(2 row(s) affected)
```

```
Average Sales Per State For Month:
SalesPerState                                  StateCode
-------------------------------------------    ---------
4630000.000000                                 CA
926000.000000                                  OR
(2 row(s) affected)
```

Listing 5-5:   The stored procedures produce different results.

Clearly the average sales size for the state of California (4,630,000) is many times greater than the total sales for the same state (10,000), which makes no sense at all. In this example, I have deliberately used test data that makes the discrepancy obvious. In general, however, such discrepancies may be more subtle and difficult to spot, so they can lurk around for a long time.

As this example clearly demonstrates, when we cut and paste code, we expose our code to the possibility of bugs if our requirements change, and we fail to change each of the multiple implementations of one and the same logic in exactly the same way. In short, copy-and-paste coding is a direct violation of the DRY (Don't Repeat Yourself) principle, which is so fundamental in software engineering.

> *The DRY principle...*
>
> *...was originally stated by Andy Hunt see* HTTP://EN.WIKIPEDIA.ORG/WIKI/ANDY. HUNT (AUTHOR) *and Dave Thomas see* HTTP://EN.WIKIPEDIA.ORG/WIKI/DAVE THO- MAS (AUTHOR) *in their book The Pragmatic Programmer. For details, go to* HTTP:// EN.WIKIPEDIA.ORG/WIKI/THE PRAGMATIC PROGRAMMER. *I encourage you to read this book; it is very relevant to every programmer.*

The code to implement a given logic should be implemented once, and once only, and reused by all applications that need it. However, of course, due care must be taken when reusing SQL code. Careless reuse of code can lead to maintenance and performance issues, especially when this reuse takes the form of scalar UDFs. We cannot reuse code without first verifying that it runs fast enough. We shall discuss this in more detail later in the chapter.

How Reusing Code Improves its Robustness

Rather than repeat the same logic in multiple places, we need to refactor the common functionality out of our two stored procedures. We can implement the definition of "sales for a given month" in an inline UDF, as shown in Listing 5-6.

```
CREATE   FUNCTION dbo.SalesForMonth (@AsOfDate DATETIME)
RETURNS TABLE
AS
RETURN
  ( SELECT   SalesID ,
             StateCode ,
             SaleDateTime ,
             Amount
    FROM     dbo.Sales
    WHERE    SaleDateTime >= DATEADD(day, -29, @AsOfDate)
             AND SaleDateTime <= @AsOfDate
  ) ;
```

Listing 5-6: Implementing the definition of "sales for a given month" in an inline UDF.

This new inline UDF can then be used in both stored procedures.

```
ALTER PROCEDURE dbo.SelectTotalSalesPerStateForMonth
   @AsOfDate DATETIME
AS
  BEGIN
    SELECT   SUM(Amount) AS SalesPerState ,
             StateCode
    FROM     dbo.SalesForMonth(@AsOfDate)
    GROUP BY StateCode ;
  END ;
GO
ALTER PROCEDURE dbo.SelectAverageSalesPerStateForMonth
   @AsOfDate DATETIME
AS
```

```
BEGIN
  SELECT  AVG(Amount) AS SalesPerState ,
          StateCode
  FROM    dbo.SalesForMonth(@AsOfDate)
  GROUP BY StateCode ;
END ;
```

Listing 5-7: Utilizing the new inline function in our two stored procedures.

After this refactoring, our two stored procedures are guaranteed to have the same defini-tion of "for a given month." We can rerun Listing 5-5 and try them out. If, at some later date, we change the definition of the reporting period again, we will have to modify only one module, SalesForMonth.

Can we reuse the definition of the reporting period in other queries against other tables? We can at least try to go one step further and have one module define our reporting period and do nothing else. As usual, we should verify that the performance is still acceptable. The code in Listing 5-8 shows how to implement the definition of reporting period as an inline UDF.

```
CREATE FUNCTION dbo.MonthReportingPeriodStart
                       (@AsOfDate DATETIME )
RETURNS TABLE
AS
RETURN
  ( SELECT  DATEADD(day, -29, @AsOfDate) AS PeriodStart
  ) ;
```

Listing 5-8: An inline UDF that implements the definition of a reporting period.

We can utilize this inline UDF when we implement the "sales for a given month" functionality.

```
ALTER FUNCTION dbo.SalesForMonth ( @AsOfDate DATETIME )
RETURNS TABLE
AS
RETURN
```

```
( SELECT   SalesID ,
           StateCode ,
           SaleDateTime ,
           Amount
   FROM    dbo.Sales AS s
           CROSS APPLY
           dbo.MonthReportingPeriodStart(@AsOfDate) AS ps
   WHERE   SaleDateTime >= ps.PeriodStart
           AND SaleDateTime <= @AsOfDate
) ;
```

Listing 5-9: Altering SalesPerStateForMonth to utilize the new MonthReportingPeriodStart function.

You can rerun Listing 5-5 one more time to verify that both our stored procedures still
work correctly.

Alternatively, we can use a scalar UDF to implement the definition of reporting period,
as shown in Listing 5-10.

```
-- being defensive, we must drop the old implementation
-- so that reporting periods are implemented
-- only in one place
DROP FUNCTION dbo.MonthReportingPeriodStart ;
GO
CREATE FUNCTION dbo.MonthReportingPeriodStart
                         ( @AsOfDate DATETIME )
RETURNS DATETIME
AS
    BEGIN ;
      DECLARE @ret DATETIME ;
      SET @ret = DATEADD(day, -29, @AsOfDate) ;
      RETURN @ret ;
    END ;
```

Listing 5-10: Scalar UDF which implements the definition of reporting period.

We also have to change our `SalesForMonth` function, so that it utilizes our new scalar UDF, as shown in Listing 5-11.

```
ALTER FUNCTION dbo.SalesForMonth ( @AsOfDate DATETIME )
RETURNS TABLE
AS
RETURN
  ( SELECT   SalesID ,
             StateCode ,
             SaleDateTime ,
             Amount
    FROM     dbo.Sales AS s
    WHERE    SaleDateTime >=
             dbo.MonthReportingPeriodStart(@AsOfDate)
             AND SaleDateTime <= @AsOfDate
  ) ;
```

Listing 5-11: Altering `SalesForMonth` **to utilize the new scalar UDF**
`MonthReportingPeriodStart`.

Note that the new implementation of `SalesForMonth` is simpler than the previous one (Listing 5-9): instead of using the CROSS APPLY clause to utilize the inline UDF, we can just invoke the scalar UDF directly in the WHERE clause.

In fact, however, the CROSS APPLY version will perform better in many cases. As always when we reuse code, we need to benchmark the performance of each of the possible approaches before making a choice. In some cases, chaining functions can lead to bad performance so, depending on the results of our benchmarking, we might even have to abandon the `SalesForMonth` and `MonthReportingPeriodStart` UDFs and return to the simpler function from Listing 5-6.

The basic fact remains, however, that implementing the same logic in multiple places increases the possibility of bugs when our requirements change. Instead, we should aim for sensible code reuse wherever possible, and UDFs are just one of the means to achieve this.

Over the coming sections, we'll discuss other ways in which we can reuse T-SQL code, as dictated by the given circumstances. Overall, reusing code is a very important component of defensive programming, and I cannot emphasize strongly enough how much it can improve the robustness of our code.

Wrapping SELECTs in Views

In some cases, it makes sense to wrap a frequently-used query in a view, as shown in Listing 5-12.

```
CREATE VIEW dbo.TotalSalesByState
AS
SELECT SUM(Amount) AS TotalSales, StateCode
FROM dbo.Sales
GROUP BY StateCode ;
```

Listing 5-12: Wrapping a query inside a view.

You can SELECT from views in exactly the same way as you can SELECT from tables, so views are very convenient and useful. However, views do not offer the ability to provide parameters to the SELECT statements that we are reusing. When this requirement arises, we reuse SELECT statements by wrapping them either in stored procedures or in user-defined functions.

As usual, we need to consider performance whenever we choose to use views. Typically views do not cause any performance degradation at all. However, we need to use them in moderation: having to deal with too many layers of nested views may overwhelm the optimizer and cause it to choose a suboptimal plan.

Reusing Parameterized Queries: Stored Procedures versus Inline UDFs

If we want to reuse parameterized queries, it is usually preferable to wrap them in user-defined functions. It is typically less convenient to reuse parameterized queries that are wrapped in stored procedures, as the following examples will demonstrate.

Let's say we have a stored procedure that returns all sales for the month, across all states, as shown in Listing 5-13.

```
CREATE PROCEDURE dbo.SelectSalesForMonth @AsOfDate DATETIME
AS
  BEGIN ;
    SELECT  Amount ,
            StateCode
    FROM    dbo.Sales
    WHERE   SaleDateTime >= DATEADD(day, -29, @AsOfDate)
            AND SaleDateTime <= @AsOfDate ;
  END ;
GO
```

Listing 5-13: A stored procedure that returns all sales for the month.

Hopefully, you spotted the missed opportunity for code reuse in this listing. We should have reused our MonthReportingPeriodStart in the WHERE clause; I leave this as an exercise for the reader.

We now need to develop a stored procedure that retrieves the total sales **per state** for a given month, and we want to reuse the SelectSalesForMonth stored procedure, Although it's possible to do this, we will need to create a table variable or a temporary table with a structure that matches the structure of the result set returned by stored procedure, as shown in Listing 5-14.

```
CREATE PROCEDURE dbo.SelectSalesPerStateForMonth
   @AsOfDate DATETIME
AS
  BEGIN ;
    DECLARE @SalesForMonth TABLE
      (
        StateCode CHAR(2) ,
        Amount DECIMAL(10, 2)
      ) ;

    INSERT  INTO @SalesForMonth
```

```
                ( Amount ,
                  StateCode
                )
                EXEC dbo.SelectSalesForMonth @AsOfDate ;

        SELECT   SUM(Amount) AS TotalSalesForMonth ,
                 StateCode
        FROM     @SalesForMonth
        GROUP BY StateCode
        ORDER BY StateCode ;
    END ;
GO
```

Listing 5-14: The SelectSalesPerStateForMonth stored procedure, which reuses the SelectSalesForMonth stored procedure and returns total sales per state for the month.

We can run a smoke test to verify that our two stored procedures work.

```
EXEC dbo.SelectSalesForMonth @AsOfDate = '20091002' ;
EXEC dbo.SelectSalesPerStateForMonth @AsOfDate = '20091002' ;
```

Listing 5-15: Testing the new stored procedures.

So far so good; we have reused the code wrapped in SelectSalesForMonth procedure and it works. However, now suppose we want to select the state with the highest total sales for a given month. It looks as if we can simply reuse the SelectSalesPerState-ForMonth procedure, again with a slight modification to create a table variable or a temporary table, as shown in Listing 5-16.

```
CREATE PROCEDURE dbo.SelectStateWithBestSalesForMonth
    @AsOfDate DATETIME
AS
    BEGIN ;
      DECLARE @SalesForMonth TABLE
        (
          TotalSales DECIMAL(10, 2) ,
```

```
        StateCode CHAR(2)
    ) ;

    INSERT  INTO @SalesForMonth
            ( TotalSales ,
              StateCode
            )
            EXEC dbo.SelectSalesPerStateForMonth @AsOfDate ;

    SELECT TOP (1)
            TotalSales ,
            StateCode
    FROM    @SalesForMonth
    ORDER BY TotalSales DESC ;
  END ;
```

Listing 5-16: Reusing SelectSalesPerStateForMonth procedure to get the state with most sales.

Unfortunately, although the procedure creates, it does not work.

```
EXEC dbo.SelectStateWithBestSalesForMonth
  @AsOfDate = '20091002' ;

Msg 8164, Level 16, State 1, Procedure
SelectSalesPerStateForMonth, Line 10
An INSERT EXEC statement cannot be nested.
```

Listing 5-17: An INSERT...EXEC statement cannot be nested. Note that the exact error message may vary depending on the version of your SQL Server.

Unfortunately, the INSERT...EXEC approach that we used in SelectSalesPerState-ForMonth procedure cannot be nested. This is a very serious limitation.

The two inline UDFs shown in Listing 5-18 implement the same requirements. Note that the TotalSalesPerStateForMonth function implements the same functionality as our previous SelectTotalSalesPerStateForMonth stored procedure.

As per our rules of code reuse, we would only ever implement one or the other, not both, in our solutions.

```
CREATE FUNCTION dbo.TotalSalesPerStateForMonth
   ( @AsOfDate DATETIME )
RETURNS TABLE
AS
RETURN
   ( SELECT   StateCode ,
             SUM(Amount) AS TotalSales
     FROM    dbo.SalesPerStateForMonth(@AsOfDate)
     GROUP BY StateCode
   ) ;
GO

CREATE FUNCTION dbo.StateWithBestSalesForMonth
   ( @AsOfDate DATETIME )
RETURNS TABLE
AS
RETURN
   ( SELECT TOP (1)
             StateCode ,
             TotalSales
     FROM    dbo.TotalSalesPerStateForMonth(@AsOfDate)
     ORDER BY TotalSales DESC
   ) ;
```

Listing 5-18: Implementing the same functionality via inline UDFs.

In contrast to what we saw in Listing 5-17, our attempt to reuse result sets returned from nested inline UDFs works just fine.

```
SELECT * FROM dbo.TotalSalesPerStateForMonth ( '20091002' ) ;
SELECT * FROM dbo.StateWithBestSalesForMonth ( '20091002' ) ;
```

```
StateCode  TotalSales
---------  ------------------------------------------
CA         140010000.00
OR         28002000.00

(2 row(s) affected)

StateCode  TotalSales
---------  ------------------------------------------
CA         140010000.00

(1 row(s) affected)
```

Listing 5-19: Testing the inline UDFs.

It is often easier to reuse code when it is wrapped in inline UDFs than when it is wrapped in stored procedures. I should emphasize that I refer only to inline UDFs, not to all three varieties of UDF. Whenever we are deciding whether to use stored procedures or UDFs, we also need to consider the following:

- INSERT EXEC requires you to create a table variable or temporary table before doing the call; stored procedures can have multiple and/or varying result sets, depending on code path, causing all kinds of problems with INSERT EXEC

- some functionality, such as data modifications and TRY...CATCH blocks, is not allowed in UDFs

- the inline UDF, like a view, is expanded in the execution plan, giving the optimizer the choice to take shortcuts, or even remove joined tables if their columns are not used.

Let's discuss performance considerations and see why it might not be a good idea to use scalar UDFs.

Scalar UDFs and Performance

Hopefully, the examples so far have demonstrated that laying out code in simple reusable modules can simplify maintenance, and reduce the chance of bugs when requirements change.

Although the emphasis of this book is on writing correct and robust code, we must, in this chapter, discuss performance. The reason is simple: careless code reuse can seriously hurt performance. For example, in some cases scalar UDFs may perform very poorly, and I will provide an example that demonstrates this, for SQL Server 2005 and 2008. Of course, in future versions of SQL Server the relative performance of the different flavors of UDFs may change, so it's essential that you always benchmark the performance impact of code refactoring, and rerun these benchmarks when you upgrade to a new SQL Server version.

For this example, we'll need to create a test table with a reasonable number of rows, so let's first set up a 128K-row helper table, Numbers, as shown in Listing 5-20, which we can use to populate the test table.

These helper tables are a must-have in database development and, in fact, if you have been working sequentially through the chapters, you will have already created an almost-identical 1-million row Numbers table in Chapter 2 (Listing 2-2). If so, or if you already have your own version that suits the same purpose, then feel free to use that instead.

```
CREATE TABLE dbo.Numbers
  (
    n INT NOT NULL ,
    CONSTRAINT PK_Numbers PRIMARY KEY ( n )
  ) ;
GO
DECLARE @i INT ;
SET @i = 1 ;
INSERT  INTO dbo.Numbers
        ( n )
VALUES  ( 1 ) ;
WHILE @i < 100000
```

```
BEGIN ;
  INSERT  INTO dbo.Numbers
            ( n )
            SELECT   @i + n
            FROM     dbo.Numbers ;
    SET @i = @i * 2 ;
END ;
```

Listing 5-20: Creating and populating the `Numbers` **helper table.**

Next, in Listing 5-21, we create the sample `Packages` table and populate it using our `Numbers` helper table.

```
CREATE TABLE dbo.Packages
  (
    PackageID INT NOT NULL ,
    WeightInPounds DECIMAL(5, 2) NOT NULL ,
    CONSTRAINT PK_Packages PRIMARY KEY ( PackageID )
  ) ;
 GO

INSERT  INTO dbo.Packages
          ( PackageID ,
            WeightInPounds
          )
          SELECT   n ,
                   1.0 + ( n % 900 ) / 10
          FROM     dbo.Numbers ;
```

Listing 5-21: Create the `Packages` **table and populate it with test data.**

Suppose that the cost of shipping for a package is $1 if it weighs less than 5 pounds and $2 if it weighs 5 pounds or more. Listing 5-22 shows how to implement this simple algorithm, both as a scalar and as an inline UDF.

```
CREATE FUNCTION dbo.GetShippingCost
  (
    @WeightInPounds DECIMAL(5, 2)
  )
RETURNS DECIMAL(5, 2)
AS
    BEGIN
      DECLARE @ret DECIMAL(5, 2) ;
      SET @ret = CASE WHEN @WeightInPounds < 5 THEN 1.00
                      ELSE 2.00
                END ;
      RETURN @ret ;
    END ;
GO


CREATE FUNCTION dbo.GetShippingCost_Inline
  (
    @WeightInPounds DECIMAL(5, 2)
  )
RETURNS TABLE
AS
RETURN
  ( SELECT   CAST(CASE WHEN @WeightInPounds < 5 THEN 1.00
                      ELSE 2.00
                END AS DECIMAL(5, 2)) AS ShippingCost
  ) ;
```

Listing 5-22: Calculating the shipping cost using a scalar UDF, GetShippingCost, and an inline UDF, GetShippingCost_Inline.

Now, we are ready to examine the comparative performance of each function, using the simple benchmark shown in Listing 5-23.

```
SET STATISTICS TIME ON ;
SET NOCOUNT ON ;

PRINT 'Using a scalar UDF' ;
```

```
SELECT   SUM(dbo.GetShippingCost(WeightInPounds))
    AS TotalShippingCost
FROM     dbo.Packages ;

PRINT 'Using an inline UDF' ;
SELECT   SUM(s.ShippingCost) AS TotalShippingCost
FROM     dbo.Packages AS p CROSS APPLY
             dbo.GetShippingCost_Inline(p.WeightInPounds) AS s
;

PRINT 'Not using any functions at all' ;
SELECT   SUM(CASE WHEN p.WeightInPounds < 5 THEN 1.00
                  ELSE 2.00
             END) AS TotalShippingCost
FROM     dbo.Packages AS p ;

SET STATISTICS TIME OFF ;
```

Listing 5-23: A simple benchmark to compare the performance of the scalar and inline UDFs vs. the performance of the copy-and-paste approach.

Although both functions implement exactly the same algorithm, the performance is dramatically different. When we run this benchmark on SQL Server 2005 or 2008, the query that uses our scalar UDF runs dramatically slower. Also, in this particular case, the query which uses the inline UDF performs very well, although not as fast as the query that does not use any UDFs at all, as shown in Listing 5-24. Of course, when you run these benchmarks on your system, you may get different results.

```
Using a scalar UDF

...<snip>...

SQL Server Execution Times:
   CPU time = 1531 ms,  elapsed time = 1552 ms.

Using an inline UDF
```

```
...<snip>...

SQL Server Execution Times:
   CPU time = 109 ms,  elapsed time = 82 ms.

Not using any functions at all

...<snip>...

 SQL Server Execution Times:
   CPU time = 32 ms,  elapsed time = 52 ms.
```

Listing 5-24: The performance of the query using our scalar UDF is dramatically slower than the performance of other equivalent queries.

I am not saying that using inline UDFs never incurs any performance penalties; blanket statements do not belong in database programming, and we always need to consider the performance of each particular case separately. However, in many cases, inline UDFs perform very well.

Multi-statement Table-valued UDFs

Besides scalar and inline UDFs, there are multi-statement table-valued UDFs. I will not discuss or benchmark them here, because I feel I've already proved the point that we need to consider performance when we refactor code. However, it's worth noting that, in general, while inline UDFs tend to be "performance neutral," scalar and multi-statement ones tend to hurt performance if not used carefully, and should be rigorously tested and benchmarked. Be especially wary of using a multi-statement table-valued UDF in an APPLY, since that may force the optimizer to re-execute the UDF for each row in the table the UDF is applied against.

If you are interested in learning about different flavors of UDF, I encourage you to read Books Online and Itzik Ben Gan's T-SQL Programming book (www.amazon.co.uk/Inside-Microsoft-Server-2008-Pro-Developer/dp/0735626022/).

Reusing Business Logic: Stored Procedure, Trigger, Constraint or Index?

There are several ways in which we can choose to implement our business logic. For example, we could use:

- stored procedures

- constraints

- triggers

- unique filtered indexes.

Over the coming sections we'll discuss the sort of situations where each approach may, or may not be appropriate

Use constraints where possible

In many cases, constraints are the easiest and simplest to use. To demonstrate this point, consider the Teams table shown in Listing 5-25, with a primary key constraint on the TeamID column.

```
CREATE TABLE dbo.Teams
  (
    TeamID INT NOT NULL ,
    Name VARCHAR( 50 ) NOT NULL ,
    CONSTRAINT PK_Teams PRIMARY KEY ( TeamID )
  ) ;
```

Listing 5-25: Creating the Teams table.

Since we wish to forbid access to the base tables, teams will be inserted into the table, one at a time, by calling a stored procedure. Our business rule is simple: team names must be unique. So, we need to decide where to implement this business rule. One choice is to enforce it in the stored procedure, as shown in Listing 5-27.

```
CREATE PROCEDURE dbo.InsertTeam
   @TeamID INT ,
   @Name VARCHAR(50)
AS
   BEGIN ;
           -- This is not a fully-functional stored
           -- procedure. Error handling is skipped to keep
           -- the example short.
           -- Also potential race conditions
           -- are not considered in this simple module
       INSERT   INTO dbo.Teams
                 ( TeamID ,
                   Name
                 )
                 SELECT   @TeamID ,
                          @Name
                 WHERE    NOT EXISTS ( SELECT *
                                        FROM    dbo.Teams
                                        WHERE   Name = @Name ) ;
             -- we also need to raise an error if we
           -- already have a team with such a name
   END ;
```

Listing 5-26: The InsertTeam stored procedure inserts a team, if the team name does not already exist in the table.

So, we have a stored procedure that enforces our rule, at least in the absence of high concurrency. However, what happens when we need another stored procedure that modifies a single row in the **Teams** table, or one that merges a batch of new rows into that table? We'll need to re-implement this same logic for every stored procedure that modifies this table. This is a form of copy-and-paste and is both time consuming and error prone.

Besides, unless you can guarantee that no applications can run modifications directly against the **Teams** table, it's likely that your business rule will be bypassed at some point, and inconsistent data will be introduced.

157

It is much easier and safer to just create the business rule once, in one place, as a UNIQUE constraint, as shown in Listing 5-27.

```
ALTER TABLE dbo.Teams
  ADD CONSTRAINT UNQ_Teams_Name UNIQUE(Name) ;
```

Listing 5-27: The UNQ_Teams_Name constraint enforces the uniqueness of team names.

We can now let the database engine make sure that this business rule is always enforced, regardless of the module or command that modifies the table.

Turn to triggers when constraints are not practical

As we have seen, constraints are extremely useful in many simple cases. However, our business rules are often more complex, and it is sometimes not possible or not practical to use constraints. To demonstrate this point, let's add one more table, TeamMembers, which references the Teams table through the TeamID column, as shown in Listing 5-28.

```
CREATE TABLE dbo.TeamMembers
  (
    TeamMemberID INT NOT NULL ,
    TeamID INT NOT NULL ,
    Name VARCHAR(50) NOT NULL ,
    IsTeamLead CHAR(1) NOT NULL ,
    CONSTRAINT PK_TeamMembers PRIMARY KEY ( TeamMemberID ) ,
    CONSTRAINT FK_TeamMembers_Teams
      FOREIGN KEY ( TeamID ) REFERENCES dbo.Teams ( TeamID )
,
    CONSTRAINT CHK_TeamMembers_IsTeamLead
      CHECK ( IsTeamLead IN ( 'Y', 'N' ) )
  ) ;
```

Listing 5-28: Creating the TeamMembers table.

Suppose that we need to implement the following business rule: no team can have more than two members. Implementing this business rule in a trigger is quite straightforward, as shown in Listing 5-29, and you only have to do it once. It is possible, but much more complex, to implement this rule via constraints.

```
CREATE TRIGGER dbo.TeamMembers_TeamSizeLimitTrigger
    ON dbo.TeamMembers
  FOR INSERT, UPDATE
AS
  IF EXISTS ( SELECT  *
              FROM   ( SELECT   TeamID ,
                                TeamMemberID
                       FROM     inserted
                       UNION
                       SELECT   TeamID ,
                                TeamMemberID
                       FROM     dbo.TeamMembers
                       WHERE    TeamID IN ( SELECT   TeamID
                                            FROM     inserted )
                     ) AS t
              GROUP BY TeamID
              HAVING  COUNT(*) > 2 )
    BEGIN ;
      RAISERROR('Team size exceeded limit',16, 10) ;
      ROLLBACK TRAN ;
    END ;
```

Listing 5-29: The TeamMembers_TeamSizeLimitTrigger trigger ensures that the teams do not exceed the maximum size.

With our business rule implemented in only one place, we can comprehensively test just one object. In order to test this trigger, we need some test data in our parent table, as shown in Listing 5-30.

```
INSERT   INTO dbo.Teams
         ( TeamID ,
           Name
         )
         SELECT  1 ,
                    'Red Bulls'
         UNION ALL
         SELECT  2 ,
                    'Blue Tigers'
         UNION ALL
         SELECT  3 ,
                    'Pink Panthers' ;
```

Listing 5-30: Adding some test data to the Teams table.

The script shown next, in Listing 5-31, verifies that we can successfully add new team members, as long as the teams' sizes do not exceed the limit imposed by our trigger.

```
-- adding team members to new teams
INSERT   INTO dbo.TeamMembers
         ( TeamMemberID ,
           TeamID ,
           Name ,
           IsTeamLead
         )
         SELECT  1 ,
                    1 ,
                    'Jill Hansen' ,
                    'N'
         UNION ALL
         SELECT  2 ,
                    1 ,
                    'Sydney Hobart' ,
                    'N'
         UNION ALL
         SELECT  3 ,
                    2 ,
```

```
                  'Hobart Sydney' ,
                  'N' ;

-- add more team members to existing teams
BEGIN TRANSACTION ;
INSERT  INTO dbo.TeamMembers
        ( TeamMemberID ,
          TeamID ,
          Name ,
          IsTeamLead
        )
        SELECT  4 ,
                2 ,
                'Lou Larry' ,
                'N' ;
ROLLBACK TRANSACTION ;
```

Listing 5-31: Testing the `_TeamSizeLimitTrigger` **trigger with valid INSERTs.**

The script shown next, in Listing 5-32, verifies that we can successfully transfer team members between teams, as long as the teams' sizes do not exceed the limit.

```
BEGIN TRANSACTION ;
UPDATE  dbo.TeamMembers
SET     TeamID = TeamID + 1 ;
ROLLBACK ;

BEGIN TRANSACTION ;
UPDATE  dbo.TeamMembers
SET     TeamID = 3 - TeamID ;
ROLLBACK ;
```

Listing 5-32: Testing the `_TeamSizeLimitTrigger` **trigger with valid UPDATEs.**

So, we've proved that our trigger allows modifications that do not violate our business rules. Now we need to make sure that it does **not** allow modifications that do violate our business rules; there are quite a few cases, and we need to verify them all. First of all,

Listing 5-33 verifies that we cannot add new team members if the resulting teams' sizes are too big. All the statements in the script must, and do, fail.

```
-- attempt to add too many team members
-- to a team which already has members
INSERT   INTO dbo.TeamMembers
         ( TeamMemberID ,
           TeamID ,
           Name ,
           IsTeamLead
         )
         SELECT   4 ,
                  2 ,
                  'Calvin Lee' ,
                  'N'
         UNION ALL
         SELECT   5 ,
                  2 ,
                  'Jim Lee' ,
                  'N' ;
GO
     -- attempt to add too many team members to an empty team
INSERT   INTO dbo.TeamMembers
         ( TeamMemberID ,
           TeamID ,
           Name ,
           IsTeamLead
         )
         SELECT   4 ,
                  3 ,
                  'Calvin Lee' ,
                  'N'
         UNION ALL
         SELECT   5 ,
                  3 ,
                  'Jim Lee' ,
                  'N'
```

```
            UNION ALL
            SELECT   6 ,
                     3 ,
                     'Jake Lee' ,
                     'N' ;
```

Listing 5-33: Testing the _TeamSizeLimitTrigger **trigger with invalid INSERTs.**

Also, we need to make sure that we cannot transfer team members if the resulting teams' sizes are too big, as shown in Listing 5-34. Again, all the following statements fail as expected.

```
-- attempt to transfer members from other teams
-- to a team which is full to capacity
UPDATE   dbo.TeamMembers
SET      TeamID = 1
WHERE    TeamMemberID = 3 ;
GO
    -- attempt to transfer too many team members
    -- to a team that is not full yet
UPDATE   dbo.TeamMembers
SET      TeamID = 2
WHERE    TeamMemberID IN ( 1, 2 ) ;
GO
    -- attempt to transfer too many team members
    -- to an empty team
UPDATE   dbo.TeamMembers
SET      TeamID = 3 ;
```

Listing 5-34: Testing the _TeamSizeLimitTrigger **trigger with invalid UPDATEs.**

The amount of testing needed to ensure that a trigger works as expected can be quite substantial. However, this is the easiest alternative; if we were to re-implement this business rule in several stored procedures, then the same amount of testing required for the single trigger would be required for each of these procedures, in order to ensure that every one of them implements our business rule correctly.

Unique filtered indexes (SQL Server 2008 only)

Last, but not least, in some cases filtered indexes also allow us to implement business rules. For example, suppose that we need to make sure that each team has at most one team lead. If you are using SQL Server 2008 and upwards, then a filtered index can easily implement this business rule, as shown in Listing 5-35. I encourage you to try out this index and see for yourself that it works.

```
CREATE UNIQUE NONCLUSTERED INDEX TeamLeads
ON dbo.TeamMembers(TeamID)
WHERE IsTeamLead='Y' ;
```

Listing 5-35: The `TeamLeads` **filtered index ensures that each team has at most one team lead.**

Summary

The aim of this chapter is to prove to you that a copy-and-paste approach to code reuse will lead to multiple, inconsistent versions of the same logic being scattered throughout your code base, and a maintenance nightmare.

It has also demonstrated how common logic can be refactored into a single reusable code unit, in the form of a constraint, stored procedure, trigger, UDF or index. This careful reuse of code will reduce the possibility of bugs and greatly improve the robustness of our code.

Unfortunately, performance considerations may prevent us from reusing our code to the fullest. Yet, with careful benchmarking, we can usually find a nice compromise and develop code that is easy to maintain but still performs well enough.

Specifically, I hope the chapter has taught you the following lessons in defensive programming:

- views are useful for simple reuse of non-parameterized queries
- for reuse of parameterized queries, inline UDFs are often preferable to stored procedures

- be wary of performance issues with scalar and multi-statement table-valued UDFs

- if possible, enforce reusable business logic in a simple constraint, or possibly a filtered index in SQL 2008 and upwards

- for more complex logic, triggers often offer the most convenient means of promoting reuse, but they require extensive testing.

Chapter 6: Common Problems with Data Integrity

SQL Server provides built-in tools, in the form of constraints and triggers, which are designed to enforce data integrity rules in the database. Alternatively, we can choose to enforce data integrity in our applications. Which approach is best? To make an informed decision, we need to understand the advantages and potential difficulties involved in each approach, as well as the downstream ramifications of making the wrong choice.

In this chapter, we shall discuss benefits and common problems associated with each of the following approaches:

- using our applications to enforce data integrity rules
- using constraints to enforce data integrity rules
- using triggers to enforce data integrity rules.

Triggers are usually used to implement those business rules or data integrity rules that are just too complex to easily enforce using constraints. In this chapter, we'll examine a few of the most common problems that can beset triggers and show how to make the trigger code more robust. Ultimately, however, no matter how defensively we code, only constraints can fully guarantee data integrity. In the next chapter we'll discuss some advanced ways of using constraints to enforce complex business rules.

Enforcing Data Integrity in the Application Layer

In this example, consider the Boxes table, shown in Listing 6-1, which our application needs to populate.

```
CREATE TABLE dbo.Boxes
    (
      Label VARCHAR(30) NOT NULL
                        PRIMARY KEY ,
      LengthInInches DECIMAL(4, 2) NULL ,
```

```
    WidthInInches DECIMAL(4, 2) NULL ,
    HeightInInches DECIMAL(4, 2) NULL
) ;
```

Listing 6-1: Creating the Boxes table, which is populated by our application.

Our application has already loaded some data into our table, as represented by the script shown in Listing 6-2.

```
INSERT   INTO dbo.Boxes
         (
             Label,
             LengthInInches,
             WidthInInches,
             HeightInInches
         )
VALUES   (
             'School memorabilia',
             3,
             4,
             5
         ) ;
```

Listing 6-2: Loading some existing data into the Boxes table.

However, suppose that we then develop a new version of our application, in which we have started to enforce the following rule when inserting rows into the Boxes table:

The height of a box must be less than, or equal to, the width; and the width must be less than, or equal to, the length.

At some later point, we are asked to develop a query that returns all the boxes with at least one dimension that is greater than 4 inches. With our new business rule in place we know (or at least we think we know) that the longest dimension of any box is the length, so all we have to do in our query is check for boxes with a length of more than 4 inches. Listing 6-3 meets these requirements.

```
SELECT  Label,
        LengthInInches,
        WidthInInches,
        HeightInInches
FROM    dbo.Boxes
WHERE   LengthInInches > 4 ;
```

Listing 6-3: A query to retrieve all boxes with at least one dimension greater than 4 inches.

Unfortunately, we have failed to ensure that our existing data meets our business rule. This query will not return the existing row, even though its largest dimension is 5 inches.

As usual, we can either eliminate our assumption, which will involve writing a more complex query that does not rely on it, or we can clean up our data, assume that it will stay clean, and leave our query alone. Unfortunately, the assumption that the data will "stay clean" is a dangerous one, when enforcing data integrity rules in the application. Our application may have bugs and, in some cases, may fail to enforce the rule. Some clients may continue to run the old version of the application, which does not enforce the new business rule at all. Some data may be loaded by means other than the application, such as through SSMS, therefore bypassing the rule enforcement altogether. All too many developers completely overlook these possibilities, assuming that enforcing business rules only in the application is safe. In reality, data integrity logic housed in the application layer is frequently bypassed.

As a result, it is quite possible that we will have data in the Boxes table that does not meet our business rule, and that we're likely to have to repeat any "data clean up" process many times. Some shops run such data clean-ups weekly or even daily. In short, although we can use our applications to enforce our data integrity rules, and although this may seem to be the fastest way to get things done in the short term, it is an approach that is inefficient in the long run.

Most of the arguments covered here may also apply to enforcing data integrity logic in stored procedures, unless you are able to implement a design whereby access of your stored procedure layer is enforced, by forbidding all direct table access.

Over the following sections, we'll discuss how to use constraints and triggers, which are usually the preferred ways to protect data integrity.

Enforcing Data Integrity in Constraints

It is well known that using constraints is the most reliable way to enforce data integrity rules. So how do we go about enforcing our previous business rule (the height of a box must be less than, or equal to, the width; and the width must be less than, or equal to, the length) in a constraint?

Our first attempt might look as shown in Listing 6-4.

```
ALTER TABLE dbo.Boxes
ADD CONSTRAINT Boxes_ConsistentDimensions
CHECK(HeightInInches <= WidthInInches
   AND WidthInInches <= LengthInInches) ;
```

Listing 6-4: The flawed Boxes_ConsistentDimensions constraint.

The attempt to add this constraint fails, because some data in the table does not validate against it.

```
Msg 547, Level 16, State 0, Line 1
The ALTER TABLE statement conflicted with the CHECK
constraint "Boxes_ConsistentDimensions". The conflict
occurred in database "TEST3", table "dbo.Boxes".
```

Listing 6-5: Existing data violates the constraint.

First, we need to remove the offending data, as shown in Listing 6-6. In real life, we would probably want to clean up that data instead of just deleting it, but we shall skip this step for brevity.

```
DELETE   FROM dbo.Boxes
WHERE    NOT ( HeightInInches <= WidthInInches
              AND WidthInInches <= LengthInInches
            ) ;
```

Listing 6-6: Deleting invalid data.

If we rerun Listing 6-4, the constraint creates. Now, if we try to insert some invalid data, by running Listing 6-2, the constraint enforces our rule and the INSERT operation fails.

Unfortunately, in its current form our constraint is still flawed, as demonstrated by the fact that Listing 6-7 succeeds in adding a box that is taller than it is long.

```
INSERT   INTO dbo.Boxes
            ( Label ,
              LengthInInches ,
              WidthInInches ,
              HeightInInches

            )
VALUES    ( 'School memorabilia' ,
              3 ,
              NULL ,
              5
            ) ;
```

Listing 6-7: Adding a box with height greater than length.

In order to use constraints effectively, we need to understand how they work; otherwise we may end up, as here, with a false sense of security and some dirty data in our database.

The problem here, as you may have guessed, is a failure to handle NULL values correctly. This is one of several very common mistakes that are made when using constraints, and over the coming sections we'll learn what they are, and how to avoid them. Along the way, we'll fix our constraint so that it works reliably.

Handling nulls in CHECK constraints

Logical conditions in CHECK constraints work differently from logical conditions in the WHERE clause. If a condition in a CHECK constraint evaluates to "unknown," then the row can still be inserted, but if a condition in a WHERE clause evaluates to "unknown," then the row will not be included in the result set. To demonstrate this difference, add another CHECK constraint to our Boxes table, as shown in Listing 6-8.

```
ALTER TABLE dbo.Boxes
ADD CONSTRAINT CHK_Boxes_PositiveLength
  CHECK ( LengthInInches > 0 ) ;
```

Listing 6-8: The CHK_Boxes_PositiveLength constraint ensures that boxes cannot have zero or negative length.

However, the condition used in the CHECK constraint will not prevent us from inserting a row with NULL length, as demonstrated in Listing 6-9.

```
INSERT   INTO dbo.Boxes
         (
           Label,
           LengthInInches,
           WidthInInches,
           HeightInInches
         )
VALUES   (
           'Diving Gear',
           NULL,
           20,
           20
         ) ;
```

Listing 6-9: The CHK_Boxes_PositiveLength check constraint allows us to save rows with NULL length.

However, this row will not validate against exactly the same condition in a
WHERE clause.

```
SELECT  Label,
        LengthInInches,
        WidthInInches,
        HeightInInches
FROM    dbo.Boxes
WHERE   LengthInInches > 0 ;
```

Listing 6-10: This SELECT statement does not return rows with NULL length.

Many SQL developers get into trouble because they fail to consider how NULL evaluates
in logical expressions. For example, we've already proven that our constraint Boxes_
ConsistentDimensions does not quite work; it validated a box with height greater
than length.

Now we know enough to understand how that happened: the constraint will only
forbid rows where the CHECK clause (HeightInInches <= WidthInInches AND
WidthInInches <= LengthInInches) evaluates to FALSE. If either condition in
the clause evaluates to UNKNOWN, and another evaluates to UNKNOWN or TRUE, then
the overall clause evaluates to UNKNOWN and the row can be inserted. In this case, both
conditions in our CHECK constraint evaluated as UNKNOWN.

```
SELECT  CASE WHEN LengthInInches >= WidthInInches THEN 'True'
             WHEN LengthInInches < WidthInInches THEN 'False'
             ELSE 'Unknown'
        END AS LengthNotLessThanWidth ,
        CASE WHEN WidthInInches >= HeightInInches THEN 'True'
             WHEN WidthInInches < HeightInInches THEN 'False'
             ELSE 'Unknown'
        END AS WidthNotLessThanHeight
FROM    dbo.Boxes
WHERE   Label = 'School memorabilia' ;
```

```
LengthNotLessThanWidth WidthNotLessThanHeight
---------------------- ----------------------
Unknown                Unknown
```

Listing 6-11: Both conditions in `Boxes_ConsistentDimensions` evaluate
as "unknown."

When we develop constraints, we must take added care if the columns involved are nullable. The script in Listing 6-11 fixes our `Boxes_ConsistentDimensions` constraint.

```
DELETE  FROM dbo.Boxes
WHERE   HeightInInches > WidthInInches
        OR WidthInInches > LengthInInches
        OR HeightInInches > LengthInInches ;
GO

ALTER TABLE dbo.Boxes
DROP CONSTRAINT Boxes_ConsistentDimensions ;
GO

ALTER TABLE dbo.Boxes
ADD CONSTRAINT Boxes_ConsistentDimensions
CHECK ( (HeightInInches <= WidthInInches
        AND WidthInInches <= LengthInInches
        AND HeightInInches <= LengthInInches)
      ) ;
```

Listing 6-12: The fixed `Boxes_ConsistentDimensions` constraint.

Rerun Listing 6-7 and you'll find that, this time, the constraint will prevent invalid data
from saving. The lesson here is simple: when testing CHECK constraints, always include
in your test cases rows with NULLs.

Foreign key constraints and NULLs

It is a common misconception that foreign keys always prevent orphan rows, that is, rows in the child table that do not have corresponding rows in the parent table. In fact, if the columns involved in the foreign key constraint are nullable, then we may have orphan rows.

Let's see for ourselves. Listing 6-13 creates a parent and child pair of tables.

```
CREATE TABLE dbo.ParkShelters
  (
    Latitude DECIMAL(9, 6) NOT NULL ,
    Longitude DECIMAL(9, 6) NOT NULL ,
    ShelterName VARCHAR(50) NOT NULL ,
    CONSTRAINT PK_ParkShelters
      PRIMARY KEY ( Latitude, Longitude )
  ) ;
GO

CREATE TABLE dbo.ShelterRepairs
  (
    RepairID INT NOT NULL PRIMARY KEY ,
    Latitude DECIMAL(9, 6) NULL ,
    Longitude DECIMAL(9, 6) NULL ,
    RepairDate DATETIME NOT NULL ,
    CONSTRAINT FK_ShelterRepairs_ParkShelters
      FOREIGN KEY ( Latitude, Longitude )
        REFERENCES dbo.ParkShelters ( Latitude, Longitude )
  ) ;
```

Listing 6-13: Create a parent table (ParkShelters) and a child table (ShelterRepairs).

We have a composite FOREIGN KEY constraint on the Latitude and Longitude columns in the child table, but since both of these columns are nullable, we can add a child row without a matching parent row into the child table, even though the parent table is empty at this time, as Listing 6-14 demonstrates.

```
INSERT INTO dbo.ShelterRepairs
        ( RepairID ,
          Latitude ,
          Longitude ,
          RepairDate
        )
VALUES  ( 0 , -- RepairID - int
          12.34 , -- Latitude - decimal
          NULL , -- Longitude - decimal
          '2010-02-06T21:07:52'  -- RepairDate - datetime
        ) ;
```

Listing 6-14: Adding repairs even though there is no such shelter.

The database engine will verify whether or not there is a matching row in the parent table if, and only if, neither the Latitude nor Longitude column in the child table contains a NULL. Listing 6-15, for example, will fail.

```
INSERT INTO dbo.ShelterRepairs
        ( RepairID ,
          Latitude ,
          Longitude ,
          RepairDate
        )
VALUES  ( 1 , -- RepairID - int
          12.34 , -- Latitude - decimal
          34.56 , -- Longitude - decimal
          '20100207'  -- RepairDate - datetime
        ) ;
```

Listing 6-15: We cannot add repairs if both Latitude and Longitude columns in the child table are not null, and there is no matching shelter.

This demonstrates that, if we need to make sure that every row in the child table has a matching row in the parent table, it is not enough to simply create a FOREIGN KEY; in such cases, we also need to ensure that the columns involved in the FOREIGN KEY, in the child table, are not nullable. Use of nullable columns in FOREIGN KEY constraints must be reserved only for the cases when it is acceptable to have rows in the child table without matching rows in the parent one.

Understanding disabled, enabled, and trusted constraints

Not all types of constraints behave in the same way. UNIQUE and PRIMARY KEY constraints always ensure that all the data is valid with respect to them but a FOREIGN KEY or CHECK constraint can exist in the database in one of three states:

- **disabled** – exists in the database, is exposed via system views, and can be scripted out; but does not do anything

- **enabled but not trusted** – validates all modifications, but does not guarantee that all existing data conforms to its rules

- **enabled and trusted** – validates all modifications, and guarantees that all existing data is valid.

Note that only CHECK constraints and FOREIGN KEY constraints can be disabled. Under the hood PRIMARY KEY and UNIQUE constraints are implemented as UNIQUE indexes. As such, neither PRIMARY KEY nor UNIQUE constraints can be disabled, and will always be trusted.

We can demonstrate the differences between disabled, enabled, and trusted constraints with a simple example, involving a FOREIGN KEY constraint. Listing 6-16 drops and recreates our Boxes table and then creates a child table, Items.

```
DROP TABLE dbo.Boxes ;
GO
CREATE TABLE dbo.Boxes
    (
        BoxLabel VARCHAR(30) NOT NULL ,
        LengthInInches DECIMAL(4, 2) NOT NULL ,
        WidthInInches DECIMAL(4, 2) NOT NULL ,
        HeightInInches DECIMAL(4, 2) NOT NULL ,
        CONSTRAINT PK_Boxes PRIMARY KEY ( BoxLabel )
```

```
    ) ;
GO
CREATE TABLE dbo.Items
    (
        ItemLabel VARCHAR(30) NOT NULL ,
        BoxLabel VARCHAR(30) NOT NULL ,
        WeightInPounds DECIMAL(4, 2) NOT NULL ,
        CONSTRAINT PK_Items PRIMARY KEY ( ItemLabel ) ,
        CONSTRAINT FK_Items_Boxes FOREIGN KEY ( BoxLabel )
            REFERENCES dbo.Boxes ( BoxLabel )
    ) ;
```

Listing 6-16: Dropping and recreating the Boxes table, and creating Items table.

Listing 6-17 populates each table with some valid test data, as per our FK_Items_Boxes constraint.

```
INSERT  INTO dbo.Boxes
        (
            BoxLabel,
            LengthInInches,
            WidthInInches,
            HeightInInches
        )
VALUES  (
            'Camping Gear' ,
            40,
            40,
            40
        ) ;
GO
INSERT  INTO dbo.Items
        (
            ItemLabel,
            BoxLabel,
            WeightInPounds
        )
```

```
VALUES    (
              'Tent',
              'Camping Gear',
              20
          ) ;
```

Listing 6-17: Populating `Boxes` and `Items` tables with valid test data.

Listing 6-18 confirms that the constraint prevents invalid data from saving.

```
INSERT    INTO dbo.Items
          (
              ItemLabel,
              BoxLabel,
              WeightInPounds
          )
VALUES    (
              'Yoga mat',
              'No Such Box',
              2
          ) ;


Msg 547, Level 16, State 0, Line 1
The INSERT statement conflicted with the FOREIGN KEY
constraint "FK_Items_Boxes". The conflict occurred in
database "TEST", table "dbo.Boxes", column 'BoxLabel'.
The statement has been terminated.
```

Listing 6-18: FK_Items_Boxes prohibits orphan rows.

Disabled constraints do...nothing

Say we need to bulk load data into these two tables, and that the loading must complete as quickly as possible; this is a very common requirement. Assuming we know that the data comes from a trusted source, and that all the data in that source is clean, it is quite a common practice to disable the FOREIGN KEY constraint, so that we can start loading data into both tables simultaneously without having to make sure that parent rows load before their child ones.

Disabling the constraint is shown in Listing 6-19.

```
ALTER TABLE dbo.Items
        NOCHECK CONSTRAINT FK_Items_Boxes ;
```

Listing 6-19: Disabling the FK_Items_Boxes constraint.

We can confirm that the constraint is disabled, by running the query in Listing 6-20.

```
SELECT  CAST(name AS char(20)) AS Name,
        is_disabled
FROM    sys.foreign_keys
WHERE   name = 'FK_Items_Boxes' ;


Name                     is_disabled
--------------------     -----------
FK_Items_Boxes           1
```

Listing 6-20: Confirming that the FK_Items_Boxes constraint is disabled.

To determine if a CHECK constraint is disabled...

...we need to query another system view, named sys.check_constraints.

Our disabled constraint no longer prevents us from saving orphan rows. If we rerun Listing 6-18 it will succeed, and an orphan row will be inserted into the child table, as shown in Listing 6-21.

```
SELECT  ItemLabel ,
        BoxLabel
FROM    dbo.Items AS i
WHERE   NOT EXISTS ( SELECT *
                     FROM    dbo.Boxes AS b
```

```
                    WHERE   i.BoxLabel = b.BoxLabel ) ;

ItemLabel                      BoxLabel
------------------------------ ------------------------
Yoga mat                       No Such Box
```

Listing 6-21: Exposing the orphan row.

In short, a disabled constraint does not actually do anything, although it still exists, and you can still script it out.

Enabled constraints do not validate existing data

For the following reasons, it is quite possible that, at the end of our bulk load, the row inserted by Listing 6-18 will still be an orphan:

- the source of our data has failed to maintain data integrity

- parent rows were exported before child ones, so the data being loaded does not represent a consistent point-in-time snapshot

- our load has partially failed.

Once the bulk load has finished, we can re-enable the FOREIGN KEY constraint, as shown in Listing 6-22.

```
ALTER TABLE dbo.Items
        CHECK CONSTRAINT FK_Items_Boxes ;
```

Listing 6-22: Re-enabling the FK_Items_Boxes constraint.

Having successfully re-enabled the constraint (rerun Listing 6-20 to verify), we cannot insert any more invalid data.

```
INSERT  INTO dbo.Items
        (
            ItemLabel,
            BoxLabel,
```

```
            WeightInPounds
        )
VALUES  (
            'Camping Stove',
            'No Such Box',
            2
        ) ;

Msg 547, Level 16, State 0, Line 1
The INSERT statement conflicted with the FOREIGN KEY
constraint "FK_Items_Boxes". The conflict occurred in
database "TEST3", table "dbo.Boxes", column 'BoxLabel'.
The statement has been terminated.
```

Listing 6-23: The FK_Items_Boxes constraint stops insertion of further orphan rows.

However, we still have an orphan row in the Items table. In short, enabled constraints prevent entering invalid data, but they do not guarantee that all existing data is valid.

Trusted constraints guarantee that existing data is valid

The problem we have is that when we enabled our FOREIGN KEY constraint, in Listing 6-22, we did not validate existing data against the constraint, and so SQL Server marks it as "not trusted," as shown in Listing 6-24.

```
SELECT  CAST(name AS char(20)) AS Name,
        is_disabled,
        is_not_trusted
FROM    sys.foreign_keys
WHERE   name = 'FK_Items_Boxes' ;

Name                     is_disabled   is_not_trusted
---------------------    -----------   -------------
FK_Items_Boxes           0             1
```

Listing 6-24: The constraint FK_Items_Boxes is enabled but not trusted.

To perform this validation, simply use the WITH CHECK option when enabling the constraint, as shown in Listing 6-25. The command fails, as it should, because we have an orphan row.

```
ALTER TABLE [dbo].[Items]
        WITH CHECK
        CHECK CONSTRAINT FK_Items_Boxes ;

Msg 547, Level 16, State 0, Line 1
The ALTER TABLE statement conflicted with the FOREIGN KEY
constraint "FK_Items_Boxes". The conflict occurred in
database "test", table "dbo.Boxes", column 'Label'.
```

Listing 6-25: A failed attempt to validate the FK_Items_Boxes constraint.

Let us delete that orphan row, as shown in Listing 6-26.

```
DELETE   FROM dbo.Items
WHERE    NOT EXISTS (SELECT *
                     FROM    dbo.Boxes AS b
                     WHERE Items.BoxLabel = b.BoxLabel );
```

Listing 6-26: Deleting the orphan row.

Now rerun Listing 6-25 and it will succeed, and the constraint will now be trusted (which can be verified by rerunning 6-24).

Only PRIMARY KEY and UNIQUE constraints are always trusted. A CHECK or FOREIGN KEY constraint may become non-trusted as a result, for example, of disabling it, and then re-enabling it without validating the existing data. Even if the data were completely valid, the constraint will still not be trusted unless the WITH CHECK option is used when it is enabled.

Only when a constraint is trusted can we know for certain that all the data in the table is valid with respect to that constraint. An added advantage of trusted constraints is that they can be used by the optimizer when devising execution plans. Conversely, the optimizer will ignore non-trusted constraints, meaning that valuable information will go unused, and could lead to suboptimal plans.

Problems with UDFs wrapped in CHECK constraints

Some complex business rules are difficult or impossible to implement via regular constraints. In such cases, it seems intuitive to develop a scalar UDF and wrap it in a CHECK constraint.

For example, suppose that we need to enforce a data integrity rule that states:

> *We can have any number of* NULLs *in the Barcode column, but the* NOT NULL *values must be unique.*

Clearly, we cannot use a UNIQUE index or constraint in this situation, because it would only allow a single NULL value, and we need to support multiple NULL values in this column.

The behavior of UNIQUE **in SQL Server is not ANSI standard**

ANSI specifies that a UNIQUE *constraint should enforce uniqueness for non-*NULL *values only. Microsoft's implementation of the* UNIQUE *constraint deviates from this standard definition.*

To set up the example, we just need to add a **Barcode** column to our **Items** table, as shown in Listing 6-27.

```
ALTER TABLE dbo.Items
ADD Barcode VARCHAR(20) NULL ;
```

Listing 6-27: Adding a Barcode column to the Items table.

To enforce our business rule, it is technically possible to develop a scalar UDF and invoke it from a CHECK constraint, as demonstrated in Listing 6-28.

```
CREATE FUNCTION dbo.GetBarcodeCount
        ( @Barcode varchar(20) )
RETURNS int
AS
   BEGIN ;
    DECLARE @barcodeCount int ;
    SELECT   @barcodeCount = COUNT(*)
    FROM     dbo.Items
    WHERE    Barcode = @Barcode ;
    RETURN @barcodeCount ;
   END ;
GO
ALTER TABLE dbo.Items
ADD CONSTRAINT UNQ_Items_Barcode
        CHECK ( dbo.GetBarcodeCount(Barcode) < 2 ) ;
GO
```

Listing 6-28: Creating GetBarcodeCount, a scalar UDF, and invoking it from a CHECK constraint.

This solution looks intuitive and it works fine for INSERTs. Listing 6-29 verifies that we can INSERT more than one NULL barcode.

```
--  DELETE FROM dbo.Items

INSERT   INTO dbo.Items
        (
           ItemLabel,
           BoxLabel,
           WeightInPounds,
           Barcode
        )
VALUES  (
           'Sleeping Bag',
           'Camping Gear',
           4,
           NULL
```

```
            ) ;
GO
INSERT   INTO dbo.Items
            (
                ItemLabel,
                BoxLabel,
                WeightInPounds,
                Barcode
            )
VALUES   (
                'Sleeping Mat',
                'Camping Gear',
                1,
                NULL
            ) ;
```

Listing 6-29: The CHECK constraint UNQ_Items_Barcode allows us to insert more than one row with a NULL barcode.

Listing 6-30 verifies that we can INSERT items with NOT NULL barcodes, as long as we do not INSERT duplicates.

```
INSERT   INTO dbo.Items
            (
                ItemLabel,
                BoxLabel,
                WeightInPounds,
                Barcode
            )
VALUES   (
                'Big Flashlight',
                'Camping Gear',
                2,
                '12345678'
            ) ;
GO
```

```
INSERT   INTO dbo.Items
         (
           ItemLabel,
           BoxLabel,
           WeightInPounds,
           Barcode
         )
VALUES   (
           'Red Flashlight',
           'Camping Gear',
           1,
           '12345679'
         ) ;
```

Listing 6-30: UNQ_Items_Barcode allows us to insert more rows with NOT NULL barcodes, as long as there are no duplicate barcodes.

Finally, Listing 6-31 verifies that we cannot INSERT a duplicate NOT NULL barcode.

```
INSERT   INTO dbo.Items
         (
           ItemLabel,
           BoxLabel,
           WeightInPounds,
           Barcode
         )
VALUES   (
           'Cooking Pan',
           'Camping Gear',
           2,
           '12345679'
         ) ;

Msg 547, Level 16, State 0, Line 1
```

187

```
The INSERT statement conflicted with the CHECK constraint
"UNQ_Items_Barcode". The conflict occurred in database
"test", table "dbo.Items", column 'Barcode'.
The statement has been terminated.
```

Listing 6-31: UNQ_Items_Barcode **prevents duplicate** NOT NULL **barcodes.**

So, as long as we only insert rows, the CHECK constraint UNQ_Items_Barcode works. Similarly, we can test it for a single-row UPDATE. The constraint allows a single-row UPDATE if there is no collision, as shown in Listing 6-32.

```
-- this update succeeds
BEGIN TRAN ;
UPDATE    dbo.Items
SET       Barcode = '12345677'
WHERE     Barcode = '12345679' ;
ROLLBACK TRAN ;
```

Listing 6-32: The check constraint UNQ_Items_Barcode **allows us to modify a NOT NULL barcode, as long as there is no collision.**

Finally, Listing 6-33 shows that the constraint prevents a single-row UPDATE if it would result in a collision, as expected.

```
BEGIN TRAN ;
UPDATE    dbo.Items
SET       Barcode = '12345678'
WHERE     Barcode = '12345679' ;
ROLLBACK ;
Msg 547, Level 16, State 0, Line 2
The UPDATE statement conflicted with the CHECK constraint
"UNQ_Items_Barcode". The conflict occurred in database
"test", table "dbo.Items", column 'Barcode'.
The statement has been terminated.
```

Listing 6-33: The check constraint UNQ_Items_Barcode **does not allow modification of a NOT NULL barcode if it would result in a collision.**

Apparently our CHECK constraint meets our requirements, correct? Not exactly. Unfortunately, the CHECK constraint may prevent a perfectly valid UPDATE, if that UPDATE modifies more than one row at a time.

In fact, this technique has the following three problems:

- such constraints may produce false negatives; they may prohibit a valid update

- such constraints may produce false positives; they may allow an invalid modification

- such constraints are very slow.

False negatives: failure during multi-row updates

A valid UPDATE can fail to validate against a scalar UDF wrapped in a CHECK constraint. To demonstrate this, we'll attempt to swap two NOT NULL barcodes that are already saved into our table and are clearly unique, as shown in Listing 6-34. Unfortunately, somehow, the UPDATE fails with exactly the same error message as we saw in Listing 6-33.

```
UPDATE   dbo.Items
SET      Barcode = CASE
                      WHEN Barcode = '12345678'
                         THEN '12345679'
                         ELSE '12345678'
                   END
WHERE    Barcode IN ( '12345678', '12345679' ) ;

Msg 547, Level 16, State 0, Line 10
The UPDATE statement conflicted with the CHECK constraint
"UNQ_Items_Barcode". The conflict occurred in database
"test", table "dbo.Items", column 'Barcode'.
The statement has been terminated.
```

Listing 6-34: The failed attempt to swap two unique Barcode items.

Let us verify that this UPDATE does not result in a collision. To accomplish that, we'll have to disable the constraint so that the UPDATE can complete, as shown in Listing 6-35.

```
ALTER TABLE dbo.Items
        NOCHECK CONSTRAINT UNQ_Items_Barcode ;
GO
UPDATE   dbo.Items
SET      Barcode = CASE
                        WHEN Barcode = '12345678'
                            THEN '12345679'
                            ELSE '12345678'
                 END
WHERE    Barcode IN ( '12345678', '12345679' ) ;
```

Listing 6-35: Disabling the constraint UNQ_Items_Barcode so that the update completes.

Listing 6-36 verifies that we do not have duplicate NOT NULL barcodes.

```
SELECT   Barcode,
         COUNT(*)
FROM     dbo.Items
WHERE    Barcode IS NOT NULL
GROUP BY Barcode
HAVING   COUNT(*) > 1 ;

(0 row(s) affected)
```

Listing 6-36: Verifying that we do not have duplicate NOT NULL barcodes.

We can re-enable the constraint and make sure that it is trusted, as shown in Listing 6-37.

```
ALTER TABLE dbo.Items
        WITH CHECK
        CHECK CONSTRAINT UNQ_Items_Barcode ;

SELECT  CAST(name AS char(20)) AS Name,
        is_disabled,
        is_not_trusted
FROM    sys.check_constraints
WHERE   name = 'UNQ_Items_Barcode' ;


Name                     is_disabled    is_not_trusted
--------------------     -----------    ---------------
UNQ_Items_Barcode        0              0
```

Listing 6-37: Re-enabling the constraint and making sure that it is trusted.

Clearly, the CHECK constraint recognizes that, after the UPDATE, all the data in Items table is valid; otherwise the ALTER TABLE command would have failed and the constraint would not be trusted

So, why did the constraint prevent a perfectly correct UPDATE from completing? The reason, 1 believe, is as follows: CHECK constraints evaluate earlier than other types of constraint. As soon as a single row is modified, the CHECK constraint, UNQ_Items_Barcode, verifies that the modified row is valid. This verification occurs before other rows are modified. In this particular case, two rows need to be modified. We do not know which row is modified first but suppose, for the sake of argument, that it is the row with barcode 12345679. When this row is modified, the new barcode for that row is 12345678. Immediately, the CHECK constraint, UNQ_Items_Barcode, invokes the scalar UDF, dbo.GetBarcodeCount, which returns 2, because there is another, as yet unmodified row with the same barcode, 12345678.

> **Note**
>
> *In this particular case we are discussing an update that touches a very small table and modifies only two rows. As such, we are not considering the possibility that this update will execute on several processors in parallel.*

As a result, our CHECK constraint provides a false negative; it erroneously prohibited a perfectly valid multi-row update. Note that the behavior described here is arguably a bug in SQL Server. As such, it could be fixed in future versions of SQL Server.

False positives: allowing an invalid modification

With this technique, a more common problem than the false negative is the false positive, i.e. allowing an invalid modification. This problem occurs because people forget that CHECK constraints only fire if the columns they protect are modified. To demonstrate this, we need to change the implementation of our scalar UDF and rewrap it in a CHECK constraint, as shown in Listing 6-38. Before the change, the UDF took Barcode as a parameter; now it takes ItemLabel.

```
ALTER TABLE dbo.Items
        DROP CONSTRAINT UNQ_Items_Barcode ;
GO
ALTER FUNCTION dbo.GetBarcodeCount
    ( @ItemLabel VARCHAR(30) )
RETURNS INT
AS
    BEGIN ;
        DECLARE @barcodeCount INT ;
        SELECT  @barcodeCount = COUNT(*)
        FROM    dbo.Items AS i1
                INNER JOIN dbo.Items AS i2
                    ON i1.Barcode = i2.Barcode
        WHERE   i1.ItemLabel = @ItemLabel ;
        RETURN @barcodeCount ;
    END ;
GO
ALTER TABLE dbo.Items
ADD CONSTRAINT UNQ_Items_Barcode
CHECK ( dbo.GetBarcodeCount(ItemLabel) < 2 ) ;
GO
```

Listing 6-38: Modifying the GetBarcodeCount scalar UDF and CHECK constraint.

This new implementation looks equivalent to the previous one. To test it, simply rerun Listings 6-29 (including the initial DELETE), 6-30, and 6-31; they should all work exactly as before. However, this new constraint allows an UPDATE that results in a duplicate barcode.

```
BEGIN TRANSACTION ;

UPDATE    dbo.Items
SET       Barcode = '12345678'
WHERE     Barcode = '12345679' ;

SELECT    Barcode ,
          COUNT ( * )
FROM      dbo.Items
GROUP BY Barcode ;

ROLLBACK ;

Barcode
-------------------- -----------
NULL                 2
12345678             2
```

Listing 6-39: An invalid UPDATE succeeds, resulting in a duplicate barcode.

What happened? Why did the constraint not prevent the duplicate? If we fire up Profiler, and set it to track individual statements, we can see that the UDF was not executed at all. From the optimizer's point of view, this makes perfect sense: apparently this CHECK constraint only uses ItemLabel, so there is no point invoking the constraint if ItemLabel has not been changed.

Note that, as usual, there is no guarantee that your optimizer will make the same choice as mine did. This means that Listing 6-39 may, or may not, work on your server exactly as it worked on mine.

Listing 6-40 tricks the optimizer into thinking that ItemLabel has been changed. This time, the CHECK constraint is invoked and prevents a duplicate.

193

```
BEGIN TRANSACTION ;

UPDATE    dbo.Items
SET       Barcode = '12345678' ,
          ItemLabel = ItemLabel + ''
WHERE     Barcode = '12345679' ;

ROLLBACK ;
```

Listing 6-40: The optimizer thinks that ItemLabel has been changed.

```
Msg 547, Level 16, State 0, Line 3
The UPDATE statement conflicted with the CHECK constraint
"UNQ_Items_Barcode". The conflict occurred in database
"TEST3", table "dbo.Items", column 'ItemLabel'.
The statement has been terminated.
```

Listing 6-41: This slightly different update fails, as it should.

As we have seen, UDFs wrapped in CHECK constraints can give us both false positives and false negatives. Fortunately, there are safer and better approaches, described in the following two sections.

The unique filtered index alternative (SQL Server 2008 only)

In SQL Server 2008, a filtered index is a perfect solution for this problem. Listing 6-42 drops our CHECK constraint and replaces it with a filtered index.

```
ALTER TABLE dbo.Items
    DROP CONSTRAINT UNQ_Items_Barcode ;
GO
CREATE UNIQUE NONCLUSTERED INDEX UNQ_Items_Barcode
    ON dbo.Items ( Barcode )
    WHERE Barcode IS NOT NULL ;
```

Listing 6-42: Creating the UNQ_Items_Barcode filtered index.

194

To verify that the filtered index works, we can empty the Items table and rerun all the steps which we took to test our CHECK constraint, which is all the scripts from Listing 6-29 to Listing 6-33. We can also rerun the scenarios where we were getting false positives and false negatives, and verify that our unique filtered index works as expected.

Before moving on, drop the filtered index, so that it does not interfere with the forthcoming examples.

```
DROP INDEX dbo.Items.UNQ_Items_Barcode ;
```

Listing 6-43: Dropping the filtered index.

The indexed view alternative

Prior to SQL Server 2008, we cannot use filtered indexes, but we can use an indexed view to accomplish the same goal.

```
CREATE VIEW dbo.Items_NotNullBarcodes
WITH SCHEMABINDING
AS
SELECT Barcode
FROM dbo.Items
WHERE Barcode IS NOT NULL ;
GO
CREATE UNIQUE CLUSTERED INDEX UNQ_Items_Barcode
ON dbo.Items_NotNullBarcodes ( Barcode ) ;
GO


-- after testing, uncomment the command and
-- drop the view, so that it does not
--interfere with forthcoming examples
--DROP VIEW dbo.Items_NotNullBarcodes;
```

Listing 6-44: Creating an indexed view.

To test, empty the `Items` table, and then run Listings 6-29 to 6-33, as well as Listings 6-34 and 6-39.

Enforcing Data Integrity Using Triggers

Constraints are robust but, as we've discussed, they are often not suitable for implementing more complex data integrity rules. When such requirements arise, many developers turn to triggers. Triggers allow a lot of flexibility; we can tuck pretty much any code into the body of a trigger. Also, in most cases (though not all, as we will see) triggers automatically fire when we modify data.

However, triggers do have limitations with regard to what functionality can be achieved, and are also hard to code, and therefore prone to weaknesses. As such, they are the cause of many common data integrity issues. Some of the typical data integrity problems related to triggers are as follows:

- some triggers falsely assume that only one row at a time is inserted/updated/deleted

- some triggers falsely assume that the primary key columns will never be modified

- under some circumstances, triggers do not fire

- triggers may undo changes made by other triggers

- some triggers do not work under snapshot isolation levels.

Some of these problems can be fixed by improving the triggers. However, not all of these problems mean that the trigger was poorly coded – some are inherent limitations of triggers in general. For example, in some cases the database engine does not fire a trigger, and there is nothing we can change in the trigger to fix that problem.

We'll discuss each of these problems in detail over the coming sections.

Problems with multi-row modifications

In the following example, our goal is to record in a "change log" table any updates made to an item's `Barcode`. Listing 6-45 creates the change log table, `ItemBarcodeChangeLog`. Note that there is no FOREIGN KEY on purpose, because the change log has to be kept even after an item has been removed.

```
CREATE TABLE dbo.ItemBarcodeChangeLog
    (
        ItemLabel varchar(30) NOT NULL,
        ModificationDateTime datetime NOT NULL,
        OldBarcode varchar(20) NULL,
        NewBarcode varchar(20) NULL,
        CONSTRAINT PK_ItemBarcodeChangeLog
            PRIMARY KEY ( ItemLabel, ModificationDateTime )
    ) ;
```

Listing 6-45: Creating a table to log changes in the Barcode column of the Items table.

The FOR UPDATE trigger shown in Listing 6-46 is designed to populate the ItemBarcodeChangeLog table, whenever a barcode is updated. When an UPDATE statement runs against the Items table, the trigger reads the Barcode value as it existed before the update, from the deleted virtual table, and stores it in a variable. It then reads the post-update Barcode value from the inserted virtual table and compares the two values. If the values are different, it logs the change in ItemBarcodeChangeLog. I have added a lot of debugging output, to make it easier to understand how it works.

```
CREATE TRIGGER dbo.Items_LogBarcodeChange ON dbo.Items
    FOR UPDATE
AS
    BEGIN ;
        PRINT 'debugging output: data before update' ;
        SELECT  ItemLabel ,
                Barcode
        FROM    deleted ;

        PRINT 'debugging output: data after update' ;
        SELECT  ItemLabel ,
                Barcode
        FROM    inserted ;

        DECLARE @ItemLabel VARCHAR(30) ,
            @OldBarcode VARCHAR(20) ,
```

```
        @NewBarcode VARCHAR(20) ;
-- retrieve the barcode before update
    SELECT   @ItemLabel = ItemLabel ,
             @OldBarcode = Barcode
    FROM     deleted ;
-- retrieve the barcode after update
    SELECT   @NewBarcode = Barcode
    FROM     inserted ;
    PRINT 'old and new barcode as stored in variables' ;
    SELECT   @OldBarcode AS OldBarcode ,
             @NewBarcode AS NewBarcode ;
-- determine if the barcode changed
    IF ( ( @OldBarcode <> @NewBarcode )
         OR ( @OldBarcode IS NULL
              AND @NewBarcode IS NOT NULL
            )
         OR ( @OldBarcode IS NOT NULL
              AND @NewBarcode IS NULL
            )
       )
      BEGIN ;
        INSERT   INTO dbo.ItemBarcodeChangeLog
                 ( ItemLabel ,
                   ModificationDateTime ,
                   OldBarcode ,
                   NewBarcode


                 )
        VALUES   ( @ItemLabel ,
                   CURRENT_TIMESTAMP ,
                   @OldBarcode ,
                   @NewBarcode
                 ) ;
      END ;
  END ;
```

Listing 6-46: The Items_LogBarcodeChange **trigger logs changes made to the** Barcode **column of the** Items **table.**

198

Listing 6-47 demonstrates how this trigger works when we perform a single-row update.

```
TRUNCATE TABLE dbo.Items ;
TRUNCATE TABLE dbo.ItemBarcodeChangeLog ;
INSERT   dbo.Items
         ( ItemLabel ,
           BoxLabel ,
           WeightInPounds ,
           Barcode
         )
VALUES   ( 'Lamp' ,              -- ItemLabel - varchar(30)
           'Camping Gear' ,      -- BoxLabel - varchar(30)
           5 ,                   -- WeightInPounds - decimal
           '123456'             -- Barcode - varchar(20)
         ) ;
GO
UPDATE   dbo.Items
SET      Barcode = '123457' ;
GO
SELECT   ItemLabel ,
         OldBarcode ,
         NewBarcode
FROM     dbo.ItemBarcodeChangeLog ;

(1 row(s) affected)
debugging output: data before update
ItemLabel                       Barcode
------------------------------- -------------------------------
Lamp                            123456

(1 row(s) affected)
```

```
debugging output: data after update
ItemLabel                           Barcode
------------------------------- -------------------------------
Lamp                                123457

(1 row(s) affected)

old and new barcode as stored in variables
OldBarcode              NewBarcode
-------------------- --------------------
123456                  123457

(1 row(s) affected)
(1 row(s) affected)
(1 row(s) affected)

ItemLabel          OldBarcode           NewBarcode
--------------- -------------------- --------------------
Lamp               123456               123457

(1 row(s) affected)
```

Listing 6-47: One row is modified and our trigger logs the change.

Our trigger works for single-row updates, but how does it handle multi-row updates?
Listing 6-48 empties the change log table, adds one more row to the Items table,
updates **two rows** in the Items table, and then interrogates the log table,
dbo.ItemBarcodeChangeLog, to see what has been saved.

```
SET NOCOUNT ON ;
BEGIN TRANSACTION ;

DELETE  FROM dbo.ItemBarcodeChangeLog ;

INSERT  INTO dbo.Items
        ( ItemLabel ,
          BoxLabel ,
```

```
          Barcode ,
          WeightInPounds
        )
VALUES  ( 'Flashlight' ,
          'Camping Gear' ,
          '234567' ,
          1
        ) ;

UPDATE  dbo.Items
SET     Barcode = Barcode + '9' ;

SELECT  ItemLabel ,
        OldBarcode ,
        NewBarcode
FROM    dbo.ItemBarcodeChangeLog ;

-- roll back to restore test data
ROLLBACK ;

debugging output: data before update
ItemLabel                       Barcode
------------------------------- -------------------------------
Lamp                            123457
Flashlight                      234567

debugging output: data after update
ItemLabel                       Barcode
------------------------------- -------------------------------
Lamp                            1234579
Flashlight                      2345679

old and new barcode as stored in variables
OldBarcode           NewBarcode
-------------------- --------------------
234567               2345679
```

ItemLabel	OldBarcode	NewBarcode
Flashlight	234567	2345679

Listing 6-48: Trigger fails to record all changes when two rows are updated.

Our trigger does not handle the multi-row update properly; it silently inserts only
one row into the log table. Note that I say "inserts only one row," rather than "logs
only one change." The difference is important: if we modify two or more rows, there
is no guarantee that our trigger will record the OldBarcode and NewBarcode values
associated with a single modified row. When we update more than one row, both the
inserted and deleted virtual tables have more than one row, as shown by the
debugging output in Listing 6-48.

The SELECT that populates the OldBarcode variable in our trigger will randomly
pick one of the two values, 123457 or 234567, listed in the "debugging output:
data before update" section. The SELECT that populates NewBarcode works in
the same way; it can choose either 1234579 or 2345679. In this case, it happens that the
OldBarcode and NewBarcode do come from one and the same modified row, and so
the net effect is that the trigger appears to log only one of the updates, albeit correctly.
In fact, this was just chance; it could equally well have taken the OldBarcode from
one row and the NewBarcode from the other, the net effect being an erroneous, single
log record.

In short, this logic used in this trigger does not work for multi-row updates; it contains
a "hidden" assumption that only one row at a time will be updated. We cannot easily get
rid of that incorrect assumption; in fact, since enforcing the assumption does not seem
feasible in this situation, we need to rewrite the trigger from scratch in order to remove
it, as shown in Listing 6-49. This time, rather than store the old and new values in
variables, we use the inserted and deleted virtual tables directly, and then populate
the change log table via a set-based query that joins those virtual tables, and correctly
handles multi-row updates.

```
ALTER TRIGGER dbo.Items_LogBarcodeChange ON dbo.Items
   FOR UPDATE
AS
   BEGIN ;
```

```
PRINT 'debugging output: data before update' ;
SELECT   ItemLabel ,
         Barcode
FROM     deleted ;

PRINT 'debugging output: data after update' ;
SELECT   ItemLabel ,
         Barcode
FROM     inserted ;

INSERT   INTO dbo.ItemBarcodeChangeLog
         ( ItemLabel ,
           ModificationDateTime ,
           OldBarcode ,
           NewBarcode

         )
         SELECT   d.ItemLabel ,
                  CURRENT_TIMESTAMP ,
                  d.Barcode ,
                  i.Barcode
         FROM     inserted AS i
                  INNER JOIN deleted AS d
                      ON i.ItemLabel = d.ItemLabel
         WHERE    ( ( d.Barcode <> i.Barcode )
                    OR ( d.Barcode IS NULL
                         AND i.Barcode IS NOT NULL
                       )
                    OR ( d.Barcode IS NOT NULL
                         AND i.Barcode IS NULL
                       )
                  ) ;
END ;
```

Listing 6-49: Altering our trigger so that it properly handles multi-row updates.

Rerunning Listing 6-48 verifies that our altered trigger now handles multi-row updates.

203

```
(snip)
ItemLabel          OldBarcode              NewBarcode
---------------    --------------------    --------------------
Flashlight         234567                  2345679
Lamp               123457                  1234579
```

Listing 6-50: Our altered trigger properly handles multi-row updates.

The first lesson here is that, when developing triggers, the defensive programmer should always use proper set-based logic, rather than iterative logic.

Mishandling updates that affect the primary key

We have fixed one problem in our trigger, but it has another serious bug; it does not handle the case when the primary key column is also modified. Listing 6-51 demonstrates the problem. This time, the code also updates the ItemLabel column, which forms part of our Primary Key, as well as the Barcode column.

```
BEGIN TRAN ;
DELETE   FROM dbo.ItemBarcodeChangeLog ;
UPDATE   dbo.Items
SET      ItemLabel = ItemLabel + 'C' ,
         Barcode = Barcode + '9' ;

SELECT   ItemLabel ,
         OldBarcode ,
         NewBarcode
FROM     dbo.ItemBarcodeChangeLog ;
ROLLBACK ;

debugging output: data before update
ItemLabel                       Barcode
----------------------------    --------------------------
Lamp                            123457
```

```
debugging output: data after update
ItemLabel                      Barcode
----------------------------   ----------------------------
LampC                          1234579


ItemLabel        OldBarcode           NewBarcode
---------------  -------------------  --------------------
```

Listing 6-51: Our altered trigger does not handle the case when we modify both the primary key column and the barcode.

In this case, the modified row does not get inserted into the log table. The problem is that our trigger relies on the implicit assumption that the primary key column in the Items table is immutable, and so can be relied on to uniquely identify a row. If the PK column is modified, the trigger has no way to relate the old value of Barcode to the new one.

As usual, we need either to enforce this assumption or to eliminate it. If we choose to ensure that our primary key column cannot change, we must modify our trigger to enforce it, as shown in Listing 6-52.

```
ALTER TRIGGER dbo.Items_LogBarcodeChange ON dbo.Items
  FOR UPDATE
AS
  BEGIN
    IF UPDATE(ItemLabel)
      BEGIN ;
        RAISERROR ( 'Modifications of ItemLabel
                                Not Allowed', 16, 1 ) ;
        ROLLBACK ;
        RETURN ;
      END ;

    INSERT  INTO dbo.ItemBarcodeChangeLog
            ( ItemLabel ,
              ModificationDateTime ,
              OldBarcode ,
```

```
          NewBarcode

    )
    SELECT  d.ItemLabel ,
            CURRENT_TIMESTAMP ,
            d.Barcode ,
            i.Barcode
    FROM    inserted AS i
            INNER JOIN deleted AS d
                ON i.ItemLabel = d.ItemLabel
    WHERE   ( ( d.Barcode <> i.Barcode )
            OR ( d.Barcode IS NULL
                AND i.Barcode IS NOT NULL
                )
            OR ( d.Barcode IS NOT NULL
                AND i.Barcode IS NULL
                )
            ) ;
END ;
```

Listing 6-52: Altering our trigger so that is does not allow modification of the primary key column.

To test this trigger, we can rerun Listings 6-48 and 6-51. If, however, our business rules allow changes to be made to labels on items, then we need some other immutable column; some column that cannot be changed, and so can uniquely identify a row.

This is one of those cases when IDENTITY columns are so useful. Listing 6-53 adds an IDENTITY column and creates a UNIQUE constraint to make sure that the IDENTITY column is always unique.

```
ALTER TABLE dbo.Items
ADD ItemID int NOT NULL
            IDENTITY(1, 1) ;
GO
```

```
ALTER TABLE dbo.Items
  ADD CONSTRAINT UNQ_Items_ItemID#
    UNIQUE ( ItemID ) ;
```

Listing 6-53: Creating an IDENTITY column that holds only unique values.

This new IDENTITY column, ItemID, is immutable; it is not possible to modify an IDENTITY column, as Listing 6-54 demonstrates.

```
UPDATE   dbo.Items
SET      ItemID = -1
WHERE    ItemID = 1 ;


Msg 8102, Level 16, State 1, Line 1
Cannot update identity column 'ItemID'.
```

Listing 6-54: It is not possible to modify IDENTITY columns.

We can now use our immutable ItemId column so that it does not have to assume that the primary key will never change, and so fixes the weakness in our trigger, as shown in Listing 6-55.

```
ALTER TRIGGER dbo.Items_LogBarcodeChange ON dbo.Items
  FOR UPDATE
AS
  BEGIN  ;
    INSERT   INTO dbo.ItemBarcodeChangeLog
             ( ItemLabel ,
               ModificationDateTime ,
               OldBarcode ,
               NewBarcode

             )
             SELECT   i.ItemLabel ,
                      CURRENT_TIMESTAMP,
                      d.Barcode ,
                      i.Barcode
```

```
            FROM      inserted AS i
                      INNER JOIN deleted AS d
                         ON i.ItemID = d.ItemID
            WHERE     ( ( d.Barcode <> i.Barcode )
                        OR ( d.Barcode IS NULL
                              AND i.Barcode IS NOT NULL
                            )
                        OR ( d.Barcode IS NOT NULL
                              AND i.Barcode IS NULL
                            )
                      ) ;
    END ;
```

Listing 6-55: The Items_LogBarcodeChange trigger now uses an immutable column, ItemID.

Again, to test this trigger, we can rerun Listings 6-48 and 6-51.

When developing triggers, we need to beware of assuming that the primary key column(s) cannot change. We have learned how to enforce this assumption when it makes sense, and how to eliminate this assumption when it does not make sense.

Sometimes triggers do not fire

Even if we have a "bug-free" trigger, it does not mean that it will fire every time our data changes. There are certain settings and actions that can prevent a trigger from firing:

- disabling a trigger
- use of the IGNORE_TRIGGERS hint in an INSERT statement when the BULK option is used with OPENROWSET
- when the nested triggers or recursive_triggers setting prevents a trigger from firing
- the TRUNCATE TABLE command does not fire FOR DELETE or INSTEAD OF DELETE triggers
- when the BULK INSERT command runs without the FIRE_TRIGGERS option

- if a trigger is dropped and later recreated, then any modifications made to the table in the interim will not have been subject to the trigger's logic

- if a table is dropped and recreated

- when parent and child tables are in different databases, and an old backup of the parent database is restored.

The final item in this list requires some elaboration. When parent and child tables are in different databases, we cannot use a FOREIGN KEY constraint to ensure that there are no orphan rows in our child table. In this case, it is very tempting to use triggers. However, suppose that we need to restore the database that contains our parent table, after a failure. Clearly, when a database is restored, triggers do not fire. This means that nothing protects us from the following scenario:

- back up the parent database

- add a new parent row

- add some child rows referring to that new parent row

- restore the parent database to the backup that does not have the latest parent row.

All of this means that we cannot necessarily assume our trigger fires every time the table it protects is modified. If our system is subject to any of the cases when triggers do not fire, then we need to have a script that will clean up our data. For example, if we have a parent and a child table in different databases, we need a script that deletes orphan rows.

Accidentally overriding changes made by other triggers

When using triggers, it is important to realize that it is possible to have more than one trigger on one and the same table, for one and the same operation. For example, consider the FOR UPDATE trigger shown in Listing 6-50.

```
CREATE TRIGGER dbo.Items_EraseBarcodeChangeLog
ON dbo.Items
  FOR UPDATE
AS
  BEGIN ;
    DELETE  FROM dbo.ItemBarcodeChangeLog ;
  END ;
```

**Listing 6-56: Creating a second FOR UPDATE trigger,
Items_EraseBarcodeChangeLog, on table Items.**

This new trigger creates without any warnings, and we may not realize that we already have another FOR UPDATE trigger on the same table. We can rerun the script in Listing 6-48 and see for ourselves that this new trigger and the previous one do the opposite things and, as such, they should not coexist. Of course, this is a simplified example, but the point is that when we have multiple triggers for the same operation on the same table, then it's a recipe for bugs and data integrity issues.

As a defensive technique, before you start coding a trigger, it's well worth running a quick check to find out if any other triggers exist on the target table. To be even safer, after adding a trigger it is a good practice to check for multiple triggers on the same table for the same operation. Listing 6-57 shows a script that finds all the tables on which there is more than one trigger for the same operation.

```
SELECT   OBJECT_NAME(t.parent_id),
         te.type_desc
FROM     sys.triggers AS t
         INNER JOIN sys.trigger_events AS te
ON t.OBJECT_ID = te.OBJECT_ID
GROUP BY OBJECT_NAME(t.parent_id),te.type_desc
HAVING   COUNT(*) > 1 ;
```

**Listing 6-57: Selecting all the tables on which there is more than one trigger for the
same operation.**

Multiple triggers for the same operation, on the same table, not only introduce the chances of conflicting changes, they also introduce the chance of redundant actions, or of unwanted and maybe unknown dependencies on undocumented execution orders.

If we want to make sure that there is not more than one trigger for one operation on one table, we can wrap the query in Listing 6-57 in a unit test and have our test harness verify that it never returns anything.

Before moving on to other examples, let us get rid of the triggers we no longer need, as shown in Listing 6-58.

```
DROP TRIGGER dbo.Items_EraseBarcodeChangeLog ;
GO
DROP TRIGGER dbo.Items_LogBarcodeChange ;
```

Listing 6-58: Dropping the triggers.

Problems with triggers under snapshot isolation levels

In Chapter 4, we discussed in detail how triggers can fail when running under snapshot isolation. As we demonstrated there, when our triggers are selecting from other rows or other tables, in some cases we are implicitly assuming that they will not run under snapshot isolation level. In such cases, it is necessary to use the READCOMMITTEDLOCK hint to eliminate this assumption.

Summary

We have discussed several cases where incorrect assumptions may lead to compromised data integrity, and we have investigated ways to improve the integrity of data by proper use of constraints and triggers.

Data integrity logic in the application layer is too easily bypassed. The only completely robust way to ensure data integrity is to use a trusted constraint. Even then, we need to test our constraints, and make sure that they handle nullable columns properly.

Triggers are dramatically more flexible than constraints, but we need to be very careful when we use them. We need to make sure that they properly handle multi-row modifications, modifications of primary key columns, and snapshot isolation. Also we need to be aware that sometimes triggers do not fire, and to be ready to clean up data if that actually happens.

Following is a brief summary of the defensive techniques learned in this chapter with regard to protecting data integrity.

- When testing CHECK constraints, always include in your test cases rows with NULLs.

- Don't make assumptions about the data, based on the presence of FOREIGN KEY or CHECK constraints, unless they are all trusted.

- UDFs wrapped in CHECK constraints are sometimes unreliable as a means to enforce data integrity rules. Filtered Indexes or Indexed Views are safer alternatives.

- When developing triggers:

  - always use proper set-based logic; never assume that only one row at a time can be modified

  - if your code assumes that the primary key won't be modified, make sure that is true, or use an IDENTITY column that is, by definition, immutable

  - query the sys.triggers system view to make sure there are no existing triggers on the table with which your one may interfere

  - make appropriate use of the READCOMMITTEDLOCK hint if the trigger needs to run under snapshot isolation levels.

Chapter 7: Advanced Use of Constraints

In the previous chapter, as well as in Chapter 4, we discussed some of the common problems with enforcing data integrity logic in triggers. Some developers have a tendency to hide all sorts of twisted logic inside the body of a trigger, in order to enforce complex business rules. Once implemented, a trigger tends to sink quietly into the background and get forgotten...until it suddenly begins misfiring and causing seemingly inexplicable data integrity issues. For example, as we proved in Chapter 4, a trigger that works when using the standard `READ COMMITTED` isolation level may fail under the snapshot isolation levels.

Constraints are, in general, a safer haven. As long as a constraint is trusted, then we know for sure that all our data complies with the rules that it dictates. However, received wisdom suggests that constraints can enforce only a very limited set of simple rules. In fact, in many cases developers give up on constraints far too easily; they allow us to solve far more complex problems than many people realize.

In this chapter, we'll revisit some of the problems discussed in previous chapters, and imperfectly solved using a trigger, and show how to solve each one using only constraints. My intention is not to lay out brain-teasers, or try to solve Sudoku puzzles in T-SQL. On the contrary, my goal is very pragmatic: to demonstrate rock-solid constraints-only solutions for typical problems. When data integrity is important, such solutions may be strongly preferable to the alternatives that use triggers.

Unlike in Chapter 4, in this chapter we shall not need to worry about the effect of isolation levels. Constraints are completely robust and ensure the integrity of data regardless of the isolation level at the time when we run the modification.

The Ticket-Tracking System

In Chapter 4, we implemented a trigger-based solution to the problem of assigning tickets in a ticket-tracking system. Our **AFTER UPDATE** trigger, dbo.Developers_Upd, enforced the following two business rules:

- developers cannot go on vacation if they have active tickets assigned to them

- inactive tickets cannot be changed to active status if they are assigned to developers that are on vacation.

Here, we'll re-implement these business rules using only constraints and, in addition, we'll be able to enforce the rule that "newly added active tickets cannot be assigned to a developer on vacation," which would have required an additional **AFTER INSERT** trigger. To ensure that we are all on the same page, we'll drop the original tables from Chapter 4 and start again from scratch.

```
IF EXISTS ( SELECT   *
            FROM     sys.objects
            WHERE    OBJECT_ID
                     = OBJECT_ID(N'dbo.Tickets') )
  BEGIN ;
    DROP TABLE dbo.Tickets ;
  END ;
GO


IF EXISTS ( SELECT   *
            FROM     sys.objects
            WHERE    OBJECT_ID
                     = OBJECT_ID(N'dbo.Developers') )
  BEGIN ;
    DROP TABLE dbo.Developers ;
  END ;
GO


CREATE TABLE dbo.Developers
  (
    DeveloperID INT NOT NULL ,
```

```
    FirstName VARCHAR(30) NOT NULL ,
    Lastname VARCHAR(30) NOT NULL ,
    DeveloperStatus VARCHAR(8) NOT NULL ,
    CONSTRAINT PK_Developers PRIMARY KEY (DeveloperID) ,
    CONSTRAINT CHK_Developers_Status
        CHECK (DeveloperStatus
          IN ( 'Active', 'Vacation' ) )
) ;

CREATE TABLE dbo.Tickets
  (
    TicketID INT NOT NULL ,
    AssignedToDeveloperID INT NULL ,
    Description VARCHAR(50) NOT NULL ,
    TicketStatus VARCHAR(6) NOT NULL ,
    DeveloperStatus VARCHAR(8) NOT NULL ,
    CONSTRAINT PK_Tickets PRIMARY KEY ( TicketID ) ,
    CONSTRAINT FK_Tickets_Developers
        FOREIGN KEY ( AssignedToDeveloperID )
            REFERENCES dbo.Developers ( DeveloperID ) ,
    CONSTRAINT CHK_Tickets_Status
        CHECK ( TicketStatus IN ( 'Active', 'Closed' ) )
) ;
```

Listing 7-1: Recreating the Developers and Tickets tables.

Enforcing business rules using constraints only

The Developers table is identical to one we used in Chapter 4, but the Tickets table is different; it has an extra column, DeveloperStatus, which we will use in a CHECK constraint that attempts to enforce both our business rules, as shown in Listing 7-2.

```
ALTER TABLE dbo.Tickets
  ADD CONSTRAINT CHK_Tickets_ValidStatuses
    CHECK(    (TicketStatus = 'Active'
              AND DeveloperStatus = 'Active')
           OR TicketStatus = 'Closed'
        ) ;
```

Listing 7-2: The `CHK_Tickets_ValidStatuses` **constraint enforces both business rules.**

However, this constraint makes a serious assumption, and we do not know yet if we can enforce it. Can we really guarantee that the `Tickets.DeveloperStatus` column will **always** match the `Developers.DeveloperStatus` column, for the assigned developer?

The answer is "maybe." **FOREIGN KEY** constraints are supposed to guarantee that columns in different tables match and the one shown in Listing 7-3 attempts to do just that. We'll discuss why we need the **ON UPDATE CASCADE** clause shortly.

```
ALTER TABLE dbo.Tickets
  ADD CONSTRAINT FK_Tickets_Developers_WithStatus
    FOREIGN KEY (AssignedToDeveloperID, DeveloperStatus)
      REFERENCES dbo.Developers
         ( DeveloperID, DeveloperStatus )
  ON UPDATE CASCADE ;
```

Listing 7-3: `FK_Tickets_Developers_WithStatus` **attempts to ensure that, for a given developer, the relevant column values match.**

Unfortunately, when we run Listing 7-3, it fails. Fortunately, the error message is very explicit and clear.

```
Msg 1776, Level 16, State 0, Line 1
There are no primary or candidate keys in the referenced
table 'dbo.Developers' that match the referencing column list
in the foreign key 'FK_Tickets_Developers_WithStatus'.
Msg 1750, Level 16, State 0, Line 1
Could not create constraint. See previous errors.
```

Listing 7-4:   A very clear error message.

As the error states, the column, or combination of columns, to which a FOREIGN KEY refers in the parent table, in this case (DeveloperID, DeveloperStatus), must be unique. The uniqueness can be enforced very easily using a UNIQUE constraint or, as shown in Listing 7-5, a UNIQUE index.

```
CREATE UNIQUE INDEX UNQ_Developers_IDWithStatus
ON dbo.Developers( DeveloperID, DeveloperStatus ) ;
```

Listing 7-5:   Enforcing the uniqueness of (DeveloperID, DeveloperStatus) in the Developers table.

The reason I chose to use an index here, rather than a constraint, is because I try to use the latter strictly to enforce business rules, and the former for performance or other issues. In this case, we are not enforcing a business rule (as DeveloperID by itself is already a candidate key) so much as overcoming a SQL Server technicality, and therefore I chose to use an index.

Now Listing 7-3 will complete successfully. Before testing our solution, let's summarize the changes we have made so far.

- Added a new column, DeveloperStatus, to the Tickets table.

- Added a CHECK constraint, CHK_Tickets_ValidStatuses, to enforce our business rules.

- Created a UNIQUE index on (DeveloperID, DeveloperStatus) in the Developers table, which allowed these two columns to be used as the parent columns in a foreign key relationship.

- Created a dual-key FOREIGN KEY constraint on the Tickets table, FK_Tickets_ Developers_WithStatus, which includes an ON UPDATE CASCADE clause.

We need to realize that in this solution one and the same information, the status of a developer, can be stored in more than one place: both in a row in the Developers table and, if the developer has tickets, in each corresponding row in the Tickets table. Clearly this is de-normalization. Usually de-normalization is common practice in data warehousing environments, but is frowned upon in OLTP systems. However, in this particular case, de-normalization is very useful.

Note that, at this time, we have two FOREIGN KEY constraints referring from Tickets to Developers:

- **FK_Tickets_Developers**, which relates a single column, AssignedToDeveloperID, in Tickets to its equivalent in Developers

- **FK_Tickets_Developers_WithStatus**, which relates two columns, (AssignedToDeveloperID, DeveloperStatus), in Tickets to their equivalent in Developers.

The reason why we need them both will soon become clear. Let's see how our constraints work. Listing 7-6 adds a single developer to our system, who is on vacation.

```
INSERT  INTO dbo.Developers
          ( DeveloperID ,
            FirstName ,
            Lastname ,
            DeveloperStatus
          )
VALUES  ( 1 ,
            'Justin' ,
            'Larsen' ,
            'Vacation'
          ) ;
```

Listing 7-6: Adding a developer who is on vacation.

Listing 7-7 shows that our CHECK constraint prevents an attempt to assign an active ticket to a developer on vacation.

```
INSERT INTO dbo.Tickets
         ( TicketID ,
           AssignedToDeveloperID ,
           Description ,
           TicketStatus ,
           DeveloperStatus
         )
VALUES  ( 1 ,
           1 ,
           'Cannot print TPS report' ,
           'Active' ,
           'Vacation'
         ) ;

Msg 547, Level 16, State 0, Line 1
The INSERT statement conflicted with the CHECK constraint
"CHK_Tickets_ValidStatuses". The conflict occurred in
database "test2", table "dbo.Tickets".
The statement has been terminated.
```

Listing 7-7: We cannot add an active ticket assigned to a developer on vacation.

Also, our dual-column FOREIGN KEY prevents us from cheating the system by adding a ticket with a DeveloperStatus that does not match the status of the assigned developer.

```
INSERT INTO dbo.Tickets
         ( TicketID ,
           AssignedToDeveloperID ,
           Description ,
           TicketStatus ,
           DeveloperStatus
         )
```

```
VALUES   ( 1 ,
            1 ,
            'Cannot print TPS report' ,
            'Active' ,
            'Active'
          ) ;


Msg 547, Level 16, State 0, Line 1
The INSERT statement conflicted with the FOREIGN KEY
constraint "FK_Tickets_Developers_WithStatus". The conflict
occurred in database "test2", table "dbo.Developers".
The statement has been terminated.
```

Listing 7-8: The DeveloperStatus **must match the** Status **of the**
assigned developer.

Listing 7-9 shows that we can add a closed ticket, but cannot reopen it, while the
developer is still on vacation.

```
INSERT   INTO dbo.Tickets
          ( TicketID ,
            AssignedToDeveloperID ,
            Description ,
            TicketStatus,
            DeveloperStatus
          )
VALUES   ( 1 ,
            1 ,
            'Cannot print TPS report' ,
            'Closed' ,
            'Vacation'
          ) ;


(1 row(s) affected)

UPDATE   dbo.Tickets
SET      TicketStatus = 'Active'
```

```
WHERE     TicketID = 1 ;

Msg 547, Level 16, State 0, Line 1
The UPDATE statement conflicted with the CHECK constraint
"CHK_Tickets_ValidStatuses". The conflict occurred in
database "test2", table "dbo.Tickets".
The statement has been terminated.
```

Listing 7-9: Adding a closed ticket and a failed attempt to reopen it.

Thanks to the ON UPDATE CASCADE clause on our FOREIGN KEY constraint, when our developer returns from vacation and is active again, his changed status, as reflected in the Developers table, is automatically propagated to the DeveloperStatus column of the Tickets table, as demonstrated in Listing 7-10.

```
PRINT 'DeveloperStatus when Justin is on vacation' ;
SELECT  TicketID ,
        DeveloperStatus
FROM    dbo.Tickets ;

UPDATE  dbo.Developers
SET     DeveloperStatus = 'Active'
WHERE   DeveloperID = 1 ;

PRINT 'DeveloperStatus when Justin is active' ;
SELECT  TicketID ,
        DeveloperStatus
FROM    dbo.Tickets ;

DeveloperStatus when Justin is on vacation
TicketID     DeveloperStatus
-----------  ----------------
1            Vacation

(1 row(s) affected)
```

```
DeveloperStatus when Justin is active
TicketID      DeveloperStatus
----------    ----------------
1             Active


(1 row(s) affected)
```

Listing 7-10: Justin's changed status is propagated to the ticket assigned to him.

This automatic propagation of values in the `Developer.DeveloperStatus` column to the `Tickets.DeveloperStatus` column, via the cascading update in the `FOREIGN KEY` constraint, is the bedrock of this technique. Now, if we attempt to reopen the ticket, by rerunning the `UPDATE` statement from Listing 7-9, it will succeed because the `DeveloperStatus` column for the ticket correctly indicates that the developer is active.

Continuing our testing, we need to ensure that our developer cannot go on vacation if any active tickets are assigned to him, as verified by Listing 7-11.

```
UPDATE  dbo.Developers
SET     DeveloperStatus = 'Vacation'
WHERE   DeveloperID = 1 ;


Msg 547, Level 16, State 0, Line 1
The UPDATE statement conflicted with the CHECK constraint
"CHK_Tickets_ValidStatuses". The conflict occurred in
database "test2", table "dbo.Tickets".
The statement has been terminated.
```

Listing 7-11: Justin has an active ticket, so he cannot go on vacation.

If we close the ticket, Justin can begin his vacation.

```
BEGIN TRANSACTION ;


UPDATE  dbo.Tickets
SET     TicketStatus = 'Closed'
```

```
WHERE    TicketID = 1 ;

UPDATE   dbo.Developers
SET      DeveloperStatus = 'Vacation'
WHERE    DeveloperID = 1 ;

-- we shall need the test data intact
-- to use in other examples,
-- so we roll the changes back

ROLLBACK ;
```

Listing 7-12: Closing the ticket allows Justin to take a vacation.

Alternatively, we can assign the ticket to another developer.

```
BEGIN TRANSACTION ;

INSERT   INTO dbo.Developers
         ( DeveloperID ,
           FirstName ,
           Lastname ,
           DeveloperStatus
         )
VALUES ( 2 ,
           'Peter' ,
           'Yang' ,
           'Active'
         ) ;

UPDATE   dbo.Tickets
SET      AssignedToDeveloperID = 2
WHERE    TicketID = 1 ;

UPDATE   dbo.Developers
SET      DeveloperStatus = 'Vacation'
WHERE    DeveloperID = 1 ;
```

```
-- we shall need the test data intact
-- to use in other examples,
-- so we roll the changes back

ROLLBACK ;
```

Listing 7-13: Reassigning an active ticket.

Also we need to verify that our system works when we modify Developers. DeveloperID column, as shown in Listing 7-14.

```
BEGIN TRANSACTION ;
PRINT 'Original Data in Tickets table' ;
SELECT   TicketID ,
            AssignedToDeveloperID ,
         DeveloperStatus
FROM     dbo.Tickets ;

UPDATE   dbo.Developers
SET      DeveloperID = -1
WHERE    DeveloperID = 1 ;

PRINT 'Data in Tickets table after DeveloperID was modified'
;
SELECT   TicketID ,
            AssignedToDeveloperID ,
         DeveloperStatus
FROM     dbo.Tickets ;

ROLLBACK ;

Original Data in Tickets table
TicketID     AssignedToDeveloperID DeveloperStatus
-----------  --------------------- ----------------
1            1                     Active
```

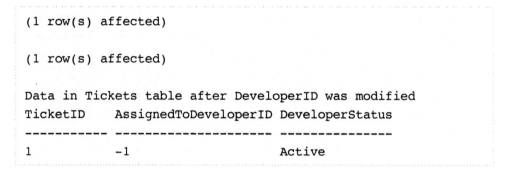

```
(1 row(s) affected)

(1 row(s) affected)

Data in Tickets table after DeveloperID was modified
TicketID     AssignedToDeveloperID DeveloperStatus
-----------  --------------------- ----------------
1                -1                    Active
```

Listing 7-14: The modified Developers.DeveloperID **value propagates into the** Tickets **table.**

As we have seen, when we modify Developers.DeveloperID, the change propagates into the Tickets table. This was not one of our requirements, but is a side effect of the ON UPDATE CASCADE clause. We'll modify our solution later, and this side effect will be gone.

So far, our constraints have worked as expected in all the cases. Of course, if we were rolling out a production system, our testing would be far from complete. For example, we should test cases when more than one ticket is assigned to a developer, cases where we modify more than one row, and the case where we modify the Developers.DeveloperID column for more than one row. However, we shall not demonstrate complete testing here; the solution presented here passes complete testing, and I encourage you to try out different test cases as an exercise.

Removing the performance hit of ON UPDATE CASCADE

We need to discuss in a little more detail the ON UPDATE CASCADE behavior and its performance implications. Whenever a developer's status changes, the corresponding DeveloperStatus column in the Tickets table changes automatically, for all the tickets assigned to that developer. This behavior definitely gets the job done, and our business rules are robustly enforced. However, we need to ask ourselves the following question: why do we need to update the DeveloperStatus column for closed tickets? Clearly our CHECK constraint only needs to use DeveloperStatus if the ticket is open.

Why should we care if the `DeveloperStatus` column is updated for closed tickets? The reason is simple: performance. In our test cases, with just one or two developers and only one ticket, it does not matter whether or not we update the `DeveloperStatus` column for closed tickets. However, in real life, a developer might have hundreds or even thousands of closed tickets assigned to him or her, but just a handful of active ones. If we can avoid modifying those closed tickets every time a developer goes on vacation, then we can significantly improve the performance of the system.

Let us change our solution, so that the `DeveloperStatus` column is not updated for closed tickets. In order to do this, we need to ensure that `Tickets.DeveloperStatus` is NULL for all closed tickets. Since open tickets can never be assigned to a developer on vacation, the result will be that `Tickets.DeveloperStatus` can now only be `Active` or NULL, and so the ON UPDATE CASCADE clause becomes redundant.

Execute the script in Listing 7-15, which performs the following steps:

- deletes the contents of both the Tickets and `Developers` tables (of course, in a production system we would take steps to preserve our data rather than delete it outright)

- makes the `Tickets.DeveloperStatus` column nullable, because we need it to be NULL for closed tickets

- modifies our `CHK_Tickets_ValidStatuses` constraint to enforce the rules that `DeveloperStatus` is NULL for all closed tickets, and is `Active` for all active ones

- drops the `FK_Tickets_Developers_WithStatus` constraint and recreates it without the ON UPDATE CASCADE clause, which is now redundant.

```
DELETE FROM dbo.Tickets ;
DELETE FROM dbo.Developers ;
GO


ALTER TABLE dbo.Tickets
DROP CONSTRAINT FK_Tickets_Developers_WithStatus ;
GO


ALTER TABLE dbo.Tickets
ALTER COLUMN DeveloperStatus VARCHAR(8) NULL ;
```

```
GO

ALTER TABLE dbo.Tickets
DROP CONSTRAINT CHK_Tickets_ValidStatuses ;
GO

ALTER TABLE dbo.Tickets
ADD CONSTRAINT CHK_Tickets_ValidStatuses
  CHECK((TicketStatus = 'Active'
         AND DeveloperStatus = 'Active'
         AND DeveloperStatus IS NOT NULL )
         OR (TicketStatus = 'Closed'
         AND DeveloperStatus IS NULL)) ;
GO

ALTER TABLE dbo.Tickets
  ADD CONSTRAINT FK_Tickets_Developers_WithStatus
    FOREIGN KEY (AssignedToDeveloperID, DeveloperStatus)
      REFERENCES dbo.Developers
        ( DeveloperID, DeveloperStatus ) ;
```

Listing 7-15: Making the DeveloperStatus column nullable and adding a new CHK_Tickets_ValidStatuses constraint to ensure the column is NULL for all closed tickets.

We are now ready to run some tests against our changed implementation. Listing 7-16 inserts some fresh test data, including a closed ticket with NULL DeveloperStatus.

```
INSERT    INTO dbo.Developers
          ( DeveloperID ,
            FirstName ,
            Lastname ,
            DeveloperStatus
          )
VALUES  ( 1 ,
            'Justin' ,
            'Larsen' ,
```

```
                'Active'
            ) ;

INSERT INTO dbo.Tickets
            ( TicketID ,
              AssignedToDeveloperID ,
              Description ,
              TicketStatus ,
              DeveloperStatus
            )
VALUES    ( 1 ,
              1 ,
              'Cannot print TPS report' ,
              'Active' ,
              'Active'
            ) ;

INSERT INTO dbo.Tickets
            ( TicketID ,
              AssignedToDeveloperID ,
              Description ,
              TicketStatus ,
              DeveloperStatus
            )
VALUES    ( 2 ,
              1 ,
              'TPS report for June hangs' ,
              'Closed' ,
              NULL
            ) ;
```

Listing 7-16: Repopulating Developers and Tickets tables.

If we rerun Listing 7-11, it will raise an error, confirming that Justin cannot go on vacation, because there is an active ticket assigned to him

Now, when we close an open ticket, we also need to set DeveloperStatus to NULL, as shown in Listing 7-17.

```
UPDATE   dbo.Tickets
SET      TicketStatus = 'Closed' ,
         DeveloperStatus = NULL
WHERE    TicketID = 1 ;
```

Listing 7-17: Closing the ticket.

At this moment, both tickets assigned to Justin are closed, and DeveloperStatus is NULL for both those tickets. This means that, for these tickets, the pair of columns (AssignedDeveloperID, DeveloperStatus) does not refer to any row in the Developers table, because DeveloperStatus is NULL. Note that, even for closed tickets, we still need to ensure that Tickets.AssignedDeveloperID refers to a valid Developers.DeveloperID; this is why we have another FOREIGN KEY constraint (FK_Tickets_Developers) on AssignedDeveloperID only.

Let's proceed with the testing. If Justin goes on vacation, we expect that no rows in the Tickets table should be modified, as verified by Listing 7-18.

```
-- we need a transaction
-- so that we can easily restore test data
BEGIN TRANSACTION ;
GO
SELECT   TicketID ,
         AssignedToDeveloperID ,
         Description ,
         TicketStatus ,
         DeveloperStatus
FROM     dbo.Tickets ;
GO
UPDATE   dbo.Developers
SET      DeveloperStatus = 'Vacation'
WHERE    DeveloperID = 1 ;
GO
SELECT   TicketID ,
```

```
          AssignedToDeveloperID ,
          Description ,
          TicketStatus ,
          DeveloperStatus
FROM      dbo.Tickets ;
GO
ROLLBACK ;
```

Listing 7-18: No rows in the Tickets table are modified if Justin goes on vacation.

If Justin is on vacation we cannot reopen a ticket assigned to him, as verified by Listing 7-19.

```
BEGIN TRANSACTION ;
GO
UPDATE    dbo.Developers
SET       DeveloperStatus = 'Vacation'
WHERE     DeveloperID = 1 ;

-- attempt one: just change the ticket's status
UPDATE    dbo.Tickets
SET       TicketStatus = 'Active'
WHERE     TicketID = 1 ;

Msg 547, Level 16, State 0, Line 6
The UPDATE statement conflicted with the CHECK constraint
"CHK_Tickets_ValidStatuses"

-- attempt two: change both Status and DeveloperStatus
UPDATE    dbo.Tickets
SET       TicketStatus = 'Active' ,
          DeveloperStatus = 'Active'
WHERE     TicketID = 1 ;

Msg 547, Level 16, State 0, Line 11
The UPDATE statement conflicted with the FOREIGN KEY
constraint "FK_Tickets_Developers_WithStatus".
```

```
SELECT   *
FROM     dbo.Tickets

-- restoring test data to its original state
ROLLBACK ;
```

Listing 7-19: Trying to reopen a ticket assigned to Justin.

We have seen how three constraints work together to enforce a rather complex business rule. Originally, we used an approach that works in the simplest possible way, and then we modified it to be more efficient. We have also removed the side effect of changes in `Developers.DeveloperID` column propagating into the `Tickets` table (and our FK constraint will prohibit changes that would result in orphaned rows).

Let's move on to discuss another case where constraints really shine: inventory systems.

Constraints and Rock-Solid Inventory Systems

In the previous example, we used constraints to improve a trigger-based solution discussed in Chapter 4. This next example is completely new and involves an inventory system that is used to store the history of changes to an inventory of items. Listing 7-20 creates the `InventoryLog` table, for this purpose.

```
CREATE TABLE dbo.InventoryLog
    (
-- In a real production system
-- there would be a foreign key to the Items table.
-- We have skipped it to keep the example simple.
        ItemID INT NOT NULL ,
        ChangeDate DATETIME NOT NULL ,
        ChangeQuantity INT NOT NULL ,
-- in a highly concurrent system
-- this combination of columns
-- might not be unique, but let us keep
-- the example simple
```

```
        CONSTRAINT PK_InventoryLog
            PRIMARY KEY ( ItemID, ChangeDate )
    ) ;
```

Listing 7-20: The `InventoryLog` table, which stores the history of changes to our inventory.

To record any change in the inventory, we insert rows into the `Inventory` table. At the very beginning, when we do not have any rows in the `InventoryLog` table, we assume that we do not have any items in our inventory at all. An increase or decrease in inventory for a given item is reflected by adding new rows. For example, if we need to record the fact that we added five items of a given type to our inventory, we add a row with `ChangeQuantity=5`. If we withdraw three items, we add another row with `ChangeQuantity=-3`.

Our business rule states that, for a given item, a change in the inventory cannot be allowed if it will result in a net inventory that is less than zero. Of course, we cannot take out more of an item than we currently have in stock. In order to determine the current inventory amount for a given item, we must query the history of all inventory changes for the item, i.e. calculate the net total in the `ChangeQuantity` column, resulting from all previous transactions, and make sure that the proposed `ChangeQuantity` would not result in negative inventory. This is the sort of calculation that would traditionally be performed in a trigger but, in order to make the trigger watertight, the code would be quite complex. Instead, we'll perform the calculation as part of our `INSERT` statement, using a `HAVING` clause to prevent illegal withdrawals.

Listing 7-21 provides several examples of valid and invalid changes to the inventory. For simplicity, we disallow retrospective logging. For example, if we have recorded for Item1 an inventory change for 20100103 then we cannot subsequently log an inventory change for the same item with a date earlier than 20100103. In a production system, we would encapsulate our modification code in a stored procedure, which can be called for all changes. Here, however, we shall just use the simplest possible code that demonstrates the technique. Note that in several places we use the `HAVING` clause without `GROUP BY`. This is a perfectly correct usage; we don't really need a `GROUP BY` clause to select aggregates such as `SUM`, `MIN`, and `AVG`, as long as we only select aggregates and not column values. Likewise, we don't need a `GROUP BY` clause if we want to use such aggregates in the `HAVING` clause, as long as column values are not used in that clause.

```
SET NOCOUNT ON ;
BEGIN TRANSACTION ;

-- this is a valid change:
-- we can always add to InventoryLog
INSERT   INTO dbo.InventoryLog
        ( ItemID ,
          ChangeDate ,
          ChangeQuantity
        )
VALUES  ( 1 ,
          '20100101' ,
          5
        ) ;

DECLARE @ItemID INT ,
    @QuantityToWithdraw INT ,
    @ChangeDate DATETIME ;

SET @ItemID = 1 ;
SET @QuantityToWithdraw = 3 ;
SET @ChangeDate = '20100103' ;

-- this is a valid change:
-- we have enough units of item 1 on hand

INSERT   INTO dbo.InventoryLog
        ( ItemID ,
          ChangeDate ,
          ChangeQuantity
        )
        SELECT  @ItemID ,
                @ChangeDate ,
                -@QuantityToWithdraw
        FROM    dbo.InventoryLog
        WHERE   ItemID = @ItemID
-- we have enough units of item 1 on hand
        HAVING  COALESCE(SUM(ChangeQuantity), 0)
```

```
                                    - @QuantityToWithdraw >= 0
-- we do not have log entries for later days
                AND COUNT(CASE WHEN @ChangeDate <=
                                    ChangeDate THEN ChangeDate
                        END) = 0 ;
SELECT  *
FROM      dbo.InventoryLog ;


SET @ItemID = 1 ;
SET @QuantityToWithdraw = 15 ;
SET @ChangeDate = '20100104' ;


-- this is a invalid change:
-- we only have 2 units left of Item 1
-- so we cannot withdraw more than 2 units


INSERT  INTO dbo.InventoryLog
        ( ItemID ,
          ChangeDate ,
          ChangeQuantity
        )
        SELECT  @ItemID ,
                @ChangeDate ,
                -@QuantityToWithdraw
        FROM    dbo.InventoryLog
        WHERE   ItemID = @ItemID
-- we have enough units of item 1 on hand
        HAVING COALESCE(SUM(ChangeQuantity), 0)
                                    - @QuantityToWithdraw >= 0
-- we do not have log entries for later days
                AND COUNT(CASE WHEN @ChangeDate <=
                                    ChangeDate THEN ChangeDate
                        END) = 0 ;


IF @@ROWCOUNT = 0
  BEGIN ;
    SELECT 'Not enough inventory to withdraw '
            + CAST(@QuantityToWithdraw AS VARCHAR(20))
```

```
                        + ' units of item '
            + CAST(@ItemID AS VARCHAR(20))
            + ' or there are log entries for later days' ;
    END ;

-- this is a invalid change:
-- we do not have any quantity of item 2
-- so we cannot withdraw any quantity
SET @ItemID = 2 ;
SET @QuantityToWithdraw = 1 ;
SET @ChangeDate = '20100103' ;

INSERT  INTO dbo.InventoryLog
        ( ItemID ,
          ChangeDate ,
          ChangeQuantity
        )
        SELECT  @ItemID ,
                @ChangeDate ,
                -@QuantityToWithdraw
        FROM    dbo.InventoryLog
        WHERE   ItemID = @ItemID
-- we have enough units of item 1 on hand
        HAVING  COALESCE(SUM(ChangeQuantity), 0)
                        - @QuantityToWithdraw >= 0
-- we do not have log entries for later days
                AND COUNT(CASE WHEN @ChangeDate <=
                                ChangeDate THEN ChangeDate
                        END) = 0 ;

IF @@ROWCOUNT = 0
  BEGIN ;
    SELECT 'Not enough inventory to withdraw '
            + CAST(@QuantityToWithdraw AS VARCHAR(20))
                    + ' units of item '
            + CAST(@ItemID AS VARCHAR(20))
            + ' or there are log entries for later days' ;
    END ;
```

235

```
SELECT   ItemID ,
         ChangeDate ,
         ChangeQuantity
FROM     dbo.InventoryLog ;

ROLLBACK ;
```

Listing 7-21: Examples of possible and impossible changes to the inventory.

For the tiny number of rows in Listing 7-21, it is not a problem to perform a SUM on the ChangeQuantity column every time we change the inventory. However, for a real inventory system, with hundreds of thousands of transactions per item, this becomes a huge performance drain.

To eliminate this expensive querying of historical inventory changes, it is very tempting to store the new stock quantity of a given item that results from an inventory change, along with the change amount. Let's add one more column to InventoryLog table to store the current amount, as shown in Listing 7-22. At the same time, we add a CHECK constraint to make sure that CurrentQuantity is never negative.

```
ALTER TABLE dbo.InventoryLog
ADD CurrentQuantity INT NOT NULL ;
GO

ALTER TABLE dbo.InventoryLog
ADD
  CONSTRAINT CHK_InventoryLog_NonnegativeCurrentQuantity
    CHECK( CurrentQuantity >= 0) ;
```

Listing 7-22: Adding the CurrentQuantity column to the InventoryLog table.

Now, instead of querying the history of changes, we need only look up the Current-Quantity value for the most recent row, and add it to the proposed ChangeQuantity, as shown in Listing 7-23.

```sql
SET NOCOUNT ON ;
BEGIN TRANSACTION ;

DECLARE @ItemID INT ,
    @ChangeQuantity INT ,
    @ChangeDate DATETIME ;

SET @ItemID = 1 ;
SET @ChangeQuantity = 5 ;
SET @ChangeDate = '20100101' ;

-- this is a valid change:
-- we can always add to InventoryLog
INSERT   INTO dbo.InventoryLog
        ( ItemID ,
          ChangeDate ,
          ChangeQuantity ,
          CurrentQuantity
        )
    SELECT   @ItemID ,
             @ChangeDate ,
             @ChangeQuantity ,
             COALESCE(( SELECT TOP (1)
                                    CurrentQuantity
                        FROM      dbo.InventoryLog
                        WHERE     ItemID = @ItemID
                          AND ChangeDate < @ChangeDate
                        ORDER BY ChangeDate DESC
                      ), 0) + @ChangeQuantity
-- we do not have log entries for later days
    WHERE NOT EXISTS ( SELECT *
                        FROM      dbo.InventoryLog
                        WHERE     ItemID = @ItemID
                          AND ChangeDate > @ChangeDate ) ;

SET @ItemID = 1 ;
SET @ChangeQuantity = -3 ;
SET @ChangeDate = '20100105' ;
```

```
-- this is a valid change:
-- we have enough on hand
INSERT   INTO dbo.InventoryLog
        ( ItemID ,
          ChangeDate ,
          ChangeQuantity ,
          CurrentQuantity
        )
    SELECT   @ItemID ,
             @ChangeDate ,
             @ChangeQuantity ,
             COALESCE(( SELECT TOP (1)
                                 CurrentQuantity
                       FROM    dbo.InventoryLog
                       WHERE   ItemID = @ItemID
                         AND ChangeDate < @ChangeDate
                       ORDER BY ChangeDate DESC
                     ), 0) + @ChangeQuantity
-- we do not have log entries for later days
    WHERE NOT EXISTS ( SELECT *
                       FROM    dbo.InventoryLog
                       WHERE   ItemID = @ItemID
                         AND ChangeDate > @ChangeDate ) ;

SELECT   *
FROM     dbo.InventoryLog ;

ROLLBACK ;
```

Listing 7-23: An example of possible changes to the inventory.

This appears to suit our requirements, but unfortunately we have nothing that
guarantees that the value of CurrentQuantity in the latest row is, indeed, the correct
current quantity in stock.

To be more specific, there are currently many ways in which we can violate our business rules. To name just a few:

- we can retrospectively delete or update a row from the log, and end up invalidating the whole log trail – for example, if we retrospectively deleted the log entry for Jan 1st in Listing 7-23, it immediately invalidates the withdrawal on Jan 5th
- we can retrospectively update ChangeQuantity and fail to modify CurrentQuantity accordingly
- we can manually update CurrentQuantity, or set it to the wrong value when adding a new row.

In order to make our inventory system robust, we require a reasonably complex "network" of interacting constraints. To fully understand how it all fits together will probably require some careful thought and experimentation. With that forewarning, let's take a look at the solution.

We need to find a way to ensure that the value stored in the CurrentQuantity column is always correct, which is a bigger challenge than it may sound. In order to guarantee this, we'll need to create several more constraints, and add some additional columns to our table.

First, we need to add two new columns, PreviousQuantity and PreviousChange-Date, as shown in Listing 7-24, in order to accurately navigate the chain of rows that modify the same item.

```
-- these columns are nullable, because
-- if we store an item for the first time,
-- there is no previous quantity
-- and no previous change date
ALTER TABLE dbo.InventoryLog
ADD PreviousQuantity INT NULL ,
    PreviousChangeDate DATETIME NULL ;
```

Listing 7-24: Add the PreviousQuantity and PreviousChangeDate columns to the InventoryLog table.

In our first solution, the user simply had to enter a change quantity and a date (alongside the ID of the item). In our new system, they are required to enter two date values (the dates for the current and for the previous entries) as well as three inventory values:

- PreviousQuantity – the quantity in stock before the current change is made
- ChangeQuantity – the quantity to be added or removed
- CurrentQuantity – the quantity that will exist after the change is made.

Our system must make sure that all values entered are mutually consistent and abide by our business rules.

First, the CHK_InventoryLog_ValidChange constraint will enforce the obvious relation between previous quantity, current quantity, and the change being made, as shown in Listing 7-25.

```
ALTER TABLE dbo.InventoryLog
ADD CONSTRAINT CHK_InventoryLog_ValidChange
CHECK( CurrentQuantity = COALESCE(PreviousQuantity, 0)
                       + ChangeQuantity) ;
```

Listing 7-25: The CHK_InventoryLog_ValidChange constraint – the value entered for CurrentQuantity must be equal to the PreviousQuantity plus the ChangeQuantity.

Note that, instead of having CHK_InventoryLog_ValidChange enforce the validity of CurrentQuantity, we could implement CurrentQuantity as a persisted computed column. This is left as an advanced exercise.

Next, the CHK_InventoryLog_ValidPreviousChangeDate constraint ensures that changes occur in chronological order.

```
ALTER TABLE dbo.InventoryLog
ADD CONSTRAINT CHK_InventoryLog_ValidPreviousChangeDate
CHECK(PreviousChangeDate < ChangeDate
        OR PreviousChangeDate IS NULL) ;
```

Listing 7-26: CHK_InventoryLog_ValidPreviousChangeDate –
PreviousChangeDate **must occur before** ChangeDate.

Clearly, for a given item, the current value for PreviousQuantity must match the previous value for CurrentQuantity. We'll use a FOREIGN KEY constraint, plus the required UNIQUE constraint or index, to enforce this rule. At the same time, this will also ensure that the PreviousChangeDate is a date that actually has an inventory change for the same item.

```
ALTER TABLE dbo.InventoryLog
ADD CONSTRAINT UNQ_InventoryLog_WithQuantity
UNIQUE( ItemID, ChangeDate, CurrentQuantity ) ;
GO

ALTER TABLE dbo.InventoryLog
ADD CONSTRAINT FK_InventoryLog_Self
FOREIGN KEY
   ( ItemID, PreviousChangeDate, PreviousQuantity )
REFERENCES dbo.InventoryLog
   ( ItemID, ChangeDate, CurrentQuantity );
```

Listing 7-27: The FK_InventoryLog_Self FK constraint.

With these four constraints in place, in addition to our PRIMARY KEY constraint and original CHECK constraint (CHK_InventoryLog_NonnegativeCurrentQuantity), it's about time to run some tests.

Adding new rows to the end of the inventory trail

The simplest test case, is to INSERT new rows at the end of the inventory trail. First, let's add an initial inventory row for each of two items, as shown in Listing 7-28.

```
INSERT INTO dbo.InventoryLog
        ( ItemID ,
          ChangeDate ,
          ChangeQuantity ,
          CurrentQuantity ,
          PreviousChangeDate ,
          PreviousQuantity
        )
VALUES  ( 1 ,
          '20100101' ,
          10 ,
          10 ,
          NULL ,
          NULL
        );

INSERT INTO dbo.InventoryLog
        ( ItemID ,
          ChangeDate ,
          ChangeQuantity ,
          CurrentQuantity ,
          PreviousChangeDate ,
          PreviousQuantity
        )
VALUES  ( 2 ,
          '20100101' ,
          5 ,
          5 ,
          NULL ,
          NULL
        );
```

Listing 7-28: Adding two items to the Inventory table.

Our first real tests, shown in Listing 7-29, prove that we cannot save a row with incorrect CurrentQuantity, even if we also enter the wrong value for PreviousQuantity.

```
INSERT INTO dbo.InventoryLog
        ( ItemID ,
          ChangeDate ,
          ChangeQuantity ,
          CurrentQuantity ,
          PreviousChangeDate ,
          PreviousQuantity
        )
VALUES  ( 2 ,
          '20100102' ,
          -2 ,
          1 , -- CurrentQuantity should be 3
          '20100101' ,
          5
        );
```

```
Msg 547, Level 16, State 0, Line 1
The INSERT statement conflicted with the CHECK constraint
"CHK_InventoryLog_ValidChange". The conflict occurred in
database "test2", table "dbo.InventoryLog".
The statement has been terminated.
```

```
INSERT INTO dbo.InventoryLog
        ( ItemID ,
          ChangeDate ,
          ChangeQuantity ,
          CurrentQuantity ,
          PreviousChangeDate ,
          PreviousQuantity
        )
VALUES  ( 2 ,
          '20100102' ,
          -2 ,
          1 ,
          '20100101' ,
          3     -- PreviousQuantity should be 5
        );
```

```
Msg 547, Level 16, State 0, Line 1
The INSERT statement conflicted with the FOREIGN KEY SAME
TABLE constraint "FK_InventoryLog_Self". The conflict
occurred in database "test2", table "dbo.InventoryLog".
The statement has been terminated.
```

Listing 7-29: A row with incorrect current quantity does not save.

Also, we cannot withdraw more of an item than is currently in stock.

```
INSERT INTO dbo.InventoryLog
        ( ItemID ,
          ChangeDate ,
          ChangeQuantity ,
          CurrentQuantity ,
          PreviousChangeDate ,
          PreviousQuantity
        )
VALUES  ( 2 ,
          '20100102' ,
          -6 ,
          -1 , -- CurrentQuantity cannot be negative
          '20100101' ,
          5
        );
```

```
Msg 547, Level 16, State 0, Line 1
The INSERT statement conflicted with the CHECK constraint
"CHK_InventoryLog_NonnegativeCurrentQuantity". The conflict
occurred in database "test2", table "dbo.InventoryLog",
column 'CurrentQuantity'.
The statement has been terminated.
```

Listing 7-30: We cannot withdraw more than the available amount.

However, we can take out a valid quantity of stock.

```
INSERT INTO dbo.InventoryLog
        ( ItemID ,
          ChangeDate ,
          ChangeQuantity ,
          CurrentQuantity ,
          PreviousChangeDate ,
          PreviousQuantity
        )
VALUES  ( 2 ,
          '20100102' ,
          -1 ,
          4 ,
          '20100101' ,
          5
        );
```

Listing 7-31: Taking out a valid amount succeeds.

So far our system has worked as expected. However, it still has loopholes. The command shown in Listing 7-32 succeeds in withdrawing more stock of a given item than is available, by failing to provide a value for PreviousChangeDate.

```
BEGIN TRANSACTION ;

INSERT INTO dbo.InventoryLog
        ( ItemID ,
          ChangeDate ,
          ChangeQuantity ,
          CurrentQuantity ,
          PreviousChangeDate ,
          PreviousQuantity
        )
VALUES  ( 2 ,
          '20100103' ,
          -20 ,
          0 ,
          NULL ,
```

```
            20
        ) ;


SELECT   *
FROM     dbo.InventoryLog
WHERE    ItemID = 2 ;


-- restoring test data
ROLLBACK ;


(1 row(s) affected)


-- results of the SELECT are edited for readability


ChangeDate   ChangeQ  CurrentQ PreviousQ PreviousChangeDate
------------ -------- -------- --------- -------------------
2010-01-01   5        5        NULL      NULL
2010-01-02   -1       4        5         2010-01-01
2010-01-03   -20      0        20        NULL


(3 row(s) affected)
```

**Listing 7-32: Withdrawing more than available amount succeeds when
PreviousChangeDate is not provided.**

The fundamental problem is being caused by the need to allow NULL values in the
PreviousChangeDate column, to reflect the fact that we may be starting a brand
new branch of history entries for that item, in which case no previous change date will
exist. Our FOREIGN KEY constraint (FK_Inventory_Self) tries to match the value of
PreviousQuantity in the row being modified to the CurrentQuantity value in the
row that describes the previous modification of the same item, based on a composite
key consisting of (ItemID, PreviousChangeDate, PreviousQuantity). Since
PreviousChangeDate is NULL, no match can be made and so we can enter an
incorrect value for PreviousQuantity (20 instead of 5).

In order to fix this obvious loophole in our logic, we should require the value entered
for PreviousChangeDate to be NOT NULL if we are saving a NOT NULL value for
PreviousQuantity, as shown in Listing 7-33.

```
ALTER TABLE dbo.InventoryLog
ADD CONSTRAINT CHK_InventoryLog_Valid_Previous_Columns
  CHECK((PreviousChangeDate IS NULL
           AND PreviousQuantity IS NULL)
        OR (PreviousChangeDate IS NOT NULL
              AND PreviousQuantity IS NOT NULL)) ;
```

Listing 7-33: Closing the loophole.

If we rerun Listing 7-32 now, the INSERT command fails. However, there is one more problem we still need to address. Although we already have some history of changes for item #2, we can start another trail of history for the same item by failing to provide either a PreviousChangeDate or PreviousQuantity, as shown in Listing 7-34.

```
BEGIN TRANSACTION ;

INSERT  INTO dbo.InventoryLog
          ( ItemID ,
            ChangeDate ,
            ChangeQuantity ,
            CurrentQuantity ,
            PreviousChangeDate ,
            PreviousQuantity
          )
VALUES  ( 2 ,
            '20100104' ,
            10 ,
            10 ,
            NULL ,
            NULL
          ) ;

SELECT  SUM(ChangeQuantity) AS TotalQuantity
FROM    dbo.InventoryLog
WHERE   ItemID = 2 ;

SELECT  ChangeDate ,
```

247

```
            ChangeQuantity ,
            CurrentQuantity
FROM        dbo.InventoryLog
WHERE       ItemID = 2 ;

-- restoring test data
ROLLBACK ;

(1 row(s) affected)
TotalQuantity
-------------
14

(1 row(s) affected)

ChangeDate                   ChangeQuantity CurrentQuantity
----------------------       -------------- ----------------
2010-01-01                   5              5
2010-01-02                   -1             4
2010-01-04                   10             10

(3 row(s) affected)
```

Listing 7-34: **We have managed to start a new history trail for item #2.**

In order to solve this problem, we need to find a way to prevent two rows with the same ItemID having a NULL value for PreviousChangeDate. Listing 7-35 creates a UNIQUE constraint to solve this problem.

```
ALTER TABLE dbo.InventoryLog
ADD CONSTRAINT UNQ_InventoryLog_OneHistoryTrailPerItem
  UNIQUE(ItemID,PreviousChangeDate ) ;
```

Listing 7-35: **Only one history trail per item is allowed.**

When we rerun Listing 7-34, the INSERT fails, as it should, and the problem has been fixed.

SQL Server UNIQUE *constraints and the ANSI Standard*

In SQL Server, a UNIQUE *constraint disallows duplicate* NULLs. *However, according to the ANSI standard it should allow them. Therefore, the* UNIQUE *constraint in Listing 7-35 will work on SQL Server but will not port to a RDBMS that implements ANSI-compliant* UNIQUE *constraints.*

Updating existing rows

In all previous examples, we have used INSERT commands to add new inventory rows. Now we need to consider how our system will behave if we allow UPDATEs of existing rows in the inventory trail for a given item. First of all, let's add another history of changes for item #2.

```
INSERT INTO dbo.InventoryLog
          ( ItemID ,
            ChangeDate ,
            ChangeQuantity ,
            CurrentQuantity ,
            PreviousChangeDate ,
            PreviousQuantity
          )
VALUES    ( 2 ,
            '20100105' ,
            -3 ,
            1 ,
            '20100102' ,
            4
          );
```

Listing 7-36: More history for item #2.

Suppose it is discovered that the initial inventory for item #2, entered on January 1st, 2010, should have reflected a quantity of 3, rather than 5, so we need to decrease the amount added for that item.

```
UPDATE    dbo.InventoryLog
SET       ChangeQuantity = 3 ,
          CurrentQuantity = 3
WHERE     ItemID = 2
          AND ChangeDate = '20100101' ;


Msg 547, Level 16, State 0, Line 1
The UPDATE statement conflicted with the SAME TABLE REFERENCE
constraint "FK_Inventory_Self". The conflict occurred in
database "test2", table "dbo.Inventory".
The statement has been terminated.
```

Listing 7-37: We cannot update a single row if it is not the last in the history trail for the item.

This UPDATE fails, which is good news, otherwise the CurrentQuantity for any subsequent row in the history trail would be incorrect.

The correct way to UPDATE a row is to include all the downstream ramifications of the change in one command. In other words, if we need to modify the initial inventory entry, then we need to make sure that, at the same time, we correctly adjust all subsequent entries in the history trail for that item. In this case, this will mean updating three rows all at once.

The UPDATE in Listing 7-38 still fails, because decreasing the original inventory from 5 to 3 means that the final modification on January 5th, 2010 would lead to a negative value of CurrentQuantity.

```
-- BEGIN and COMMIT TRANCATION statements are to
-- preserve current data for future tests
BEGIN TRANSACTION ;
DECLARE @fixAmount INT ,
    @fixDate DATETIME ,
    @fixItem INT ;
SET @fixAmount = -2 ;
SET @fixDate = '20100101' ;
SET @fixItem = 2 ;
```

```sql
PRINT 'data before the update' ;
SELECT   ChangeQuantity ,
         CurrentQuantity ,
         PreviousQuantity
FROM     dbo.InventoryLog
WHERE    ItemID = @fixItem ;


PRINT 'how data will look like if the update succeeds' ;
SELECT ChangeQuantity + CASE WHEN ChangeDate = @fixDate
                                       THEN @fixAmount
                             ELSE 0
                        END AS NewChangeQuantity ,
       CurrentQuantity + CASE WHEN ChangeDate >= @fixDate
                                        THEN @fixAmount
                              ELSE 0
                         END AS NewCurrentQuantity,
       PreviousQuantity + CASE WHEN ChangeDate > @fixDate
                                         THEN @fixAmount
                               ELSE 0
                          END AS NewPreviousQuantity
FROM     dbo.InventoryLog
WHERE    ItemID = @fixItem ;


UPDATE   dbo.InventoryLog
SET      ChangeQuantity = ChangeQuantity
         + CASE WHEN ChangeDate = @fixDate
                  THEN @fixAmount
                ELSE 0
            END ,
         CurrentQuantity = CurrentQuantity + @fixAmount ,
         PreviousQuantity = PreviousQuantity
         + CASE WHEN ChangeDate > @fixDate
                  THEN @fixAmount
                ELSE 0
            END
WHERE    ItemID = @fixItem
         AND ChangeDate >= @fixDate ;
```

251

```
ROLLBACK ;

data before the update
ChangeQuantity CurrentQuantity PreviousQuantity
-------------- ---------------- -----------------
5               5                NULL
-1              4                5
-3              1                4


how data will look if the update succeeds
NewChangeQuantity NewCurrentQuantity NewPreviousQuantity
----------------- ------------------ -------------------
3                 3                  NULL
-1                2                  3
-3                -1                 2

Msg 547, Level 16, State 0, Line 12
The UPDATE statement conflicted with the CHECK constraint
"CHK_Inventory_NonnegativeCurrentQuantity". The conflict
occurred in database "test2", table "dbo.Inventory", column
'CurrentQuantity'.
The statement has been terminated.
```

Listing 7-38: Updating all inventory rows for a given item at the same time.

If we set @fixAmount to a valid amount, -1 instead of -2, and then rerun Listing 7-38 it will complete successfully. We can also set @fixAmount to a positive number, run the listing again, and see that again it succeeds, as it should.

Although we have now managed, with some difficulty, to modify a row in the middle of a history trail, we need to emphasize that only inserting rows at the end of history trail is fast and convenient. Correcting history is harder and may be significantly less performant. However, our solution has dramatically simplified and speeded up the most common operation, namely inserting rows at the end of history trails.

Adding rows out of date order

At the moment, our inventory system robustly handles the insertion of new rows to the end of the inventory (i.e. in date order). However, far more complex is the situation where we need to insert a row when it is not the last in the trail history. It requires two actions:

• inserting the row itself

• modifying CurrentQuantity and PreviousQuantity for all the later rows in the history trail for the item.

Both inserting and updating need to be done in a single command, so we need to use MERGE. The MERGE which gets the job done is quite complex and is shown in Listing 7-39.

```
-- DEBUG: Use transaction to enable rollback at end
BEGIN TRANSACTION ;

-- Required input: Item, date, and amount of inventory
change.
DECLARE @ItemID INT ,
    @ChangeDate DATETIME ,
    @ChangeQuantity INT ;
SET @ItemID = 2 ;
SET @ChangeDate = '20100103' ;
SET @ChangeQuantity = 1 ;

-- DEBUG: showing the data before MERGE
SELECT CONVERT(CHAR(8), ChangeDate, 112) AS ChangeDate ,
        ChangeQuantity ,
        CurrentQuantity ,
        PreviousQuantity ,
        CONVERT(CHAR(8), PreviousChangeDate, 112)
                            AS PreviousChangeDate
FROM    dbo.InventoryLog
WHERE   ItemID = @ItemID ;
```

```sql
-- Find the row to be updated (if any)
DECLARE @OldChange INT ,
    @PreviousChangeDate DATETIME ,
    @PreviousQuantity INT ;

SELECT  @OldChange = ChangeQuantity ,
        @PreviousChangeDate = PreviousChangeDate ,
        @PreviousQuantity = PreviousQuantity
FROM    dbo.InventoryLog
WHERE   ItemID = @ItemID
        AND ChangeDate = @ChangeDate ;

IF @@ROWCOUNT = 0
    BEGIN ;
  -- Row doesn't exist yet; find the previous row
        SELECT TOP ( 1 )
                @PreviousChangeDate = ChangeDate ,
                @PreviousQuantity = CurrentQuantity
        FROM    dbo.InventoryLog
        WHERE   ItemID = @ItemID
                AND ChangeDate < @ChangeDate
        ORDER BY ChangeDate DESC ;
    END ;

-- Calculate new quantity; old quantity can be NULL
-- if this is a new row and there is no previous row.
DECLARE @NewChange INT ;
SET @NewChange = COALESCE(@OldChange, 0) + @ChangeQuantity ;

-- One MERGE statement to do all the work
MERGE INTO dbo.InventoryLog AS t
    USING
        ( SELECT @ItemID AS ItemID ,
                 @ChangeDate AS ChangeDate ,
                 @NewChange AS ChangeQuantity ,
                 @PreviousChangeDate AS PreviousChangeDate ,
                 @PreviousQuantity AS PreviousQuantity
        ) AS s
```

254

```
ON    s.ItemID = t.ItemID
     AND s.ChangeDate = t.ChangeDate
-- If row did not exist, insert it
   WHEN NOT MATCHED BY TARGET
       THEN INSERT (
                     ItemID ,
                     ChangeDate ,
                     ChangeQuantity ,
                     CurrentQuantity ,
                     PreviousChangeDate ,
                     PreviousQuantity
                   )
         VALUES    ( s.ItemID ,
                     s.ChangeDate ,
                     s.ChangeQuantity ,
                     COALESCE(s.PreviousQuantity, 0)
                             + s.ChangeQuantity ,
                     s.PreviousChangeDate ,
                     s.PreviousQuantity
                   )
-- If row does exist and change quantity becomes 0, delete it
   WHEN MATCHED AND t.ItemID = @ItemID
       AND @NewChange = 0
       THEN DELETE
-- If row does exist and change quantity does not become
-- 0, update it
   WHEN MATCHED AND t.ItemID = @ItemID
       THEN UPDATE
         SET   ChangeQuantity = @NewChange ,
               CurrentQuantity = t.CurrentQuantity
                                 + @ChangeQuantity
-- Also update all rows with a later date
   WHEN NOT MATCHED BY SOURCE AND t.ItemID = @ItemID
       AND t.ChangeDate > @ChangeDate
       THEN UPDATE
         SET   CurrentQuantity = t.CurrentQuantity
                                 + @ChangeQuantity ,
               PreviousQuantity =
```

255

```
                        CASE
-- Special case: New first row after first row was deleted
                        WHEN @NewChange = 0
                             AND t.PreviousChangeDate
                                        = @ChangeDate
                             AND @PreviousChangeDate IS NULL
                        THEN NULL
                        ELSE COALESCE(t.PreviousQuantity,0)
                                   + @ChangeQuantity
                   END ,
-- Previous change date has to be changed in some cases
              PreviousChangeDate =
                   CASE
-- First row after row that was inserted
                        WHEN @NewChange = @ChangeQuantity
                             AND ( t.PreviousChangeDate =
                                    @PreviousChangeDate
                             OR ( t.PreviousChangeDate
                                             IS NULL
                             AND @PreviousChangeDate
                                             IS NULL
                                  )
                                  ) THEN @ChangeDate
-- First row after row that was deleted
                        WHEN @NewChange = 0
                             AND t.PreviousChangeDate =
                                    @ChangeDate
                        THEN @PreviousChangeDate
-- Otherwise no change
                        ELSE t.PreviousChangeDate
                   END ;


-- DEBUG: showing the data after MERGE
SELECT  CONVERT(CHAR(8), ChangeDate, 112) AS ChangeDate ,
        ChangeQuantity ,
        CurrentQuantity ,
        PreviousQuantity ,
        CONVERT(CHAR(8), PreviousChangeDate, 112)
```

```
                              AS PreviousChangeDate
FROM      dbo.InventoryLog
WHERE     ItemID = @ItemID ;


-- DEBUG: Roll back changes so we can repeat tests
ROLLBACK TRANSACTION ;
```

ChangeDate	ChangeQ	CurrentQ	PreviousQ	PreviousChangeDate
20100101	5	5	NULL	NULL
20100102	-1	4	5	20100101
20100105	-3	1	5	20100102

ChangeDate	ChangeQ	CurrentQ	PreviousQ	PreviousChangeDate
20100101	5	5	NULL	NULL
20100102	-1	4	5	20100101
20100103	1	5	4	20100102
20100105	-3	2	5	20100103

```
(4 row(s) affected)
```

Listing 7-39: Inserting a row in the middle of a history trail.

This code handles inserting rows before the first date, inbetween dates, and after the last date. More importantly, it will also handle the case when there is already a row with the same ItemID and ChangeDate, automatically modifying that row (and all "later" rows for the same item) to reflect the new net change, which is computed as the old change plus the new change. Finally, it will also automatically delete a row if the new net change equals zero (no change).

As we have seen, modifying anywhere other than in the very end of a history trail may be quite involved, but the integrity of our data is never compromised. In many cases, such as inventory systems, this complexity of modifications in the middle of a history is perfectly acceptable, because under normal circumstances we just never need to do it. However, this approach is not for everyone; we need to decide whether to use it on a case-by-case basis.

257

Summary

There are two options for business rules that are too complex for simple constraints. The most common option is to use triggers, as they are generally easier to write and maintain. However, although trigger logic is quite easy to write, it is not always easy, and sometimes impossible, to ensure that the resulting triggers are entirely robust. Chapter 6 discussed several common problems with triggers, including cases where they simply do not fire. Also, in Chapter 4, we saw that triggers do not always work as expected under snapshot isolation levels.

The alternative solution, as presented in this chapter, uses several constraints, working together to enforce complex business rules so that data integrity is never compromised. The solution presented is complex but if data integrity is a top priority then such constraints-only solutions should be considered.

The solution presented here entails data de-normalization, and so some redundant data storage. It is robust under all circumstances but, in such situations, we must take extreme care, as we did here, to avoid ending up with inconsistent data and to ensure that the performance of such systems is acceptable. Nevertheless, it should be noted that redundant storage may have some negative impact on the overall performance of your queries.

Chapter 8: Defensive Error Handling

The ability to handle errors is essential in any programming language and, naturally, we have to implement safe error handling in our T-SQL if we want to build solid SQL Server code. SQL Server 2005 (and later) superseded the old-style @@Error error handling, with the TRY...CATCH blocks that are more familiar to Java and C# programmers.

While use of TRY...CATCH certainly is the best way to handle errors in T-SQL, it is not without difficulties. Error handling in T-SQL can be very complex, and its behavior can sometimes seem erratic and inconsistent. Furthermore, error handling in Transact SQL lacks many features that developers who use languages such as Java and C# take for granted. For example, in SQL Server 2005 and 2008, we cannot even re-throw an error without changing its error code. This complicates handling errors, because we have to write separate conditions for detecting exceptions caught for the first time, and for detecting re-thrown exceptions.

This chapter will demonstrate simple SQL Server error handling, using XACT_ABORT and transactions; it will describe the most common problems with TRY...CATCH error handling, and advocate that the defensive programmer, where possible, should implement only simple error checking and handling in SQL Server, with client-side error handling used to enforce what is done on the server.

Prepare for Unanticipated Failure

Any statement can, and at some point inevitably will, fail. This may seem to be a statement of the obvious, but too many programmers seem to assume that, once their code "works," then the data modifications and queries that it contains will always succeed.

In fact, data modifications can and do fail unexpectedly. For example, the data may not validate against a constraint or a trigger, or the command may become a deadlock victim. Even if the table does not have any constraints or triggers at the time the code is developed, they may be added later. It is wise to assume that our modifications will not always succeed.

Many queries, too, can fail. Just as a modification can become a deadlock victim, so can a SELECT (unless that SELECT is running under either of the two snapshot isolation levels). If a SELECT statement utilizes a user-defined function, then errors may occur in that function that will cause the query to fail. Other common causes of failure are queries that attempt to use a temporary table that does not exist, or contain subqueries that return more than one value.

Listing 8-1 demonstrates a very simple case of a SELECT statement that may succeed or fail, depending on locale settings.

```
CREATE VIEW dbo.NextNewYearEve AS
SELECT DATEADD
          (YEAR,
           DATEDIFF(year, '12/31/2000', CURRENT_TIMESTAMP),
           '12/31/2000'
          ) AS NextNewYearEve ;
GO


SET LANGUAGE us_english ;
SELECT    NextNewYearEve
FROM      dbo.NextNewYearEve ;

Changed language setting to us_english.
NextNewYearEve
-----------------------
2009-12-31 00:00:00.000

SET LANGUAGE Norwegian ;
SELECT    NextNewYearEve
FROM      dbo.NextNewYearEve ;
GO
```

```
Changed language setting to Norsk.
NextNewYearEve
-----------------------
Msg 241, Level 16, State 1, Line 2
Conversion failed when converting date and/or time from
character string.

DROP VIEW dbo.NextNewYearEve ;
```

Listing 8-1: Language settings can cause certain date queries to fail.

The main point is clear: when we develop T-SQL code, we cannot assume that our queries or data modifications will always succeed, and we need to be prepared for such failures and handle them gracefully. When an unexpected error occurs during data modification, it is essential that execution of the statement is terminated, the database is returned to the state it was in before the statement started, and a message is sent to the calling client, giving some details of the error that occurred and the action taken as a result. Likewise, if a SELECT fails that is part of a longer transaction that has already modified data, then these modifications must be undone as well.

Using Transactions for Data Modifications

In many cases, during data modifications, we cannot take our database from one consistent state to another in a single statement. If a data modification requires more than one statement to effect the required change, then explicit transactions should be used to ensure that these statements succeed or fail as a unit, and that our error handling can handle them as a unit.

For example, suppose that we need to log, in one table, all the modifications made to another table. Listing 8-2 shows the code to create the table to be modified (Codes) and the table in which the modifications will be logged (CodeDescriptionsChangeLog).

```
IF EXISTS ( SELECT   *
            FROM     INFORMATION_SCHEMA.TABLES
            WHERE    TABLE_NAME = 'Codes'
            AND TABLE_SCHEMA = 'dbo' )
  BEGIN;
    -- we used a Codes table in a previous chapter
    -- let us make sure that is does not exist any more
    DROP TABLE dbo.Codes ;
  END ;
GO
CREATE TABLE dbo.Codes
  (
    Code VARCHAR(10) NOT NULL ,
    Description VARCHAR(40) NULL ,
    CONSTRAINT PK_Codes PRIMARY KEY CLUSTERED ( Code )
  ) ;
GO


-- we did not use this table name before in this book,
-- so there is no need to check if it already exists
CREATE TABLE dbo.CodeDescriptionsChangeLog
    (
        Code VARCHAR(10) NOT NULL ,
        ChangeDate DATETIME NOT NULL ,
        OldDescription VARCHAR(40) NULL ,
        NewDescription VARCHAR(40) NULL ,
        CONSTRAINT PK_CodeDescriptionsChangeLog PRIMARY KEY (
Code, ChangeDate )
    ) ;
```

Listing 8-2: The Codes and CodeDescriptionsChangeLog tables.

Note that the log table does not have a FOREIGN KEY constraint referring to the Codes table, because the log records need to be kept even if we delete the corresponding rows in Codes.

The procedure shown in Listing 8-3 modifies the Codes table, and logs the change in the CodeDescriptionsChangeLog table.

262

```
CREATE PROCEDURE dbo.ChangeCodeDescription
    @Code VARCHAR(10) ,
    @Description VARCHAR(40)
AS
    BEGIN ;
        INSERT  INTO dbo.CodeDescriptionsChangeLog
                ( Code ,
                  ChangeDate ,
                  OldDescription ,
                  NewDescription
                )
                SELECT  Code ,
                        CURRENT_TIMESTAMP ,
                        Description ,
                        @Description
                FROM    dbo.Codes
                WHERE   Code = @Code ;

        UPDATE  dbo.Codes
        SET     Description = @Description
        WHERE   Code = @Code ;
    END ;
```

Listing 8-3: The ChangeCodeDescription stored procedure.

Listing 8-4 runs a simple smoke test on the new procedure.

```
INSERT  INTO dbo.Codes
        ( Code, Description )
VALUES  ( 'IL', 'Ill.' ) ;
GO

EXEC dbo.ChangeCodeDescription
  @Code = 'IL',
  @Description = 'Illinois' ;
GO
```

```
SELECT   Code ,
         OldDescription + ',  ' + NewDescription
FROM     dbo.CodeDescriptionsChangeLog ;


Code

---------- -------------------------------------------
IL          Ill., Illinois
```

Listing 8-4: A smoke test on the `ChangeCodeDescription` stored procedure.

It looks like the procedure works, right? Note, however, that this stored procedure does not attempt to determine whether or not either of the two modifications failed, and it does not handle possible errors. Of course, one might argue that this stored procedure could be a component of a perfectly valid system, if it is invoked by an application that does all the error handling. However, that does not make it, as is, a valid component. There's a huge risk that a developer who builds another application may find this procedure and decide to call it, unaware of the required error handling in the calling procedure.

It may seem that nothing could possibly go wrong during these two trivial modifications, but we still cannot assume that both modifications will always succeed. In fact, even in this trivial example, we can devise a case where one modification can fail: if two modifications occur simultaneously, we may get a primary key violation on the `CodeDescriptionsChangeLog` table.

Rather than reproduce that case here, we can prove the same point simply by creating a `CHECK` constraint that prohibits inserts and updates against the `CodeDescriptionsChangeLog` table, and demonstrating what happens when one of our modifications fails and we do nothing to detect and handle it.

```
SET XACT_ABORT OFF ;
-- if  XACT_ABORT OFF were set to ON ,
-- the code below would behave differently.
-- We shall discuss it later in this chapter.


DELETE    FROM dbo.CodeDescriptionsChangeLog ;
```

```
BEGIN TRANSACTION ;
GO


-- This constraint temporarily prevents all inserts
-- and updates against the log table.
-- When the transaction is rolled back, the constraint
-- will be gone.
ALTER TABLE dbo.CodeDescriptionsChangeLog
ADD CONSTRAINT CodeDescriptionsChangeLog_Immutable
    CHECK(1<0) ;
GO


EXEC dbo.ChangeCodeDescription
  @Code = 'IL',
  @Description = 'other value' ;
GO


-- dbo.Codes table has been updated
SELECT    Code ,
          Description
FROM      dbo.Codes ;


-- dbo.CodeDescriptionsChangeLog has not been updated
SELECT    Code ,
          OldDescription + ', ' + NewDescription
FROM      dbo.CodeDescriptionsChangeLog ;
GO


ROLLBACK ;

Msg 547, Level 16, State 0, Procedure ChangeCodeDescription,
Line 6
The INSERT statement conflicted with the CHECK constraint
"CodeDescriptionsChangeLog_Immutable". The conflict occurred
in database "Test", table "dbo.CodeDescriptionsChangeLog".
The statement has been terminated.

(1 row(s) affected)
```

265

```
Code          Description
----------    -------------------------------------
IL            other value


(1 row(s) affected)

Code
----------    -------------------------------------

(0 row(s) affected)
```

Listing 8-5: An INSERT into CodeDescriptionsChangeLog fails, but the UPDATE of Codes succeeds, and we end up with an UPDATE that has not been logged.

In order to avoid this situation, we need to begin a transaction, attempt to do both modifications, determine whether or not both completed successfully, and commit the transaction only if both modifications succeeded. If either modification failed, we need to roll back the transaction, as part of our error handling. T-SQL allows several ways to accomplish that. Let's begin with the simplest approach: using transactions along with the XACT_ABORT setting.

Using Transactions and XACT_ABORT to Handle Errors

In many cases, we do not need sophisticated error handling. Quite frequently, all we need to do in case of an error, is roll back all the changes and throw an exception, so that the client knows that there is a problem and will handle it. In such situations, a perfectly reasonable approach is to make use of the XACT_ABORT setting.

By default, in SQL Server this setting is OFF, which means that in some circumstances SQL Server can continue processing when a T-SQL statement causes a run-time error. In other words, for less severe errors, it may be possible to roll back only the statement that caused the error, and to continue processing other statements in the transaction.

If **XACT_ABORT** is turned on, SQL Server stops processing as soon as a T-SQL run-time error occurs, and the entire transaction is rolled back. When handling unexpected, unanticipated errors, there is often little choice but to cease execution and roll back to a point where there system is in a "known state." Otherwise, you risk seeing partially completed transactions persisted to your database, and so compromising data integrity. In dealing with such cases, it makes sense to have **XACT_ABORT** turned ON.

Data modifications via OLE DB

*Note that, in some cases, **XACT_ABORT** is already set to ON by default. For example, OLE DB will do that for you. However, it is usually preferable to explicitly set it, because we do not know in which context our code will be used later.*

Listing 8-6 illustrates a basic error-handling approach, whereby our modifications take place within an explicit transaction, having set **XACT_ABORT** to ON. The **PRINT** commands in the procedure are for demonstration purposes only; we would not need them in production code.

```
ALTER PROCEDURE dbo.ChangeCodeDescription
    @Code VARCHAR(10) ,
    @Description VARCHAR(40)
AS
    BEGIN ;
        SET XACT_ABORT ON ;
        BEGIN TRANSACTION ;
        INSERT   INTO dbo.CodeDescriptionsChangeLog
                 ( Code ,
                   ChangeDate ,
                   OldDescription ,
                   NewDescription
                 )
        SELECT   Code ,
                 current_timestamp ,
                 Description ,
                 @Description
        FROM     dbo.Codes
        WHERE    Code = @Code ;
```

```
        PRINT 'First modifications succeeded' ;

        UPDATE  dbo.Codes
        SET     Description = @Description
        WHERE   Code = @Code ;
  -- the following commands execute only if both
  -- modifications succeeded
        PRINT 'Both modifications succeeded, committing
             the transaction' ;
        COMMIT ;
    END ;
```

Listing 8-6: Using the XACT_ABORT setting and an explicit transaction.

Note that, although we want to roll back all the changes if an error occurs, we do not need to explicitly determine if there are any errors, and we do not need to explicitly invoke ROLLBACK in our code; when XACT_ABORT is set to ON, it all happens automatically. Listing 8-7 tests our altered stored procedure.

```
SET NOCOUNT ON ;
SET XACT_ABORT OFF ;


DELETE   FROM dbo.CodeDescriptionsChangeLog ;


BEGIN TRANSACTION ;
GO


-- This constraint temporarily prevents all inserts
-- and updates against the log table.
-- When the transaction is rolled back, the constraint
-- will be gone.
ALTER TABLE dbo.CodeDescriptionsChangeLog
ADD CONSTRAINT CodeDescriptionsChangeLog_Immutable
    CHECK(1<0) ;
GO


EXEC dbo.ChangeCodeDescription
```

```
    @Code = 'IL',
    @Description = 'other value' ;
GO
-- transaction is rolled back automatically
SELECT @@TRANCOUNT AS [@@TRANCOUNT after stored procedure
call] ;

-- dbo.Codes table has not been updated
SELECT    Code ,
          Description
FROM      dbo.Codes ;

-- dbo.CodeDescriptionsChangeLog has not been updated
SELECT    Code ,
          OldDescription + ', ' + NewDescription
FROM      dbo.CodeDescriptionsChangeLog ;

Msg 547, Level 16, State 0, Procedure ChangeCodeDescription,
Line 8
The INSERT statement conflicted with the CHECK constraint
"CodeDescriptionsChangeLog_Immutable". The conflict occurred
in database "test", table "dbo.CodeDescriptionsChangeLog".
@@TRANCOUNT after stored procedure call
-------------------------------------------
0

Code          Description
----------    ----------------------------
IL            Illinois

Code
----------    ----------------------------
```

Listing 8-7: Testing the altered stored procedure.

As we have seen, the stored procedure worked perfectly well. Of course, this is just the first in a series of tests we should perform on our stored procedure.

Complete testing would include:

- making sure that, if both the modification of the Codes table and the INSERT into the CodeDescriptionsChangeLog table succeed, then the transaction commits and both changes persist

- verifying that, if an UPDATE of the Codes table fails, then the transaction rolls back. To reproduce a failure, we can use a similar technique; a CHECK constraint that makes sure all UPDATEs against the Codes table fail

- invoking the stored procedure without an outstanding transaction, when @@TRANCOUNT is 0. In that case, we shall have to explicitly drop the CHECK constraint which we create in our test.

I encourage you to tweak Listing 8-7 and try out these other tests. In many cases, this simple approach of setting XACT_ABORT to ON and using an explicit transaction for modifications gets the job done without much effort. We should use this simple and robust approach unless we really need more sophisticated functionality from our error handling.

If we really want to do some more complex error handling on the server, using T-SQL, then we should use TRY...CATCH blocks, which are available in SQL Server 2005 and upwards.

Using TRY...CATCH blocks to Handle Errors

To handle errors in T-SQL modules, in SQL Server 2005 and upwards, we can use TRY...CATCH blocks. If any command inside the TRY block raises an error, the execution of the TRY block terminates immediately, which is similar to the behavior under the XACT_ABORT setting. But, unlike with XACT_ABORT, where the whole batch terminates, only the execution of the code inside the TRY block terminates, and the CATCH block begins to execute.

In cases where you are aware that a certain specific error could occur, your error-handling strategy can be different. You may attempt to add code to your CATCH block that corrects the error, or at least allows processing to continue. In these cases, it makes more sense to have XACT_ABORT set to OFF, so that you can handle the errors, and inform the calling client of what happened, without rolling back the entire batch.

As will become clear as we progress, my current philosophy is that all but the simplest error handling should ideally be implemented in a client-side language where the error handling is more robust and feature rich than it is in SQL Server TRY...CATCH.

My goal here is, therefore, not to cover TRY...CATCH in full detail, but to set out, with examples, some of the reasons why error handling in T-SQL can be complex and a little bewildering. I really want to encourage you to either fully understand all the ins and outs of T-SQL error handling, or to avoid using it at all, except in the simplest cases.

Erland Sommarskog's website, HTTP://WWW.SOMMARSKOG.SE/, is an excellent source of information on error handling. The book entitled *Expert SQL Server 2005 Development* by Adam Machanic, Hugo Kornelis, and Lara Rubbelke is another great resource.

Finally, note that I do not cover "old-style" error handling using @@ERROR at all in this chapter. Use of @@ERROR has some well-known problems, such as the inability to handle errors raised by triggers, and the fact that sometimes SQL Server simply fails to set its value correctly. In general, my advice would be to upgrade from @@ERROR to TRY... CATCH or, even better, to client-side error handling for all but the simplest cases, as soon as possible.

A TRY...CATCH example: retrying after deadlocks

Sometimes, it may make sense to use TRY...CATCH blocks to retry the execution of a statement after a deadlock. One must exercise caution when doing so, as retrying an UPDATE statement in this manner may lead to lost updates, as we discuss in detail in Chapter 10, *Surviving Concurrent Modifications*. The defensive programmer must take all possible measures to ensure that the possibility of deadlocks is minimized but, in some cases, it may be deemed acceptable, in the short term at least, to automatically retry after a deadlock.

In order to provide an example that you can run on your server, we'll alter our ChangeCodeDescription stored procedure, as shown in Listing 8-8, so that it is highly likely to be chosen as a deadlock victim, if it embraces in a deadlock with a competing session. Our goal here is not to demonstrate how to develop stored procedures that are unlikely to embrace in deadlocks, but to see how to use a TRY...CATCH block to retry after a deadlock.

If processing switches to our CATCH block, we will attempt to re-execute our transaction once more, in response to a deadlock; otherwise we will simply re-throw the error so that the calling client is notified and can respond.

```
ALTER PROCEDURE dbo.ChangeCodeDescription
  @Code VARCHAR(10) ,
  @Description VARCHAR(40)
AS
  BEGIN ;
    DECLARE @tryCount INT ,
            @OldDescription VARCHAR(40) ;
    SET DEADLOCK_PRIORITY LOW ;
    SET XACT_ABORT OFF ;
    SET @tryCount = 1 ;
    WHILE @tryCount < 3
      BEGIN
        BEGIN TRY
          BEGIN TRANSACTION ;
          SET @OldDescription = ( SELECT  Description
                                  FROM    dbo.Codes
                                  WHERE   Code = @Code
                                ) ;

          UPDATE  dbo.Codes
          SET     Description = @Description
          WHERE   Code = @Code ;

          INSERT  INTO dbo.CodeDescriptionsChangeLog
                  ( Code ,
                    ChangeDate ,
                    OldDescription ,
                    NewDescription
                  )
                  SELECT  @Code ,
                          CURRENT_TIMESTAMP ,
                          @OldDescription ,
                          @Description ;
```

```
                PRINT 'Modifications succeeded' ;
                COMMIT ;
                RETURN 0 ;
            END TRY
            BEGIN CATCH
            -- transaction is not rolled back automatically
            -- we need to roll back explicitly
              IF @@TRANCOUNT <> 0
                BEGIN ;
                  PRINT 'Rolling back' ;
                  ROLLBACK ;
                END ;
              IF ERROR_NUMBER() <> 1205
                BEGIN
            -- if this is not a deadlock, "re-throw" the error
                  DECLARE @ErrorMessage NVARCHAR(4000) ;
                  SET @ErrorMessage = ERROR_MESSAGE() ;
                  RAISERROR('Error %s occurred in
                            SelectCodeChangeLogAndCode'
                          ,16,1,@ErrorMessage) ;
                  RETURN -1 ;
                END ;
              ELSE
                BEGIN ;
                  PRINT 'Encountered a deadlock'
                END ;
            END CATCH ;
            SET @tryCount = @tryCount + 1 ;
          END ;
        RETURN 0 ;
    END ;
```

Listing 8-8: Altering the ChangeCodeDescription **stored procedure so that it retries after a deadlock.**

Before we run our test, let's reset the test data in our Codes and CodeDescriptions-ChangeLog tables.

273

```
-- reset our test data
DELETE   FROM dbo.CodeDescriptionsChangeLog ;
DELETE   FROM dbo.Codes ;
INSERT   INTO dbo.Codes
         ( Code, Description )
VALUES   ( 'IL', 'IL' ) ;
GO

EXEC dbo.ChangeCodeDescription
    @Code = 'IL',
    @Description = 'Ill.' ;
GO

SELECT   Code ,
         Description
FROM     dbo.Codes ;

SELECT   Code ,
         OldDescription + ', ' + NewDescription
FROM     dbo.CodeDescriptionsChangeLog ;

(1 row(s) affected)

(1 row(s) affected)
Modifications succeeded
Code        Description
----------  ------------------------------------------
IL          Ill.

(1 row(s) affected)

Code
----------  ------------------------------------------
IL          IL, Ill.

(1 row(s) affected)
```

Listing 8-9: Resetting the test data.

We're now ready to run the test. From one tab in SSMS, we'll start a SERIALIZABLE transaction against the CodeDescriptionsChangeLog table, as shown in Listing 8-10.

```
SET DEADLOCK_PRIORITY HIGH ;
SET TRANSACTION ISOLATION LEVEL SERIALIZABLE ;
BEGIN TRANSACTION ;
SELECT * FROM dbo.CodeDescriptionsChangeLog ;

/*
UPDATE   dbo.Codes
SET      Description = 'Illinois'
WHERE    Code = 'IL' ;
COMMIT ;

*/
```

Listing 8-10: Tab 1, start a transaction against the CodeDescriptionsChangeLog table.

From a second tab, invoke our stored procedure, as shown in Listing 8-11. The session will "hang" in lock waiting mode, due to our SERIALIZABLE transaction accessing the CodeDescriptionsChangeLog table.

```
EXEC dbo.ChangeCodeDescription
     @code='IL',
     @Description='?' ;

SELECT    Code ,
          Description
FROM      dbo.Codes ;

SELECT    Code ,
          OldDescription + ', ' + NewDescription
FROM      dbo.CodeDescriptionsChangeLog ;
```

Listing 8-11: Tab 2, invoke the ChangeCodeDescription stored procedure.

Now return to Tab 1, and execute the commented UPDATE against the Codes table, from Listing 8-10, including the COMMIT. As soon as this code tries to execute, a deadlock is detected. SQL Server chooses our stored procedure execution from Tab 2 as the deadlock victim, since we deliberately contrived for this to be the case. The transaction in our TRY block is rolled back, but then our CATCH block is executed and we try to execute our stored procedure again. This time, since Tab 1 has now committed, the modification succeeds. The output from Tab 2 is shown in Listing 8-12.

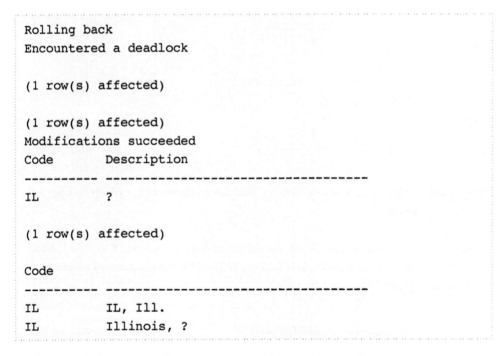

```
Rolling back
Encountered a deadlock

(1 row(s) affected)

(1 row(s) affected)
Modifications succeeded
Code          Description
----------    ------------------------------------
IL            ?

(1 row(s) affected)

Code
----------    ------------------------------------
IL            IL, Ill.
IL            Illinois, ?
```

Listing 8-12. Tab 2, output from execution of the stored procedure.

Note also, however, that the UPDATE we execute from Tab 1 is "lost;" its changes were overwritten when the retry succeeded.

From these examples, we have learned the following:

- if several modifications must succeed or fail together, use transactions, and roll the modification back, as a unit, if any one of them fails

- always anticipate that any modification may fail; use **XACT_ABORT** to ensure that transactions roll back after a failure; alternatively, we can wrap our transactions in **TRY** blocks, and roll them back in **CATCH** blocks.

Unfortunately, there are a few problems with using **TRY...CATCH** error handling that we need to discuss. In the next section, we'll look at some ways in which **TRY...CATCH** error handling is limited and its behavior surprising. We'll then see what we can achieve when using C# for error handling, instead of T-SQL.

TRY...CATCH Gotchas

T-SQL is not really an efficient language for error handling, and is certainly less robust than error handling in client-side languages such as C++, Java, and C#. As such, although in most cases **TRY...CATCH** blocks work as expected and catch errors as they should, there are also quite a few "special cases" that we need to know about, where the behavior is not as we might expect.

Furthermore, **TRY...CATCH** error handling does not really facilitate code reuse. If we want to use this approach in another stored procedure, we cannot fully reuse our T-SQL error handling code; we have to cut and paste much of it into that other stored procedure. This, as we proved in Chapter 5, *Reusing T-SQL Code*, is a recipe for bugs and inconsistencies.

Over the following sections, we'll discuss some of the special cases of which we need to be aware when using **TRY...CATCH**.

Re-throwing errors

In many cases, we do not wish to handle certain errors in our **CATCH** block, and instead want to re-throw them, so that they are handled elsewhere. In our previous example, where we wished to retry execution after a deadlock, all other errors were handled by capturing the error message, using the **ERROR_MESSAGE** function, and re-throwing the error using **RAISERROR**. However, the error message on its own is generally insufficient; we should also retrieve the information from the **ERROR_LINE**, **ERROR_NUMBER**, **ERROR_PROCEDURE**, **ERROR_SEVERITY**, and **ERROR_STATE** functions, declare variables to store this information, and then use **RAISERROR** to re-throw it. This is very verbose and, as we shall see later, we can achieve exactly the same outcome in C# by issuing one single command: throw.

However, the real problem with the TRY...CATCH approach is this: RAISERROR cannot preserve ERROR_NUMBER, so when we re-throw an error we often change its error code. For example, consider the ConversionErrorDemo stored procedure in Listing 8-13. It attempts to cast a string as an integer in the TRY block, and then in the CATCH block invokes two of the seven error handling functions and re-throws the error.

```
CREATE PROCEDURE dbo.ConversionErrorDemo
AS
    BEGIN TRY ;
        SELECT  CAST('abc' AS INT) ;
    -- some other code
    END TRY
    BEGIN CATCH ;
        DECLARE @ErrorNumber INT ,
            @ErrorMessage NVARCHAR(4000) ;
        SELECT  @ErrorNumber = ERROR_NUMBER() ,
                @ErrorMessage = ERROR_MESSAGE() ;
        IF @ErrorNumber = 245
            BEGIN ;
    -- we shall not handle conversion errors here
    -- let us try to re-throw the error, so that
    -- it is handled elsewhere.
    -- This error has number 245, but we cannot
    -- have RAISERROR keep the number of the error.
                RAISERROR(@ErrorMessage, 16, 1) ;
            END ;
        ELSE
            BEGIN ;
    -- handle all other errors here
                SELECT  @ErrorNumber AS ErrorNumber ,
                        @ErrorMessage AS ErrorMessage ;
            END ;
    END CATCH ;
GO
```

```
EXEC dbo.ConversionErrorDemo ;

(0 row(s) affected)
Msg 50000, Level 16, State 1, Procedure ConversionErrorDemo,
Line 19
Conversion failed when converting the varchar value 'abc' to
data type int.
```

Listing 8-13: An error with error number 245, which gets a different ERROR_NUMBER, 50000, when re-thrown.

The fact that re-thrown errors get a different error number means that, when we actually come to handling conversion errors, both re-thrown and original, we cannot catch then using the error number alone, as shown in Listing 8-14.

```
BEGIN TRY ;
    EXEC dbo.ConversionErrorDemo ;
    -- some other code
END TRY
BEGIN CATCH ;
    DECLARE @ErrorNumber INT ,
        @ErrorMessage NVARCHAR(4000) ;
    SELECT   @ErrorNumber = error_number() ,
             @ErrorMessage = error_message() ;
    IF @ErrorNumber = 245
        BEGIN ;
            PRINT 'Conversion error caught';
        END ;
    ELSE
        BEGIN ;
    -- handle all other errors here
            PRINT 'Some other error caught';
            SELECT  @ErrorNumber AS ErrorNumber ,
                    @ErrorMessage AS ErrorMessage ;
        END ;
END CATCH ;
GO
```

```
Some other error caught
ErrorNumber ErrorMessage
----------- -----------------
50000        Conversion failed when converting the varchar
             value 'abc' to data type int.
```

Listing 8-14: The re-thrown error is no longer assigned number 245.

To catch both the original and re-thrown error, we need to parse the error message, as shown in Listing 8-15.

```
BEGIN TRY ;
    EXEC dbo.ConversionErrorDemo ;
    -- some other code
END TRY
BEGIN CATCH ;
    DECLARE @ErrorNumber INT ,
        @ErrorMessage NVARCHAR(4000) ;
    SELECT  @ErrorNumber = ERROR_NUMBER() ,
            @ErrorMessage = ERROR_MESSAGE() ;
    IF @ErrorNumber = 245
        OR @ErrorMessage LIKE '%Conversion failed when
                                converting %'
        BEGIN ;
            PRINT 'Conversion error caught' ;
        END ;
    ELSE
        BEGIN ;
    -- handle all other errors here
            PRINT 'Some other error caught' ;
            SELECT  @ErrorNumber AS ErrorNumber ,
                    @ErrorMessage AS ErrorMessage ;
        END ;
END CATCH ;
```

Listing 8-15: Parsing the error message to catch a re-thrown error.

Although, this time, we did catch our re-thrown error, our method is not robust: we can by mistake catch other errors and handle them as if they were conversion errors, as shown in Listing 8-16.

```
BEGIN TRY ;
    RAISERROR('Error saving ticket %s',16,1,
    'Saving discount blows up: ''Conversion failed when
                                converting ...''') ;
    -- some other code
END TRY
BEGIN CATCH ;
    DECLARE @ErrorNumber INT ,
        @ErrorMessage NVARCHAR(4000) ;
    SELECT  @ErrorNumber = ERROR_NUMBER() ,
            @ErrorMessage = ERROR_MESSAGE() ;
    IF @ErrorNumber = 245
        OR @ErrorMessage LIKE '%Conversion failed when
                                converting %'
        BEGIN ;
            PRINT 'Conversion error caught' ;
        END ;
    ELSE
        BEGIN ;
    -- handle all other errors here
            PRINT 'Some other error caught' ;
            SELECT  @ErrorNumber AS ErrorNumber ,
                    @ErrorMessage AS ErrorMessage ;
        END ;
END CATCH ;
GO

Conversion error caught
```

Listing 8-16: Incorrectly handling a ticket-saving error as if it were a conversion error.

As we have seen, the inability of T-SQL to re-throw errors may prevent us from robustly handling re-thrown errors. If we need to re-throw errors, we should do it on the client.

281

TRY...CATCH blocks cannot catch all errors

Interestingly enough, sometimes TRY...CATCH blocks just do not catch errors. This sometimes represents "expected behavior;" in other words, the behavior is documented and the reason why the error is not caught, for example when a connection fails, is intuitive. However, in some other cases the behavior, while still documented, can be quite surprising.

In either case, however, it means that we cannot assume that all errors originating in the database can, or will, be handled in a TRY...CATCH. Whenever we issue an SQL statement from the client, we need to be aware that it can generate an exception, and we need to be ready to handle it on the client, in case the TRY...CATCH blocks that we use in our T-SQL code don't catch it.

Killed connections and timeouts

In some cases, it is the expected behavior that errors cannot be caught by TRY...CATCH blocks. For example, if your connection is killed, it is documented and well known that your CATCH block will not catch and handle it.

Also, we need to be aware of "attentions," also known as "timeouts," as they also cannot be caught by TRY...CATCH blocks, and this is also the expected behavior. To demonstrate this, start the script in Listing 8-17, but cancel its execution immediately by pressing the **Cancel Executing Query** button.

```
SET XACT_ABORT OFF;
BEGIN TRY ;
  PRINT 'Beginning TRY block' ;
  BEGIN TRANSACTION ;
  WAITFOR DELAY '00:10:00' ;
  COMMIT ;
  PRINT 'Ending TRY block' ;
END TRY
BEGIN CATCH ;
  PRINT 'Entering CATCH block' ;
END CATCH ;
```

```
PRINT 'After the end of the CATCH block' ;

Beginning TRY block
Query was cancelled by user.
```

Listing 8-17: TRY...CATCH **behavior when a timeout occurs.**

The execution stops immediately, without executing the CATCH block. Listing 8-18 demonstrates that the connection is still in the middle of an outstanding transaction.

```
SELECT  @@TRANCOUNT AS [@@TRANCOUNT] ;
ROLLBACK ;

@@TRANCOUNT
-----------
1

(1 row(s) affected)
```

Listing 8-18: The connection is in the middle of an outstanding transaction.

If the client initiates a timeout, the behavior is exactly the same: the execution stops immediately, the outstanding transaction is neither committed nor rolled back, and an unhandled exception is sent to the client. This is simply how timeouts work, and the only way to avoid this behavior is to turn it off altogether. For instance, we can turn off timeouts in ADO.NET by setting the CommandTimeout property to 0. Of course, we can turn XACT_ABORT on, in which case at least the transaction will be rolled back. The CATCH block, however, will still be bypassed.

Problems with TRY...CATCH scope

In some cases, the behavior in TRY...CATCH is documented, but will be surprising to developers used to error handling in languages such as C#.

Listing 8-19 demonstrates a simple case of a query, wrapped in a TRY...CATCH, which tries to use a temporary table that does not exist. However, the CATCH block is not executed, and we get an unhandled exception.

```
BEGIN TRY ;
  PRINT 'Beginning TRY block' ;
  SELECT  COUNT(*)
  FROM    #NoSuchTempTable ;
  PRINT 'Ending TRY block' ;
END TRY
BEGIN CATCH ;
  PRINT 'Entering CATCH block' ;
END CATCH ;
PRINT 'After the end of the CATCH block' ;

Beginning TRY block
Msg 208, Level 16, State 0, Line 3
Invalid object name '#NoSuchTempTable'.
```

Listing 8-19: Sometimes a CATCH block is bypassed when an error occurs.

Even more surprising for object-oriented developers is that this is not a bug; it is just the way SQL Server works in this case. According to MSDN for SQL Server 2008:

> "Errors that occur during statement-level recompilation...are not handled by a CATCH block when they occur at the same level of execution as the TRY...CATCH construct."

The issue here is that compilation errors that occur at run time (as a result of deferred name resolution) abort the rest of the scope, which is equal to the batch in directly submitted SQL, but only equal to the rest of the procedure in a stored procedure or function. So a TRY...CATCH at the same scope will not intercept these errors, but a TRY...CATCH on a different scope (regardless of being nested or not) will catch it.

My point here is simple: SQL Server does not always handle errors in a way object-oriented languages do. If we choose to use the error handling provided by SQL Server, we really need to learn it in detail or we will be in for some unpleasant surprises.

Doomed transactions

There is another serious problem with T-SQL **TRY...CATCH** blocks: in some cases an error that occurred inside a **TRY** block is considered so severe that the whole transaction is doomed, or, in other words, it cannot be committed. Theoretically, the concept of doomed transactions makes perfect sense. Unfortunately, some really trivial errors, such as conversion errors, render transactions doomed if we use **TRY...CATCH** provided by T-SQL. For example, consider the transactions shown in Listing 8-20. The first attempts to perform a 1/0 calculation, and the second, to convert a strong to an integer. We do not want to roll back the whole transaction if an error occurs, so we set **XACT_ABORT** to **OFF**.

```
SET XACT_ABORT OFF ;
SET NOCOUNT ON ;

BEGIN TRANSACTION ;
SELECT  1 ;
GO
BEGIN TRY ;
    SELECT  1 / 0 ;
END TRY
BEGIN CATCH
    PRINT 'Error occurred' ;
    SELECT error_message() AS ErrorMessage ;
END CATCH ;
GO
IF @@TRANCOUNT <> 0
    BEGIN ;
        COMMIT ;
        PRINT 'Committed' ;
    END ;
GO

BEGIN TRANSACTION ;
SELECT  1 ;
GO
BEGIN TRY ;
```

```
     SELECT  cast('abc' AS INT ) ;
END TRY
BEGIN CATCH
    PRINT 'Error occurred' ;
    SELECT error_message() AS ErrorMessage ;
END CATCH ;
GO
IF @@TRANCOUNT <> 0
    BEGIN ;
        COMMIT ;
        PRINT 'Committed' ;
    END ;


-----------
1
-----------
Error occurred
ErrorMessage
---------------------------------------
Divide by zero error encountered.

Committed


-----------
1
-----------
Error occurred
ErrorMessage
---------------------------------------
Conversion failed when converting the varchar value 'abc' to
data type int.

Msg 3998, Level 16, State 1, Line 1
Uncommittable transaction is detected at the end of the
batch. The transaction is rolled back.
```

Listing 8-20: A transaction is doomed after a trivial error such as a conversion error.

As the output demonstrates, we can commit a transaction after a divide by zero, but a conversion error renders the transaction doomed, and therefore uncommittable. The latter case demonstrates that even a seemingly trivial conversion error is considered severe enough to override the XACT_ABORT setting, and the whole transaction is automatically rolled back.

To determine whether or not our transaction is committable, within TRY...CATCH, we can use the XACT_STATE() function, as demonstrated in Listing 8-21.

```
BEGIN TRY ;
  BEGIN TRANSACTION ;
  SELECT  CAST ('abc' AS INT) ;
  COMMIT ;
  PRINT 'Ending TRY block' ;
END TRY
BEGIN CATCH ;
  PRINT 'Entering CATCH block' ;
  IF XACT_STATE () = 1
    BEGIN ;
      PRINT 'Transaction is committable' ;
      COMMIT ;
    END ;
  IF XACT_STATE () = -1
    BEGIN ;
      PRINT 'Transaction is not committable' ;
      ROLLBACK ;
    END ;
END CATCH ;
PRINT 'Ending batch' ;
GO
SELECT  @@TRANCOUNT AS [@@TRANCOUNT] ;
BEGIN TRY ;
  BEGIN TRANSACTION ;
  SELECT  1 / 0 ;
  COMMIT ;
  PRINT 'Ending TRY block' ;
END TRY
```

```
BEGIN CATCH ;
  PRINT 'Entering CATCH block' ;
  IF XACT_STATE () = 1
    BEGIN ;
      PRINT 'Transaction is committable' ;
      COMMIT ;
    END ;
  IF XACT_STATE () = -1
    BEGIN ;
      PRINT 'Transaction is not committable' ;
      ROLLBACK ;
    END ;
END CATCH ;
PRINT 'Ending batch' ;
GO


(0 row(s) affected)
Entering CATCH block
Transaction is not committable
Ending batch

(1 row(s) affected)

(0 row(s) affected)
Entering CATCH block
Transaction is committable
Ending batch
```

Listing 8-21: Using xact_state to determine if our transaction is committable or doomed.

Clearly, there are situations where the concept of a doomed transaction makes sense. For example, if the server runs out of disk space while running a transaction, there is no way the transaction could complete. Unfortunately, the current implementation of SQL Server sometimes dooms transactions for very trivial reasons. In all too many cases, this peculiar behavior of SQL Server makes it impossible to develop feature-rich error handling in T-SQL because, if a transaction is doomed, we have no choice other than to roll it back.

288

We will not cover any examples here, but this can also cause problems when attempting to use SAVEPOINTs. Consider the following, very common, requirement:

> *"If our stored procedure is invoked in the middle of an outstanding transaction, and if any command in our stored procedure fails, undo only the changes made by the stored procedure. Do not make any decisions regarding the changes done outside of our stored procedure."*

Unfortunately, there is no robust way to implement such requirements in T-SQL using a SAVEPOINT. While it will work in most cases, it will not work as intended when a transaction is doomed.

Client-side Error Handling

In order to overcome the described limitations and difficulties with error handling using SQL Server's TRY...CATCH, my advice is simple: when we need to implement feature-rich error handling to respond intelligently to an anticipated error, we should do it in a language that offers more robust error handling, such as C#.

By doing so, we avoid complications caused by doomed transactions (for example, trivial conversion errors in a C# TRY block will never doom a transaction), or by error numbers being changed when they are re-thrown, and so on. Furthermore, once error handling is implemented in a C# class it can be reused by all modules that need it, so we promote code reuse to its fullest extent.

Nowadays many of us developers use more than one language in our daily activities, and the reason is very simple and very pragmatic: in many cases it is much easier to learn a new language to accomplish a specific task, to which the language is well-suited, than it is to try to "bend" a single language to all purposes.

By way of an example, Listing 8-22 re-implements in C# our "retry after deadlock" logic, from Listing 8-8. We need only implement this logic once, and we can use this class to execute any command against SQL Server.

```csharp
class SqlCommandExecutor
{
    public static void RetryAfterDeadlock
        (SqlCommand command, int timesToRetry)
    {
        int retryCount = 0;
        while (retryCount < timesToRetry)
        {
            retryCount++;
            try
            {
                command.ExecuteNonQuery();
                Console.WriteLine
                        ("Command succeeded:" +
                                command.CommandText);
                return;
            }
            catch (SqlException e)
            {
                if (e.Number != 1205)
                {
                    throw;
                }
                Console.WriteLine
                        ("Retrying after deadlock:" +
                                command.CommandText);
            }
        }
    }
}
```

Listing 8-22. Implementing the "retry after deadlock" logic in a C# class.

Let's try this class out. First of all, we need to remove the retry logic from our Change-
CodeDescription stored procedure, but keep it just as prone to deadlocks as before.
Listing 8-23 shows how to accomplish that.

```
ALTER PROCEDURE dbo.ChangeCodeDescription
    @Code VARCHAR( 10 ) ,
    @Description VARCHAR( 40 )
AS
    BEGIN ;
        DECLARE @OldDescription VARCHAR( 40 ) ;
        SET DEADLOCK_PRIORITY LOW ;
        SET XACT_ABORT ON ;
        BEGIN TRANSACTION ;
        SET @OldDescription = ( SELECT  Description
                                FROM    dbo.Codes
                                WHERE   Code = @Code
                              ) ;

        UPDATE   dbo.Codes
        SET      Description = @Description
        WHERE    Code = @Code ;

        INSERT   INTO dbo.CodeDescriptionsChangeLog
                 ( Code ,
                   ChangeDate ,
                   OldDescription ,
                   NewDescription
                 )
                 SELECT   @Code ,
                          current_timestamp ,
                          @OldDescription ,
                          @Description ;
        PRINT 'Modifications succeeded' ;

        COMMIT ;
        RETURN 0 ;
    END ;
```

Listing 8-23: Removing the retry logic from the `ChangeCodeDescription` stored procedure.

Obviously we'd first need to test this procedure and verify that it can successfully complete; a step that I will leave as a simple exercise.

In order to test what happens when we have a deadlock, we need to first reset our test data by rerunning the script in Listing 8-9. Next, start a SERIALIZABLE transaction against the CodeDescriptionsChangeLog table, by running the script in Listing 8-10.

Rather than invoke our ChangeCodeDescription stored procedure from a second SSMS session, as before, we need to execute the C# code shown in Listing 8-24, which invokes the same stored procedure through our RetryAfterDeadlock method.

```
class RetryAfterDeadlockDemo
{
    static void Main(string[] args)
    {
        try
        {
            using (SqlConnection connection =
                new SqlConnection
                    ("server=(local);
                        trusted_connection=true;
                            database=test8;"))
            {
                connection.Open();
                SqlCommand command =
                    connection.CreateCommand();
                command.CommandText =
                    "EXEC dbo.ChangeCodeDescription
                        @code='IL', @Description='?' ;";
                command.CommandType = CommandType.Text;
                SqlCommandExecutor.
                    RetryAfterDeadlock(command, 3);
                Console.WriteLine("Command succeeded");
            }
        }
        catch (Exception e)
        {
```

```
                Console.WriteLine("Error in Main:" + e);
            }
        }
    }
```

Listing 8-24: Using the `RetryAfterDeadlock` method to invoke our stored procedure.

This method will not complete, as the table is locked by our SSMS transaction. Return to SSMS and highlight and execute the commented code, both the UPDATE command and the COMMIT. The transaction invoked from C# will be chosen as a deadlock victim and it will retry, and there is enough debugging output in our C# code to demonstrate what is happening.

Finally, let us verify that, after the retry, the modification completed, as shown in Listing 8-25.

```
EXEC dbo.ChangeCodeDescription @code='IL',
         @Description='?' ;

SELECT     Code ,
           Description
FROM       dbo.Codes ;

SELECT     Code ,
           OldDescription + ', ' + NewDescription
FROM       dbo.CodeDescriptionsChangeLog ;


Code          Description
----------    ----------------------------------------
IL            ?


(1 row(s) affected)
```

```
Code
---------- ------------------------------------
IL          IL, Ill.
IL          Illinois, ?
```

Listing 8-25: Checking that the data is in the expected state.

In short, C# allows us to implement our "retry after deadlock" logic just once and reuse it as many times as we need. As defensive programmers, we really want to reuse our code, not to cut and paste the same code all over our systems, and so we have a strong motivation to use a good modern tool such as C# for our error handling.

My message here is quite moderate. I am not suggesting that we abandon T-SQL error handling; far from it. In the simplest cases, when all we need is to roll back and raise an error, we should use **XACT_ABORT** and transactions. Notice that in Listing 8-23 we use **XACT_ABORT** and a transaction to roll back after a deadlock, but we implement all of the more complex error-handling logic in C#.

Of course, there are situations when we do need to implement error handling in T-SQL. Whenever we are considering such an option, we need to realize that error handling in T-SQL is very complex and not really intuitive to a developer with experience in other languages. Also, it has a lot of gotchas, and it lacks some features which client-side programmers consider as their birthright, such as the ability to re-throw an error exactly as it was caught.

Summary

It is essential that the defensive database programmer includes robust error handling in all production T-SQL code. However, as much as the introduction of TRY...CATCH has improved error handling in T-SQL, it still lacks the versatility, elegance and ease of use that is typical of client-side languages such as Java and C#. Ultimately, you will find that it is not possible to handle certain errors in Transact SQL at all and that we need to complement our T-SQL error handling with error handling on the client.

I hope the chapter has taught you the following specific lessons in defensive error handling:

- if you already use a modern language such as C# in your system, then it makes sense to utilize it to do complex handling of errors related to the database

- if handling errors on SQL Server, keep it simple where possible; set XACT_ABORT to ON and use transactions in order to roll back and raise an error

- if you wish to use TRY...CATCH, learn it thoroughly, and watch out in particular for the following problems:

  - one and the same code may run differently depending on the XACT_ABORT setting

  - we cannot re-throw errors exactly as we catch them

  - CATCH blocks do not catch all errors

  - some errors do not respect XACT_ABORT settings

  - some transactions may be rendered uncommittable, *a.k.a.* doomed.

Chapter 9: Concurrent Queries and Transaction Isolation Levels

When we develop queries, we usually try them out against a test database. Typically, the data in this test database is static; in other words, it is not being retrieved and modified by other connections, as we do our testing.

Unfortunately, in all too many cases, a query that works splendidly in isolation fails miserably when put to work in a live OLTP system, with real-life concurrency. To make a bad situation worse, such errors are, in many cases, subtle and intermittent, and therefore very difficult to reproduce and understand.

Even the simplest SELECT, against one table, may retrieve incorrect results when the base table is being modified at the same time. This chapter explores how the choice of transaction isolation level affects the behavior of such queries, and then moves on to discuss more complex cases, involving multi-table transactions, where the potential for transaction "interference," as well as deadlocks, when using higher isolation levels, greatly increases.

A Brief Review of Traditional Isolation Levels

Let's start by briefly reviewing the expected behavior of a single-table query, running under READ COMMITTED, REPEATABLE READ or SERIALIZABLE isolation levels, when the table in question is being concurrently modified. It will be very far from a complete explanation of the behavior of these isolation levels; the intent is merely to provide enough background to understand the more complex examples that follow. For more information, I refer you to the following books:

- *Expert SQL Server 2005 Development* by Adam Machanic, with Hugo Kornelis and Lara Rubbelke

- *Microsoft SQL Server 2008 Internals* by Kalen Delaney et al.

Before we start, the first thing we need to do is make sure that READ_COMMITTED_ SNAPSHOT is turned off in our test database, as shown in Listing 9-1.

```
-- replace OurDatabaseName
-- with the name of the database
-- where you are running the examples
ALTER DATABASE OurDatabaseName
SET READ_COMMITTED_SNAPSHOT OFF ;
```

Listing 9-1: Ensuring that READ COMMITTED SNAPSHOT is off for our database.

All of the examples in this chapter should be run in this same test database. The basis for our first set of examples is the AccountBalances table shown in Listing 9-2.

```
CREATE TABLE dbo.AccountBalances
    (
        AccountNumber INT NOT NULL
                CONSTRAINT PK_AccountBalances PRIMARY KEY ,
        Amount DECIMAL( 10, 2) NOT NULL ,
        CustomerID INT NOT NULL ,
-- I want the table to be quite wide,
-- so that scanning it takes considerable time,
-- this is why I have added a filler column
        SpaceFiller CHAR(100) NOT NULL
    ) ;
```

Listing 9-2: Creating the AccountBalances table.

Let us add some test data to this table.

```
INSERT INTO dbo.AccountBalances
        ( AccountNumber ,
          Amount ,
          CustomerID ,
          SpaceFiller
        )
```

```
VALUES   ( 101 ,
           20 ,
           1 ,
           'some information'
         ) ;

INSERT INTO dbo.AccountBalances
         ( AccountNumber ,
           Amount ,
           CustomerID ,
           SpaceFiller
         )
VALUES   ( 105 ,
           20 ,
           2 ,
           'some information'
         ) ;
```

Listing 9-3: Adding test data.

Now we are ready to see how isolation levels work.

READ COMMITTED

The easiest way to simulate concurrency is to open multiple query windows
(displayed as tabs) in SSMS. In most of this chapter, we will use two such tabs. In
Tab #1, start a transaction and select some rows, as shown in Listing 9-4, but do not
commit the transaction.

```
SET TRANSACTION ISOLATION LEVEL READ COMMITTED ;
BEGIN TRANSACTION ;
SELECT   AccountNumber ,
         Amount
FROM     dbo.AccountBalances
WHERE AccountNumber BETWEEN 101 AND 105 ;
-- COMMIT ;
```

299

```
AccountNumber Amount
------------- --------------------------------------
101           20.00
105           20.00
```

Listing 9-4: **Tab #1, start a transaction and select some data.**

In Tab #2, start a transaction to modify the same data; don't commit the changes as yet.

```
BEGIN TRANSACTION ;

-- Update account 101
UPDATE    dbo.AccountBalances
SET       Amount = Amount + 10
WHERE     AccountNumber = 101 ;

-- Delete account 105 (belonging to Customer with ID=2)
DELETE    dbo.AccountBalances
WHERE     AccountNumber = 105 ;

-- Create a new account for Customer with ID=2
INSERT    INTO dbo.AccountBalances
          ( AccountNumber ,
            Amount ,
            CustomerID ,
            SpaceFiller
          )
VALUES    ( 103 ,
            25 ,
            2 ,
            'some information'
          ) ;

-- COMMIT ;
-- ROLLBACK ;
```

Listing 9-5: **Tab #2, begin a transaction; modify the same data as queried in Tab #1.**

Under READ COMMITTED isolation level SQL Server acquires shared read locks on data being read, to prevent the data being modified while it is being queried. However, once the query has completed processing, the locks are released and the update can proceed, even if the transaction to which the query belongs is still open, i.e. neither committed nor rolled back. As such, Listing 9-5 completes immediately, even though the transaction running our query is still open.

Next, highlight just the SELECT statement in Listing 9-4 (otherwise BEGIN TRANSAC-TION will execute again as well, leaving you with a nested transaction) and press F5, or click **Execute**. The query will not complete; it stays in lock-waiting state, because the rows it intends to read are currently subject to an uncommitted modification, and so are locked. If we commit the modification running in Tab #2, by selecting just the COMMIT statement without the preceding comment marks, the query in Tab #1 will complete immediately, and return the results shown in Listing 9-6.

```
AccountNumber Amount
------------- ------------------------------------------
101           30.00
103           25.00
```

Listing 9-6: The data was modified between the two times the select was run.

Clearly, the amount in Account Number 101 is different, Account 105 is gone, and a new account, 103, is added to the range of accounts between 101 and 105.

In short, READ COMMITTED isolation level prevents us from reading uncommitted (i.e. "dirty") data but, if the same query is repeated within a given transaction, it may return different results.

Before moving on, commit (or roll back) the open transaction in Tab #1, empty the AccountBalances table, as shown in Listing 9-7, and rerun Listing 9-3 to re-establish the original test data.

```
DELETE FROM dbo.AccountBalances ;
```

Listing 9-7: Deleting the modified test data.

REPEATABLE READ

If we run a query with REPEATABLE READ isolation level, the database engine guarantees that all the rows that were read cannot be modified or deleted until the transaction which read them completes. To demonstrate this, run Listing 9-8.

```
SET TRANSACTION ISOLATION LEVEL REPEATABLE READ ;
BEGIN TRANSACTION ;
SELECT   AccountNumber ,
         Amount
FROM     dbo.AccountBalances
WHERE AccountNumber BETWEEN 101 AND 105 ;


-- COMMIT ;
```

Listing 9-8: **Start a query under** REPEATABLE READ **isolation level.**

In a second tab start, but don't commit, a modification of the same data (Listing 9-5). This time, the modification will not complete; it stays in lock-waiting state, because the rows it needs to modify are locked by our REPEATABLE READ query. Cancel the modification transaction in Listing 9-8, and issue the ROLLBACK command. In its place, run the INSERT statement in Listing 9-9.

```
INSERT INTO dbo.AccountBalances
        ( AccountNumber ,
          Amount ,
          CustomerID ,
          SpaceFiller
        )
VALUES  ( 103 , -- AccountNumber - int
          25 , -- Amount - decimal
          2 , -- CustomerID - int
          'some information'  -- SpaceFiller - char(100)
        ) ;
```

Listing 9-9: **Adding a new account.**

While **REPEATABLE READ** isolation level guarantees that a repeated read of the **same data**, within a transaction, will return consistent results, it does not prevent **new data** being added that could be returned by the query. Run just the **SELECT** command in Listing 9-8. The results returned include the new row we just added.

```
AccountNumber  Amount
-------------  ------------------------------------
101            20.00
103            25.00
105            20.00
```

Listing 9-10: A second query in the same transaction returns different results.

In this sense, the term **REPEATABLE READ** is a misnomer; repeated reads in a single transaction can return different results if new data is added that satisfies the search criteria.

Before moving, remember to **COMMIT** the open transaction in the first tab (Listing 9-8) and then restore our test data by running Listing 9-7, followed by Listing 9-3.

SERIALIZABLE

Using the **SERIALIZABLE** isolation level, the database engine guarantees that, if we rerun the same query during the same transaction, we will get **exactly** the same result. To demonstrate this, open a tab and run Listing 9-11.

```
SET TRANSACTION ISOLATION LEVEL SERIALIZABLE ;
BEGIN TRANSACTION ;
SELECT   AccountNumber ,
         Amount
FROM     dbo.AccountBalances
WHERE AccountNumber BETWEEN 101 AND 105 ;

-- COMMIT ;
```

Listing 9-11: A query with SERIALIZABLE isolation level.

303

In a second tab, rerun the INSERT statement in Listing 9-9, to add Account 103. The INSERT will not complete because, if it did, a repeated execution of our query, which selects all accounts between 101 and 105, would return a different result. Cancel the modification, and commit (or roll back) the open transaction in the first tab.

When Queries Intermittently Return Incorrect Results

As discussed in Chapter 4, the default transaction isolation level in SQL Server is READ COMMITTED and most SQL Server code is written to run in this mode. This isolation level guarantees that we select only committed data. In situations where a table is subject to frequent data modification, it is possible, perhaps even likely, that reporting queries run against this table will return incorrect and inconsistent data.

In order to avoid such interference between "competing" transactions, it may be tempting to increase the isolation level of the reporting transaction to REPEATABLE READ or SERIALIZABLE. However, this will lead to an increased risk of deadlocks. This surprises some developers, perhaps because in most textbook examples of deadlocks both transactions modify data. In fact, as we shall see, a reader and a writer can just as easily embrace in a deadlock when using either of these isolation levels and, furthermore, it can happen when only a single table is being accessed.

SQL Server 2005 introduces the snapshot isolation level, which alleviates some of these problems, but also introduces new challenges.

READ COMMITTED

Let's take a look at an example of what can happen in the default READ COMMITTED mode when a query and data modification transaction operate on the same data, at the same time. The script in Listing 9-12 populates the AccountBalances table with fresh test data; 200,000 accounts with exactly 1,000 dollars in each.

```
-- the TRUNCATE statement is there because
-- we will rerun the script multiple times
TRUNCATE TABLE dbo.AccountBalances ;
GO
DECLARE @i INT ;
-- make sure to turn NOCOUNT on
-- otherwise you will get a huge output
SET NOCOUNT ON ;
SET @i = 100000 ;
WHILE @i < 300000
    BEGIN ;
        INSERT  dbo.AccountBalances
                ( AccountNumber ,
                  Amount ,
                  CustomerID ,
                  SpaceFiller
                )
        VALUES  ( @i * 10 ,
                  1000 ,
                  @i ,
                  'qwerty'
                ) ;
        SET @i = @i + 1 ;
    END ;
GO
```

Listing 9-12: Populating the AccountBalances table with test data; depending on the server, this script may run for several minutes.

Clearly the total amount of money in all the accounts is exactly 200 million dollars, as confirmed by the query in Listing 9-13.

```
SET TRANSACTION ISOLATION LEVEL READ COMMITTED ;
SELECT   SUM(Amount) AS TotalAmount
FROM     dbo.AccountBalances ;


TotalAmount
---------------------------------------
200000000.00


(1 row(s) affected)
```

Listing 9-13: A simple query to calculate the total amount in all accounts.

Of course, this query will reliably return the correct result every time, as long as the data in the Amount column is not being concurrently modified. However, suppose that we have another transaction that transfers money from one account to another, as shown in Listing 9-14.

```
DECLARE @rc INT ,
    @succeeded INT ;
BEGIN TRAN ;
SET @succeeded = 0 ;
UPDATE   dbo.AccountBalances
SET      Amount = Amount - 10
WHERE    AccountNumber = 1234560
         AND Amount > 10 ;
SELECT   @rc = @@ROWCOUNT ;
IF @rc = 1
    BEGIN;
         UPDATE   dbo.AccountBalances
         SET      Amount = Amount + 10
         WHERE    AccountNumber = 2345670 ;
         SELECT   @rc = @@ROWCOUNT ;
         SET @succeeded = CASE WHEN @rc = 1 THEN 1
                               ELSE 0
                          END ;
    END ;
```

```
IF @succeeded = 1
    BEGIN ;
        COMMIT ;
    END ;
ELSE
    BEGIN ;
        ROLLBACK ;
    END ;
```

Listing 9-14: A transaction that transfers $10 from one account to another.

Run the script from Listing 9-14 and then, after it has completed, rerun the query from Listing 9-13. The query will return the same total, 200 million, which is correct since we only transferred money and the net total remains the same.

However, it is theoretically possible, under READ COMMITTED isolation level, for the query to return the wrong total. Consider, for example, what might happen when our query and our UPDATE transaction are operating simultaneously on the Account-Balances table, as described in Table 9-1.

Connection One	Connection Two

Begins running the following command:
 	
`SELECT SUM(Amount) AS`
`    TotalAmount`
`FROM dbo.AccountBalances;`	

Reads the page that stores account number 1234560. Adds $1,000 to the total.	
	Begins a transaction. Withdraws $10 from account 2345670. Deposits $10 to account 1234560. Commits the transaction.

Possibly waits until the update locks from Connection Two are released. Reads the page that stores account number 2345670. Adds $990 to the total.	

Table 9-1: A query could, in theory, return incorrect totals when running under READ COMMITTED isolation level.

In this case, $10 is transferred from an account the query has yet to read into one it has already read, so the total returned by the SELECT will be $10 less than the correct total. Equally possible is the case where the transfer transaction moves money from an account the query has already read, into one it has yet to read, in which case the reported total will be greater than the correct amount.

Let me demonstrate that this example is not only theoretically possible, but is easy to reproduce and, as such, may be quite likely. To reproduce the problem, we'll run our SELECT multiple times, in a loop in one session, while simultaneously, from a second session, making multiple transfers of money between accounts.

The two scripts, shown in Listing 9-15 and Listing 9-16, need to execute simultaneously from two different tabs in SSMS. The first script, Listing 9-15, transfers money between two accounts. Do not run it yet; just cut and paste it into an SSMS tab.

```
DECLARE @i INT ,
    @rc INT ,
    @AccountNumber INT ,
    @AnotherAccountNumber INT ,
    @succeeded INT ;

SET TRANSACTION ISOLATION LEVEL READ COMMITTED ;
SET NOCOUNT ON ;
SET @i = 0 ;
WHILE   @i < 100000
    BEGIN ;
    -- currently all account numbers end with zeros
        SET @AccountNumber = 100000 + RAND() * 200000 ;
        SET @AnotherAccountNumber = 100000 + RAND()*200000 ;
```

```
-- so I calculate account numbers in two simple steps
  SET @AccountNumber = @AccountNumber * 10 ;
  SET @AnotherAccountNumber=@AnotherAccountNumber*10 ;
  IF @AccountNumber <> @AnotherAccountNumber
    BEGIN ;
      SET @succeeded = 0 ;
      BEGIN TRAN ;
      UPDATE   dbo.AccountBalances
      SET    Amount = Amount - 10
      WHERE    AccountNumber = @AccountNumber
                            AND Amount > 10 ;
      SET @rc = @@ROWCOUNT ;
      IF @rc = 1
        BEGIN ;
          UPDATE   dbo.AccountBalances
          SET    Amount = Amount + 10
          WHERE AccountNumber =@AnotherAccountNumber ;
          SET @rc = @@ROWCOUNT ;
          SET @succeeded = CASE WHEN @rc = 1
                            THEN 1
                          ELSE 0
                      END ;
        END ;
      IF @succeeded = 1
        BEGIN ;
          COMMIT ;
        END ;
      ELSE
        BEGIN ;
          ROLLBACK ;
        END ;
    END ;
  SET @i = @i + 1 ;
END ;
```

Listing 9-15: The script to transfer money between randomly chosen accounts in a loop.

Our second script simulates 50 separate transactions, each calculating the total money in all accounts. For clarity, we could include BEGIN TRAN / COMMIT TRAN statements around the SELECT SUM.. but, since it's a single-statement transaction, they are not required.

Cut and paste the script in Listing 9-16 into a second SSMS tab, and start both scripts immediately, one after another.

```
SET TRANSACTION ISOLATION LEVEL READ COMMITTED ;
-- SET TRANSACTION ISOLATION LEVEL SNAPSHOT;
-- SET TRANSACTION ISOLATION LEVEL REPEATABLE READ ;
-- SET TRANSACTION ISOLATION LEVEL SERIALIZABLE ;

SET NOCOUNT ON ;
DECLARE @i INT ;
SET @i = 0 ;
DECLARE @totals TABLE ( total DECIMAL(17, 2) ) ;
WHILE  @i < 50
    BEGIN ;
        INSERT  INTO @totals
                ( total
                )
                SELECT  SUM(Amount)
                FROM    dbo.AccountBalances ;
        SET @i = @i + 1 ;
    END ;
SELECT  COUNT(*) AS [Count] ,
        total
FROM    @totals
GROUP BY total ;
```

Listing 9-16: Selecting the total amount in a loop, under READ COMMITTED isolation level.

These scripts will, by design, take some time to finish. When the script from Listing 9-16 finishes, you should see output with many incorrect results, such as that shown in Listing 9-17.

Count	Total
1	199999940
6	199999970
7	199999980
11	199999990
11	200000000
6	200000010
5	200000020
2	200000030
1	200000040

**Listing 9-17: The count of the numbers of times a given total is returned by our
SELECT query.**

Notice that, on my box, the query returns the correct result 11 times out of 50. On all
other executions it produces an incorrect result, which may be both less than, or greater
than, the correct amount. This equates to a success rate of 22%.

The exact output may be different on your machine and will vary slightly each time
you run the test, but the general outcome will be the same, i.e. the query will produce
incorrect results most of the time.

This illustrates a very important point: many problems caused by concurrency are,
by their nature, intermittent. Typically, we cannot reproduce such problems in our
test environments exactly as they happened in production. The best we can do is to
successfully simulate high concurrency in our test environments so that we may
reproduce similar cases. For example, we might have a customer complain that the
totals should be 200,000,000 but they are 200,000,040. Our test harness may reproduce
exactly this case in less than 1% of its executions, but it also can reproduce a lot of other
similar cases.

Of course, in this case, we have deliberately created circumstances under which the
SELECT is very likely to return incorrect results. However, the message is clear: if we
run our SELECTs under READ COMMITTED isolation level, we may from time to time get
incorrect results. The probability of getting incorrect results depends on our workload
and our environment. Whether or not our customers can tolerate incorrect results

depends on their requirements, but we need to be aware of this possibility whenever we run our queries under READ COMMITTED isolation level.

Can higher isolation levels, SERIALIZABLE or REPEATABLE READ, fix the problem?

REPEATABLE READ

Let us begin with REPEATABLE READ isolation level. If we reload the data, change the isolation level under which our query is running to REPEATABLE READ, and rerun the same two scripts, 9-15 and 9-16, concurrently, most likely we shall get a deadlock. Table 9-2 describes how it can happen:

Connection One	Connection Two

Begins running the following command:
`SELECT SUM(Amount) AS`
`    TotalAmount`
`FROM dbo.AccountBalances;`	

Reads the page that stores account number 1234560, keeping a shared lock for the duration of the transaction.	
	Begins a transaction. Withdraws $10 from account 2345670. Attempts to deposit $10 to account 1234560, but the row it needs to modify is locked by Connection One. Stays in lock-waiting state, waiting for Connection One to release the locks.

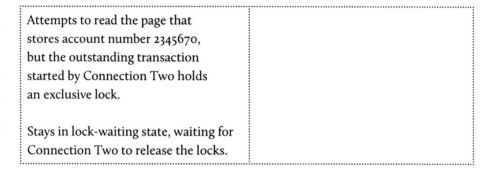

Attempts to read the page that stores account number 2345670, but the outstanding transaction started by Connection Two holds an exclusive lock.
Stays in lock-waiting state, waiting for Connection Two to release the locks.

Table 9-2: A query running under REPEATABLE READ isolation level at the same time as a data modification.

In order to avoid the potential of a non-repeatable read, the query running under REPEATABLE READ causes SQL Server to acquire shared read locks on the data and keep them until the end of the transaction, rather than just the end of the query. Therefore the UPDATE cannot proceed and the two sessions are embraced in a deadlock. The query will either return correct results or error out as the deadlock victim.

To some, perhaps used to seeing deadlocks described purely in terms of competing modifications, it may seem counterintuitive that our query may be chosen as a deadlock victim rather than the modifying transaction. In fact, SQL Server simply chooses the transaction with the lowest rollback cost as the deadlock victim.

Does all this mean that if we run our queries under REPEATABLE READ isolation level, we cannot get incorrect results? Not necessarily. All we've done so far is run our queries concurrently with one type of transaction, which transferred money between existing accounts. Let's see how our queries work when executed simultaneously with a different kind of transaction, which:

- withdraws money from an account

- creates a new account

- deposits the money in this new account.

Listing 9-18 encloses a single money transfer to a new account in a transaction, and then repeats that transaction 10,000 times.

```
DECLARE @i INT ,
  @rc INT ,
  @AccountNumber INT ,
  @AnotherAccountNumber INT ,
  @succeeded INT ;

SET TRANSACTION ISOLATION LEVEL READ COMMITTED ;
SET NOCOUNT ON ;
SET @i = 0 ;
WHILE ( @i < 10000 )
  BEGIN ;
  -- currently all account numbers end with zeros
    SET @AccountNumber = 100000 + RAND() * 200000 ;
    SET @AnotherAccountNumber = 100000 + RAND()*200000 ;
  -- so I calculate account numbers in two simple steps
    SET @AccountNumber = @AccountNumber * 10 ;
    SET @AnotherAccountNumber =@AnotherAccountNumber*10;
    IF @AccountNumber <> @AnotherAccountNumber
      BEGIN ;
        SET @succeeded = 0 ;
        BEGIN TRAN ;
        UPDATE  dbo.AccountBalances
        SET    Amount = Amount - 10
        WHERE   AccountNumber = @AccountNumber
            AND Amount > 10 ;
        SELECT  @rc = @@ROWCOUNT ;
        IF @rc = 1
          BEGIN ;
            INSERT  dbo.AccountBalances
                ( AccountNumber ,
                  Amount ,
                  CustomerID ,
                  SpaceFiller
                )
                SELECT  @AnotherAccountNumber - 5 ,
                    10 ,
                    @i ,
                    'qwerty'
```

```
            WHERE    NOT EXISTS ( SELECT 1
                          FROM    dbo.AccountBalances
                          WHERE   AccountNumber =
                                  @AnotherAccountNumber
                                - 5 ) ;
        SET @rc = @@ROWCOUNT ;
        SET @succeeded = CASE WHEN @rc = 1 THEN 1
                    ELSE 0
                END ;
      END ;
    IF @succeeded = 1
      BEGIN ;
        COMMIT ;
      END ;
    ELSE
      BEGIN ;
        ROLLBACK ;
      END ;
    END ;
  SET @i = @i + 1 ;
END ;
```

Listing 9-18: A script to transfer money in $10 increments from randomly chosen accounts into new accounts, in a loop.

We are now ready to simulate what can happen on a system under heavy load, with multiple transactions accessing the same data at almost the same moment. In order to run through this test case, follow the steps below.

- Repopulate the data with the original rows, by rerunning the script in Listing 9-12 (this step is optional; we can run our examples a few times without repopulating the test data).

- Change the isolation level in Listing 9-16 to **REPEATABLE READ** (uncomment the corresponding line and comment out the previous isolation level).

- Start the scripts from Listings 9-16 and 9-18, one immediately after the other. These two scripts must run concurrently most of the time.

Typical results returned by our queries are shown in Listing 9-19.

```
Count          Total
-----------    ------------------------------------
7              199999980.00
4              199999990.00
39             200000000.00
```

Listing 9-19: The results of the REPEATABLE READ test.

As in the previous cases, each time we run the test we should not expect to get exactly the same result, but they should be similar. Remember, again, that we have deliberately set up a case where both scripts run for a long enough time to make the chance of errors high.

In any event, this time, we get the correct result more than 75% of the time, but we still get many incorrect results, which are always less than the correct amount. This may seem counterintuitive at first: REPEATABLE READ ensures that reads of existing data are always consistent, but "phantom rows" may appear in the results. By adding in the values in these phantom rows, you might predict an answer that was erroneously high.

However, the reason that we no longer get totals that are greater than the correct amount is simple: the situation described previously, whereby $10 is withdrawn from an account that has already been read by the query, is no longer possible, because, under REPEATABLE READ, the shared locks on the pages that have been read by the query are held until the transaction is committed. Only the scenario implemented in Listing 9-18, where we subtract money from the account which has not been read yet, and transfer money into a new account in the middle of an already read page, is possible. This second scenario always results in totals smaller than the correct amount.

SERIALIZABLE

If we increase the isolation level to SERIALIZABLE, we will never get any incorrect totals, but we are very likely to get deadlocks, as we did under REPEATABLE READ isolation level, in the scenario described in Table 9-2.

To test this out for yourself, simply follow the steps described in the previous section, i.e. repopulate the table (optional), alter the isolation level in Listing 9-16 to SERIALIZABLE, and then run scripts 9-16 and 9-18 in two separate tabs.

So, although SERIALIZABLE isolation level guarantees that our queries always return correct results, the price tag is quite hefty; we have the highest probability of causing deadlocks.

SNAPSHOT

If we change the isolation level under which we run our queries to either SNAPSHOT or READ_COMMITTED_SNAPSHOT (see Chapter 4 for further details on these modes), we will always get correct totals, and we will never get any deadlocks. Of course, switching to snapshot isolation may have performance implications with regard to tempdb usage and so on. A full discussion of this topic is beyond the scope of this book but is covered in detail in the previously-referenced book by Kalen Delaney et al., *Microsoft SQL Server 2008 Internals*.

Before rerunning our tests, we need to make sure that snapshot isolation is allowed in our database, as shown in Listing 9-20.

```
-- Replace OurDatabase
-- with the name of the database
-- in which you are running the examples

ALTER DATABASE OurDatabase
    SET ALLOW_SNAPSHOT_ISOLATION ON ;
```

Listing 9-20: Enabling snapshot isolation in the test database.

To see for yourself, run through the following steps:

- repopulate the data with the original rows, by rerunning the script in Listing 9-12 (again, this step is optional)

- change the isolation level in Listing 9-16 to SNAPSHOT

- start the scripts from Listings 9-15 and 9-16 one immediately after the other; these two scripts must run concurrently most of the time.

As you will see, SNAPSHOT isolation definitely fixes the problem. Note that in this case, we can use either SNAPSHOT or READ_COMMITTED_SNAPSHOT modes; for a single statement both will guarantee a consistent point-in-time snapshot. However, if we run multiple statements in one transaction and expect a consistent point-in-time snapshot, we can use only SNAPSHOT isolation level. We shall discuss this in more detail later in this chapter.

Choosing the right isolation level

As our tests have proved, in cases where data in a table is subject to both frequent modifications and reporting queries, the READ COMMITTED isolation level for the queries is not guaranteed to return consistent and correct results. Using the REPEATABLE READ level, we can still get inconsistent and incorrect data in some cases and, because of the way that SQL implements this level, using shared read locks, it can lead to deadlocks

In SERIALIZABLE mode, our reporting transaction is guaranteed to be completely isolated from the effects of other transactions, so the correct result will always be returned, but at the expense of a much higher risk of deadlocks – see *Minimizing Deadlocks*, later in the chapter, for further discussion on this topic.

The fact that we can get deadlocks when we run our loops under REPEATABLE READ or SERIALIZABLE isolation level demonstrates two very important points.

- Even if two transactions access only one table, they still can embrace in a deadlock. It is very important to realize that we do not need to access two tables to have a deadlock.

- Even if just one transaction writes, and the other one only reads, they can still embrace in a deadlock.

If our queries must be guaranteed to return correct results under the sort of conditions described, and we wish to avoid the potential for deadlocks, then the snapshot isolation level becomes a very attractive option.

When using this level for our reporting queries:

- our readers never embrace in deadlocks with our writers (although the writers may still embrace in deadlocks with each other)

- our readers always return results consistent with a point in time, either the start of the transaction (`SNAPSHOT` mode) or the start of the current statement (`READ_COMMITTED_SNAPSHOT` mode).

Note, however, that using snapshot isolation is not "free;" it comes at a performance cost. For example:

- extra bytes in the rows result in more I/O

- the version store causes more pressure on the I/O devices for `tempdb`

- maintaining the version store slows down data modification

- extra logic to determine which row from the version store has to be used causes computational overhead.

Furthermore, as we proved in Chapter 4, developers need to be aware that in some cases switching to snapshot isolation is a breaking change.

Of course, another option would be to prohibit any concurrency at all when we select our totals by using use a hint that causes the whole table to be locked as we start selecting from it. However, this action kills concurrency, so it is almost never an option.

Querying Multiple Tables that are being Simultaneously Modified

We have just spent considerable time and effort discussing how a simple one-table query executes under different isolation levels, when various patterns of data modification are occurring simultaneously. Even in that very simple case, we saw several different ways in which data consistency could be compromised. When a query works against more than one table while those tables are being simultaneously modified, the number of potential ways in which we may end up with incorrect or inconsistent data increases dramatically.

In cases where we need to develop queries that can reliably report consistent results from tables undergoing simultaneous modification, then the snapshot isolation level is a very useful tool.

In the following example, we'll be querying two tables, `Packages` and `PackageItems`. At the same time, we'll start a transaction that modifies both of these tables. Initially, we'll examine the behavior with READ COMMITTED isolation level and prove that we can get inconsistent results. We'll then switch to SNAPSHOT isolation level to prove that this fixes the issue.

I've purposefully made the example as simple as possible, with one parent table (`Packages`) and one child table (`PackageItems`), while still demonstrating the salient points. Listing 9-21 creates these tables.

```
CREATE TABLE dbo.Packages
    (
        PackageLabel VARCHAR(30) NOT NULL ,
        LengthInInches DECIMAL(7, 2) NOT NULL ,
        WidthInInches DECIMAL(7, 2) NOT NULL ,
        HeightInInches DECIMAL(7, 2) NOT NULL ,
        CONSTRAINT PK_Packages PRIMARY KEY (PackageLabel )
    ) ;
GO

CREATE TABLE dbo.PackageItems
    (
        ItemLabel VARCHAR(30) NOT NULL ,
        PackageLabel VARCHAR(30) NOT NULL ,
        MaxSizeInInches DECIMAL(7, 2) NOT NULL ,
        CONSTRAINT PK_PackageItems PRIMARY KEY (ItemLabel ) ,
        CONSTRAINT FK_PackageItems_Packages
            FOREIGN KEY ( PackageLabel )
            REFERENCES dbo.Packages (PackageLabel )
    ) ;
```

Listing 9-21: Create the `Packages` and `PackageItems` tables.

Listing 9-22 populates these tables with some test data.

```
INSERT   INTO dbo.Packages
         ( PackageLabel ,
           LengthInInches ,
           WidthInInches ,
           HeightInInches
         )
VALUES   ( 'Gifts for in-laws' ,
           5 ,
           5 ,
           2
         ) ;
GO

INSERT   INTO dbo.PackageItems
         ( PackageLabel ,
           ItemLabel ,
           MaxSizeInInches
         )
VALUES   ( 'Gifts for in-laws' ,
           'Box of chocolates' ,
           5
         ) ;
```

Listing 9-22: Populate Packages and PackageItems tables with test data.

Behavior in READ COMMITTED mode

Our first reporting query, shown in Listing 9-23, retrieves all the data regarding our "Gifts for in-laws" package and displays it on a screen form, for user review.

```
SET TRANSACTION ISOLATION LEVEL READ COMMITTED ;

BEGIN TRANSACTION ;
```

```
SELECT    PackageLabel ,
          LengthInInches ,
          WidthInInches ,
          HeightInInches
FROM      dbo.Packages
WHERE     PackageLabel = 'Gifts for in-laws' ;


PackageLabel        LengthInInches WidthInInches HeightInInches
------------------------------------------------------------------
Gifts for in-laws 5.00             5.00          2.00
```

Listing 9-23: A query that selects data from the Packages table.

At the same time as we are selecting our data, another connection modifies the
PackageItems table by adding a new gift item, a golf club and then, in the same
transaction, updates the Packages table to increase the size of the "Gifts for in-laws"
package so that it can accommodate the golf clubs, as shown in Listing 9-24, which
should be run in a second tab.

```
BEGIN TRY ;
    BEGIN TRANSACTION ;

    INSERT  INTO dbo.PackageItems
            ( PackageLabel ,
              ItemLabel ,
              MaxSizeInInches
            )
    VALUES  ( 'Gifts for in-laws' ,
              'Golf Club' ,
              45
            ) ;

    UPDATE  dbo.Packages
    SET     LengthInInches = 48
    WHERE   PackageLabel = 'Gifts for in-laws' ;

    COMMIT ;
```

```
END TRY
BEGIN CATCH ;
    SELECT ERROR_MESSAGE ();
    ROLLBACK ;
END CATCH ;
```

Listing 9-24: While one connection queries the Packages table, another connection modifies that same data.

While this data is being modified, we have rendered the information about the package on our screen, and we are now proceeding to retrieve and display the information regarding the contents of our package, as shown in Listing 9-25, which should be executed from the first tab.

```
SELECT  ItemLabel ,
        MaxSizeInInches
FROM    dbo.PackageItems
WHERE   PackageLabel = 'Gifts for in-laws' ;

COMMIT ;


ItemLabel                          MaxSizeInInches
--------------------------------   ----------------
Box of chocolates                  5.00
Golf Club                          45.00
```

Listing 9-25: A query issued to select information regarding the contents of our package.

Clearly, the information that we see on our screen is inconsistent: the golf club is 45 inches long and, as such, it cannot fit into a small 5 x 5 x 2 package. Note that the committed data in our database has never been in an inconsistent state; the second connection added a large gift and increased the size of the package, in a single transaction. The committed data changed from one consistent state into another consistent state. It is entirely our fault that we have not ensured that our two queries reflect a consistent point-in-time snapshot of the data.

323

Some people may argue that this is a "rigged" example; that, if we had done things the right way, and queried the two tables in a single statement, using an INNER JOIN, rather than separately, then we would not see these inconsistent results.

There are two problems with this argument. Firstly, in real life it is quite common that we'll need to query more than two tables when we instantiate an object on the client. For example, to instantiate one object of a Vehicle class, we may need to query several tables, Vehicles, VehicleMaintenance, VehicleTrips, TrafficTickets, and so on. In such cases, it makes no sense to join one parent table to several child tables. We have to query these tables separately, and we have to come up with consistent point-in-time data in all our result sets.

Secondly, we can still get inconsistent data even if we do things the right way, and retrieve all the data we need in one query, instead of two separate ones. To prove this point, we'll run through the example again, using the latter approach. Let's add some fresh test data, as shown in Listing 9-26.

```
SET NOCOUNT ON ;
DELETE FROM dbo.PackageItems ;
DELETE FROM dbo.Packages ;
GO

INSERT   INTO dbo.Packages
          ( PackageLabel ,
            LengthInInches ,
            WidthInInches ,
            HeightInInches
          )
VALUES   ( 'Gifts for in-laws' ,
            5 ,
            5 ,
            2
          ) ;
GO

DECLARE @i INT ;
SET @i = 1 ;
```

```
WHILE @i < 10000
  BEGIN ;
    INSERT  INTO dbo.PackageItems
        ( PackageLabel ,
          ItemLabel ,
          MaxSizeInInches
        )
    SELECT 'Gifts for in-laws' ,
           'item # ' + CAST(@i AS VARCHAR(10)) ,
           2 ;
    SET @i = @i + 1 ;
  END ;
```

Listing 9-26: Adding fresh test data.

As in our previous examples, in one tab we'll repeatedly modify the data that is being retrieved, as shown in Listing 9-27. At the start, MaxSizeInInches and HeightIn-Inches for all items are all equal (and of value 2). The loop increases the size of an item, and the size of the corresponding box, all in one transaction. Therefore, the committed data will always have the maximum size of all items and the maximum size of all boxes, and they should always be equal. Paste the script into a tab, but do not start it yet.

```
SET NOCOUNT ON ;
-- We want to make sure that this script
-- becomes a deadlock victim
SET DEADLOCK_PRIORITY LOW ;
DECLARE @i INT ;
SET @i = 1 ;
WHILE @i < 10000
    BEGIN ;
        BEGIN TRAN ;
        UPDATE  dbo.PackageItems
        SET     MaxSizeInInches = MaxSizeInInches + 1
        WHERE   ItemLabel = 'item # 9999'
        UPDATE  dbo.Packages
        SET     HeightInInches = HeightInInches + 1
        WHERE   PackageLabel = 'Gifts for in-laws' ;
```

```
        COMMIT ;
        SET @i = @i + 1 ;
    END ;
```

Listing 9-27: Modifying the data that is being retrieved.

In a second tab, we'll run in a loop a query that accesses both of our tables, as shown in Listing 9-28. This loop joins the package to all items, then finds the highest MaxSizeInInches (for package #9999), and the highest HeightInInches (equal in all rows, but the MAX is required for valid SQL). If they are not equal, the offending row is output.

Please note that, in order to see similar behavior, READ_COMMITTED_SNAPSHOT must be turned off in your test database, as shown in Listing 9-1.

```
-- Hit Ctrl+T to run in text mode
DECLARE @res TABLE
    (
        boxSize DECIMAL(14, 2) NOT NULL ,
        itemSize DECIMAL(14, 2) NOT NULL
    ) ;
SET NOCOUNT ON ;
-- We want to make sure this script does not
-- become a deadlock victim
SET DEADLOCK_PRIORITY HIGH ;
SET TRANSACTION ISOLATION LEVEL READ COMMITTED ;
DECLARE @i INT ,
    @d INT ;
SET @i = 1 ;
WHILE @i < 1000
    BEGIN ;
        INSERT  INTO @res
                ( boxSize ,
                  itemSize
                )
        SELECT  p.HeightInInches ,
                i.MaxSizeInInches
```

```
                    FROM      dbo.Packages AS p
                       INNER JOIN dbo.PackageItems AS i
                       ON p.PackageLabel = i.PackageLabel ;
--   Are the maximum size of all items and the
--   maximum size of all boxes equal to each other?
         SELECT   @d = MAX(boxSize) - MAX(itemSize)
         FROM     @res ;
         IF @d <> 0
--  If they are not equal, this is a discrepancy
--  Let us display the discrepancy
            SELECT   boxSize ,
                       MAX(itemSize) AS MaxItemSize
            FROM     @res
            GROUP BY boxSize
            HAVING   boxSize <> MAX(itemSize) ;
         DELETE   FROM @res ;
         SET @i = @i + 1 ;
      END ;
```

Listing 9-28: Running a query against both test tables, in a loop, and detecting any inconsistent results.

Start Listing 9-27 and then Listing 9-28 immediately, one after the other. Listing 9-28 should detect inconsistent results, as demonstrated in Listing 9-29.

```
(snip)
boxSize                                   MaxItemSize
----------------------------------------- -----------
2469.00                                   2511.00

boxSize                                   MaxItemSize
----------------------------------------- -----------
2697.00                                   2733.00
```

```
boxSize                                      MaxItemSize
-----------------------------------------    -----------
2926.00                                      2962.00
(snip)
```

Listing 9-29: Typical inconsistent results detected by Listing 9-27.

Note that I ran these examples on several servers, using both SQL Server 2005 and 2008, and saw similar results in each case. Nevertheless, I cannot guarantee that these scripts will run in the same way on your server, and it is possible that you will not see any discrepancies. As usual, a lot depends on which execution plan is chosen by the optimizer, and we cannot control the choice of execution plans unless we use hints.

Of course, the fact that we do not control the choice of execution plans also means that, even if you see no inconsistent results now, you may do so after the next upgrade, or after a significant change in the statistics.

Fortunately, as we shall see next, snapshot isolation offers a way to guarantee consistent point-in-time results.

Behavior in SNAPSHOT mode

As described in Chapter 4, snapshot isolation mode is a built-in mechanism designed to provide a consistent point-in-time view of our data. When we begin a transaction and start selecting data, the database engine guarantees that our queries return a consistent view of the data, as of the time when our transaction began.

Let's repeat our initial example, where we returned the required data in two separate result sets. First, restore the original test data by deleting the existing data from the Packages and PackageItems tables, as shown in Listing 9-30, and then rerunning Listing 9-22.

```
DELETE  FROM dbo.PackageItems ;
DELETE  FROM dbo.Packages ;
```

Listing 9-30: Delete the modified data from Packages and PackageItems.

Also, if you have not already done so, run Listing 9-20 to enable snapshot isolation.

In Listing 9-31, we run the same initial reporting query against the **Packages** table as in Listing 9-23, but this time the query is running within a transaction, under snapshot isolation level.

```
SET TRANSACTION ISOLATION LEVEL SNAPSHOT ;

BEGIN TRANSACTION ;

SELECT    PackageLabel ,
          LengthInInches ,
          WidthInInches ,
          HeightInInches
FROM      dbo.Packages
WHERE     PackageLabel = 'Gifts for in-laws' ;
```

Listing 9-31: Begin a transaction under SNAPSHOT isolation level, and retrieve the data regarding our package.

In a second tab, rerun the script from Listing 9-24. Having modified the data, let us complete the retrieval of our data for our screen form, by running the query shown in Listing 9-32 in the same tab in which we ran Listing 9-31.

```
SELECT    ItemLabel ,
          MaxSizeInInches
FROM      dbo.PackageItems
WHERE     PackageLabel = 'Gifts for in-laws' ;

COMMIT ;
```

```
ItemLabel                        MaxSizeInInches
------------------------------   ------------------------------
Box of chocolates                5.00
```

Listing 9-32: The same query against `PackageItems` table, in the context of a transaction under `SNAPSHOT` isolation level, returns data consistent with the time our transaction began.

So, this time our query returns the data as of the time when we began our transaction, and so the modifications that committed after we began our transaction did not show up in our second result set.

Likewise, we can repeat our test where the data was retrieved from the two tables in a single result set, by changing the isolation level used in Listing 9-27 to `SNAPSHOT` and then rerunning this script, along with Listing 9-28. Again, you should see that no inconsistent results are detected.

SNAPSHOT versus READ_COMMITTED_SNAPSHOT

The difference between `SNAPSHOT` and `READ_COMMITTED_SNAPSHOT` isolation level is as follows:

- `READ_COMMITTED_SNAPSHOT` isolation level isolates us from the modifications which committed after our **statement** began

- `SNAPSHOT` isolation level isolates us from the modifications which committed after our **transaction** began.

This difference only manifests itself when we execute multi-statement transactions. To highlight this difference, and to demonstrate why in some cases it matters, let's rerun our multi-statement example but this time under `READ_COMMITTED_SNAPSHOT` isolation level.

First, we need to enable `READ_COMMITTED_SNAPSHOT` isolation, for our database, as shown in Listing 9-33. Note that versions prior to SQL Server 2005 do not support this isolation level, so this statement would simply return an error. The `ALTER DATABASE` command to enable this isolation level needs an exclusive database lock, so it will wait until no other connection is using the database. However, the ROLLBACK IMMEDIATE option will allow SQL Server to force all other connections out of the database, instead of waiting.

```
-- Replace OurDatabase
-- with the name of the database
-- in which you are running the scripts

ALTER DATABASE OurDatabase
SET READ_COMMITTED_SNAPSHOT ON
WITH ROLLBACK IMMEDIATE ;
```

Listing 9-33: **Enabling** READ_COMMITTED_SNAPSHOT **for our database.**

Now, run the scripts from Listings 9-30 (deleting the modified data) and 9-22 (reinsert the original data). Then, in one tab, set the isolation level to READ_COMMITTED_SNAP-SHOT and then start the transaction, as shown in Listing 9-34.

```
-- In this context READ COMMITTED
-- actually means READ_COMMITTED_SNAPSHOT
SET TRANSACTION ISOLATION LEVEL READ COMMITTED ;

BEGIN TRANSACTION ;

SELECT   PackageLabel ,
         LengthInInches ,
         WidthInInches ,
         HeightInInches
FROM     dbo.Packages
WHERE    PackageLabel = 'Gifts for in-laws' ;
```

Listing 9-34: **Begin a transaction under** READ_COMMITTED_SNAPSHOT **isolation level and run the first query.**

In a second tab, rerun the data modification script from Listing 9-24. Return to Tab #1 and run the script from Listing 9-32. The output is shown in Listing 9-34, and is identical to that which we saw in Listing 9-25.

```
ItemLabel                        MaxSizeInInches
-----------------------------    -----------------------------
Box of chocolates                5.00
Golf Club                        45.00
```

Listing 9-35: When our queries run under `READ_COMMITTED_SNAPSHOT` isolation level, the output of the second query is inconsistent with the output from the first one.

In this example, `READ_COMMITTED_SNAPSHOT` isolation level does not solve our problem. The reason is simple: `READ_COMMITTED_SNAPSHOT` isolation level isolates us from the modifications which committed after our **statement** began. On the other hand, `SNAPSHOT` isolation level isolates us from the modifications which committed after our **transaction** began. So, if we issue multiple queries and need them to return consistent point-in-time results, we need to run all our queries in one transaction and to use only `SNAPSHOT` isolation level.

Of course, in simple cases when we have only to access two tables, we can use a simple join query and retrieve all the data we need in one statement. If we rerun the test described by Listings 9-27 and 9-28, but using `READ_COMMITTED_SNAPSHOT` isolation level for the query, we will be protected from inconsistent results.

Minimizing Deadlocks

If you need to guarantee consistent results in cases where tables are subject to simultaneous reporting queries and data modifications, then you may need to consider running the reporting queries under a higher isolation level, either `REPEATABLE READ`, `SERIALIZABLE`, or one of the snapshot isolation levels.

As discussed earlier, typically both `REPEATABLE READ` and `SERIALIZABLE` isolation levels increase the chances of our queries embracing in deadlocks with transactions that are modifying the same data. Let us consider a simple example, which is a variation of the multiple table example we've been using up to now, and which causes a deadlock.

As in the previous examples, first we need to rerun the scripts from Listings 9-30 (delete the modified data) and 9-22 (reinsert the original data). In one tab, begin a transaction under REPEATABLE READ isolation level and run the first query, as shown in Listing 9-36.

```
-- We want this transaction to be chosen
-- as a deadlock victim
SET DEADLOCK_PRIORITY LOW ;

SET TRANSACTION ISOLATION LEVEL REPEATABLE READ ;
BEGIN TRANSACTION ;

SELECT  PackageLabel ,
        LengthInInches ,
        WidthInInches ,
        HeightInInches
FROM    dbo.Packages
WHERE   PackageLabel = 'Gifts for in-laws' ;
```

Listing 9-36: Begin a transaction under REPEATABLE READ isolation level and run the first query.

In a second tab, start our modification, as shown in Listing 9-37.

```
BEGIN TRANSACTION ;

INSERT  INTO dbo.PackageItems
        ( PackageLabel ,
          ItemLabel ,
          MaxSizeInInches
        )
```

```
VALUES  ( 'Gifts for in-laws' ,
            'Golf Club' ,
            45
        ) ;
```

Listing 9-37: Begin the transaction that modifies our data.

Return to the first tab and rerun the script from Listing 9-32. The script does not complete, because our query is blocked by the uncommitted modifications from the second tab. Return to the second tab and complete our modifications, as shown in Listing 9-38.

```
UPDATE  dbo.Packages
SET     LengthInInches = 48
WHERE   Label = 'Gifts for in-laws' ;

COMMIT ;
```

Listing 9-38: Complete the modifications in the second tab.

Our modification will first try to acquire locks, and enter a waiting state when it is detected that the required rows are locked by another transaction. Since a deadlock situation is detected, one of the processes, in this case our query, is chosen as the deadlock victim and killed. At this point, our modification executes and completes. Return to the first tab and you will see the evidence that our querying transaction has been chosen as the deadlock victim.

As our examples have demonstrated, even a read-only transaction can cause a deadlock, and be chosen as a deadlock victim. The easiest way to minimize deadlocks in such situations is to use snapshot isolation. We can refresh our data one more time, change the isolation level in Listing 9-36 to **SNAPSHOT**, and rerun our test case. Under snapshot isolation the script from Listing 9-32 will complete right away; it will not be blocked by the uncommitted data modification in the second tab, and there will be no deadlock.

In certain situations, however, it may not be possible or desirable to use snapshot isolation. For example, it may not be possible for performance reasons, or we may be dealing with legacy code developed prior to SQL Server 2005. If snapshot isolation is not an option, we can simply retry our queries after deadlocks. This is discussed in Chapter 8, along with other issues related to error handling.

There is another quite common recommendation for minimizing deadlocks: always access tables in one and the same order. In some cases, this recommendation makes sense. For example, if we modified the `Packages` table before the `PackageItems` table in the previous example, our two transactions would not embrace in a deadlock.

However, it is not always possible to follow this recommendation. For example, if we need to delete a package and all its items in one transaction, then we need to modify the `PackageItems` table before the `Packages` table; the `FOREIGN KEY` constraint `FK_PackageItems_Packages` makes the other order impossible. On the other hand, if we need to add a new package and all its items in one transaction, we have to modify the tables in the opposite order because of that constraint.

Also, we need to realize that when we modify data in one table, other tables may also be accessed because of constraints or triggers, and the order in which these other tables are accessed may or may not be the order that we intended.

More to the point, I have deliberately chosen to select from two tables with two different queries; this made my examples much simpler. In real life, we frequently join tables in one select query, and if we do not use hints, then there is no way we can predict which plan the optimizer will choose, and in which order the pages which store the data will be accessed. This means that trying to always modify tables in one and the same order does not always help: although we may have control over the order in which we modify data, we have less control over the order in which the data is read by SELECTs.

So, as we have seen, the recommendation to always access the tables in one and the same order is of rather limited usefulness; it might be helpful in some cases, but it is impossible to follow in others.

Conclusion

Hopefully, this chapter has convinced you that when you are querying data that is being simultaneously modified, your queries may return inconsistent results. This is true for both the `READ COMMITTED` and `REPEATABLE READ` isolation levels.

Furthermore we have demonstrated that while `SERIALIZABLE` will prevent inconsistent results, its use greatly increases the prospect that deadlocks will occur, and that our queries will be chosen as deadlock victims.

The snapshot isolation level is the only one that can guarantee consistent point-in-time results. If your transactions comprise single-statement queries then either `SNAPSHOT` mode will protect you from inconsistent results. If they comprise multiple statements, then only `SNAPSHOT`, and not `READ_COMMITTED_SNAPSHOT`, can guarantee consistency. Furthermore, it attains this consistency without causing deadlocks.

Of course, using snapshot isolation is not free. It can break some existing functionality, as we discussed in Chapter 4, *When Upgrading Breaks Code*. It can also take some effort for the DBAs to set it up, and it may affect your database performance.

Overall, however, I believe that in many cases snapshot isolation is a viable way of resolving many problems related to concurrency.

Chapter 10: Developing Modifications that Survive Concurrency

Just like queries, modifications that work perfectly well in the isolated world of the test database, can suddenly start misbehaving intermittently, when run in a production environment under conditions of concurrent access. There are a number of different problems that might occur when "competing" connections try to simultaneously update the same data, some of the most common of which are:

- **lost modifications, a.k.a. lost updates** – such problems occur when modifications performed by one connection are overwritten by another; these typically occur silently; no errors are raised

- **resource contention errors** – such as deadlocks and lock timeouts

- **primary key and unique constraint violations** – such problems occur when different modifications attempt to insert one and the same row.

The sort of situation in which a lost update or another error can occur, in other words, when the result of the operation is dependent on the sequence or timing of other events, is known as a **race condition**. It is the job of the defensive programmer to guard against potential race conditions in their software. The most common solutions for such problems include:

- serializing modifications against the same data, so that race conditions do not occur

- detecting and handling errors caused by concurrency

- rewriting code so that it better withstands race conditions or avoids them altogether.

We shall discuss a few all-too-common examples that demonstrate the sort of problems that can arise, and then show different ways of solving them. Of course, it is possible that the problems that you encounter with concurrent modifications will be different from those described here. However, the basic approaches described for solving such problems are very likely to be useful in your situation.

Understanding Lost Modifications

Lost modifications can occur when multiple connections modify the same row of data. For example, one connection (A) reads a row of data, with the intent to update that row, based on certain criteria. Meanwhile, after A has read the data, but before it updates it, a second connection (B) updates the same row. Connection A then performs its update, potentially causing the update made by B to be lost.

The classic example of a lost update involves reading data into a user form for subsequent modification. For example, an employee loads data pertaining to a particular customer into a user form, in order to update their address. Meanwhile, an automated process updates the same row, assigning to the customer a new status, such as "loyal customer." If the employee submits the address update and the application updates the whole row, rather than the column that was changed, then the customer could be reset back to their old status, and the effect of the automated process will be lost.

Aside from having a more intelligent logic attached to the form, so only the column modified is updated in the database (we'll discuss this in more detail shortly), there are essentially two concurrency control approaches that we can use in order to avoid such lost updates.

Optimistic approach. Even though we have selected a row, other sessions can modify it, but we optimistically assume that this will not happen. When the selected row is updated, we have logic in place that will test to see if the row has been modified by someone else, since it was queried. If it has, then the employee would get a message saying that the row has been changed, and asking if we still want to make the requested change. This approach is preferable when selected rows are rarely modified, or when a typical modification takes a lot of time, such as modifying data via on-screen forms.

Pessimistic approach. Here, we pessimistically assume that rows will get modified by another process between reading them and updating them, unless we do something to prevent it. When the employee selects a row, or list of rows, the system makes sure that nobody else can modify those rows. With this approach, the automated process would be blocked until the employee had made the address update (and we'd need logic in place to allow it to retry). This approach is most useful when selected rows are very likely to be modified and/or the modification does not take much time. Typically this approach is not used when users modify data via on-screen forms.

In the example we've used here, the two modifying transactions do not, from the database's perspective, overlap. The automated update starts and finishes before the employee's address update has started. In such circumstances, and given user forms are involved, we're likely to take an optimistic approach to concurrency control.

In cases where only automated processes involved, where we have quick transactions attempting to (almost) simultaneously change the same rows of data, we also risk lost updates, and we are likely to adopt a pessimistic approach to concurrency control, in order to avoid them.

Let's take a look at some fairly typical examples of when a lost update can occur.

Non-Overlapping Modifications

From the point of view of the database engine, the modifications in this example do not overlap; they occur at different times. Still, the second modification overwrites the changes made by the first one, and some information is lost.

Suppose that a ticket has been created in our bug-tracking system to report that a very important business report for our Californian office has suddenly stopped working. Listing 10-1 shows the table that stores tickets. We have already used a table named `Tickets` in previous chapters; make sure to create a new database to run the examples, or, at the very least, make sure to drop the table `Tickets` if it exists.

```
CREATE TABLE dbo.Tickets
    (
        TicketID INT NOT NULL ,
        Problem VARCHAR(50) NOT NULL ,
        CausedBy VARCHAR(50) NULL ,
        ProposedSolution VARCHAR(50) NULL ,
        AssignedTo VARCHAR(50) NOT NULL ,
        Status VARCHAR(50) NOT NULL ,
        CONSTRAINT PK_Tickets PRIMARY KEY ( TicketID )
    ) ;
```

Listing 10-1:   Creating the dbo.Tickets table.

339

Of course, in real life, this table would have more columns, such as `Priority`, and possibly some columns would have different types, and there would be some constraints. However, as usual in this book, all the details that are not relevant to this simple example are omitted. Listing 10-2 shows the ticket that was created.

```
INSERT   INTO dbo.Tickets
          ( TicketID ,
            Problem ,
            CausedBy ,
            ProposedSolution ,
            AssignedTo ,
            Status
          )
VALUES   ( 123 ,
            'TPS report for California not working' ,
            NULL ,
            NULL ,
            'TPS report team' ,
            'Opened'
          ) ;
```

Listing 10-2: **The ticket in the `dbo.Tickets` table, reporting a problem with the TPS report.**

This is a very important ticket, so two developers – let's call them Arnie and Brian – immediately start troubleshooting. Brian starts the bug-tracking GUI and opens the ticket. In the meantime, Arnie starts his investigation and quickly realizes that one of the tables used in the report is empty; possibly it has been accidentally truncated. He opens the same ticket in his on-screen form in the bug-tracking GUI and immediately updates the ticket, describing the likely cause of the problem. He also reassigns the ticket to the DBA team. The resulting SQL is shown in Listing 10-3.

```
-- Arnie loads data into form
SELECT   TicketID ,
          Problem ,
          CausedBy ,
          ProposedSolution ,
```

```
        AssignedTo ,
        Status
FROM    dbo.Tickets
WHERE   TicketID = 123
GO


-- Arnie updates the form
BEGIN TRAN ;
UPDATE  dbo.Tickets
SET  AssignedTo = 'DBA team' ,
     CausedBy = 'The dbo.Customers table is empty' ,
     Problem = 'TPS report for California not working' ,
     ProposedSolution =
            'Restore dbo.Customers table from backup'
WHERE   TicketID = 123 ;
COMMIT ;
```

Listing 10-3: The SQL that was issued by Arnie's bug-tracking form.

Meanwhile, Brian has decided to start by ascertaining whether it was just the report that had failed, or whether it was also affecting their Ohio office. He runs the report for Ohio and gets the same problem so, from his on-screen view of the ticket, which he opened before Arnie made his update, Brian updates the **Problem** field to reflect this. The resulting SQL is shown in Listing 10-4.

```
--Brian updates the form
BEGIN TRAN ;
UPDATE  dbo.Tickets
SET  AssignedTo = 'TPS report team' ,
     CausedBy = NULL ,
     Problem =
       'TPS report for California and Ohio not working' ,
     ProposedSolution = NULL
WHERE   TicketID = 123 ;
COMMIT ;
```

Listing 10-4: The SQL that was issued by Brian's bug-tracking form.

The changes saved by Arnie were completely lost. Clearly, our bug-tracking system is susceptible to lost updates, and so has a big problem. There are two approaches to this issue that we must consider in order to prevent the lost update:

- writing logic into the client/data access layer so that only columns are updated in the database, not the entire row

- using concurrency control logic.

Let's consider each in turn.

Only updating changed columns

In this simple example, the problem is pretty blatant: the SQL generated by the user form updates all the fields from the screen, not just the one `Problem` field that Brian modified. In this case, the problem could be solved by designing a better data access layer that only updates those columns that were modified in the form.

Nevertheless, this is only a partial solution and will not be adequate in every case. If Brian, in addition to recording that the TPS report for Ohio was also not working, had suggested as interim solution such as, "temporarily expose yesterday's TPS report," then Arnie's much more sensible solution would have been overwritten, regardless.

```
UPDATE   dbo.Tickets
SET      Problem =
         'TPS report for California and Ohio not working' ,
         ProposedSolution =
      'Expose yesterday''s TPS report instead of live one'
WHERE    TicketID = 123 ;
```

Listing 10-5: Brian proposes a poor solution, overwrites a much better one suggested by Arnie.

Furthermore, updating only changed columns, while feasible, is far from an ideal solution. Let's count how many different **UPDATE** statements would be required in order to modify only the columns that were actually updated on the screen. There are five columns that may be modified, which gives us a total $2^5 = 32$ different update combinations. Should we generate UPDATE commands on the fly? Should we wrap 32 updates in stored procedures? Surely, developing all this code manually is out of the question? Although generating such code would be quite easy, neither choice seems very attractive.

Using concurrency control logic

Ultimately, any system that has the potential for "update conflicts" which could result in lost updates, needs some concurrency control logic in place to either prevent such conflicts from occurring, or determine what should happen when they do.

In previous chapters, we discussed the use of isolation levels to mediate the potential interference of concurrent transactions. Unfortunately, in our bug tracking example, isolation levels alone will not help us. Although from a user's point of view the problem is caused by concurrent updates of the database, from the database's perspective the modifying transactions never overlap. The basic format of the example was:

1. Session 1 queries data into form

2. Session 2 queries same data into form

3. Session 2 starts transaction to update data

4. Session 2 completes transaction to update data

5. Session 1 starts transaction to update data

6. Session 1 completes transaction to update data

7. Session 2's update is lost.

Although the example was run in the default READ COMMITTED mode, the result would have been the same using any of the other transaction isolation levels. In order for isolation levels to have any effect, the transactions must overlap, and in order for that to happen, we'd need to adopt a pessimistic approach, and start the transactions much earlier, as soon as the data was queried into the form, and essentially lock the data from that point. As discussed earlier, this pessimistic approach is often not feasible in situations where data is held in user forms for a long time; to do so would inevitably grind the whole system to a halt. So, when the bug-tracking system opens ticket number 123 for both Arnie and Brian, it should not keep the transactions open after their screen forms have been rendered.

If it is possible to start the transactions earlier, then there may be some cases where high levels such as SERIALIZABLE, or certainly SNAPSHOT (as we will discuss shortly) can help. Note, though, that we cannot always prevent lost updates in this manner. In our previous example, we would simply be in danger of reversing the problem, and losing Brian's, rather than Arnie's, update.

If you wish to implement a pessimistic approach, without locking resources as soon as the data is queried, then the situation is difficult. Unfortunately, there is no built-in mechanism to implement pessimistic concurrency control for longer than the lifetime of a transaction. If we need to implement such an approach, we need to roll it out ourselves. For more information on how to accomplish this, refer to the book, *Expert SQL Server 2005 Development*, by Adam Machanic with Hugo Kornelis and Lara Rubbelke, where the authors show how to roll out your own locks, persist them in a table, and use triggers to verify if rows to be modified are locked.

A more straightforward approach, for examples such as this, is to implement optimistic concurrency control, where we "optimistically assume" that the rows won't be modified in the time between querying them and updating them. Of course, with no control logic, the conflicting update just proceeds, and a lost update occurs, as we saw. However, with proper application of the optimistic approach, we'd have logic in place that raised a warning and prevented the conflicting update from proceeding. So, in our previous example, at the point Brian tried to update the system, the form data would be refreshed and Brian would get a warning that the data had changed since he queried it, and his update would not proceed.

Optimistic concurrency control to detect and prevent lost updates

Let's take a look at three examples of how to implement optimistic concurrency control in our bug tracking example.

Saving the original values

To detect lost updates, our code needs to remember the values of the columns before they were modified, and submit those old values along with the modified ones. The following rather large stored procedure performs the update only if no columns were changed.

```
CREATE PROCEDURE dbo.UpdateTicket
    @TicketID INT ,
    @Problem VARCHAR(50) ,
    @CausedBy VARCHAR(50) ,
    @ProposedSolution VARCHAR(50) ,
    @AssignedTo VARCHAR(50) ,
    @Status VARCHAR(50) ,
    @OldProblem VARCHAR(50) ,
    @OldCausedBy VARCHAR(50) ,
    @OldProposedSolution VARCHAR(50) ,
    @OldAssignedTo VARCHAR(50) ,
    @OldStatus VARCHAR(50)
AS
    BEGIN ;
        SET NOCOUNT ON ;
        SET XACT_ABORT ON ;
        SET TRANSACTION ISOLATION LEVEL READ COMMITTED ;

        BEGIN TRANSACTION ;
        UPDATE  dbo.Tickets
        SET     Problem = @Problem ,
                CausedBy = @CausedBy ,
                ProposedSolution = @ProposedSolution ,
                AssignedTo = @AssignedTo ,
                Status = @Status
        WHERE   TicketID = @TicketID
                AND ( Problem = @OldProblem )
                AND ( AssignedTo = @OldAssignedTo )
                AND ( Status = @OldStatus )
                -- conditions for nullable columns
```

```
                    -- CausedBy and ProposedSolution
                    -- are more complex
                    AND ( CausedBy = @OldCausedBy
                          OR ( CausedBy IS NULL
                                AND @OldCausedBy IS NULL
                             )
                        )
                    AND ( ProposedSolution =
                                    @OldProposedSolution
                          OR ( ProposedSolution IS NULL
                             AND @OldProposedSolution IS NULL
                             )
                        ) ;

        IF @@ROWCOUNT = 0
            BEGIN ;
                ROLLBACK TRANSACTION ;
                RAISERROR('Ticket number %d not found
                or modified after it was read',
                16, 1, @TicketID) ;
            END ;
        ELSE
            BEGIN ;
                COMMIT TRANSACTION ;
            END ;
    END ;
```

Listing 10-6: Stored procedure only modifies if the ticket has not been changed.

As you can see by the size of this procedure, it takes a significant amount of code, both on the server and on the client, to implement this approach. Still, let's see how it works. We'll rerun our bug tracking example (Listings 10-3 and 10-4) using this stored procedure. First, we need to delete and reinsert test data.

```
DELETE FROM dbo.Tickets ;
```

Listing 10-7: Deleting modified test data.

To restore the test data, rerun Listing 10-2. Arnie's update, which was originally performed by Listing 10-3, is now submitted using the UpdateTicket stored procedure, as shown in Listing 10-8.

```
EXECUTE dbo.UpdateTicket
   @TicketID = 123
  ,@Problem = 'TPS report for California not working'
  ,@CausedBy = 'The Customers table is empty'
  ,@ProposedSolution =  'Restore Customers table
                          from backup'
  ,@AssignedTo = 'DBA team'
  ,@Status = 'Opened'
  ,@OldProblem = 'TPS report for California not working'
  ,@OldCausedBy = NULL
  ,@OldProposedSolution = NULL
  ,@OldAssignedTo = 'TPS report team'
  ,@OldStatus = 'Opened' ;
```

Listing 10-8: Using the UpdateTicket stored procedure to save Arnie's changes.

Brian's update from Listing 10-5 is also submitted via the same stored procedure, which detects a lost update, as shown in Listing 10-9.

```
EXECUTE dbo.UpdateTicket
  @TicketID = 123
  ,@Problem = 'TPS report for California and Ohio
                not working'
  ,@CausedBy = NULL
  ,@ProposedSolution = 'Expose yesterdays'' TPS report'
  ,@AssignedTo = 'TPS report team'
  ,@Status = 'Opened'
  ,@OldProblem = 'TPS report for California not working'
  ,@OldCausedBy = NULL
  ,@OldProposedSolution = NULL
  ,@OldAssignedTo = 'TPS report team'
  ,@OldStatus = 'Opened' ;
```

```
Msg 50000, Level 16, State 1, Procedure UpdateTicket, Line 47
Ticket number 123 modified after it was read
```

Listing 10-9: Stored procedure detects a lost update and does not save Brian's changes.

Although this approach works in detecting and preventing lost updates, there is a more efficient one, using the ROWVERSION column.

Using ROWVERSION

A ROWVERSION column in a table is simply a column with a data type of ROWVERSION, which contains a number that auto-increments every time the row is modified. In other words, there is no way to modify a row without incrementing its ROWVERSION column. We can use this feature to detect and prevent lost updates.

In the simplest case, where we load a single row into a screen form, we can retrieve the ROWVERSION along with other columns. When we save the modified data in the database, we can match the saved ROWVERSION against the current ROWVERSION of the row that we are going to modify. If the ROWVERSION value has changed, then the row must have been modified since we read it.

In order to demonstrate this approach, we first need to add a ROWVERSION column to the Tickets table, as shown in Listing 10-10.

```
ALTER TABLE dbo.Tickets
  ADD CurrentVersion ROWVERSION NOT NULL ;
```

Listing 10-10: Adding a ROWVERSION column to the Tickets table.

To populate the changed table, simply rerun scripts 10-7 and 10-2. Listing 10-11 shows how to modify our `UpdateTicket` stored procedure to use the new `ROWVERSION` column. It compares the `ROWVERSION` of the row to be modified against the original `ROWVERSION` value, passed as a parameter, and modifies the row only if these `ROWVERSION` values match.

```
ALTER PROCEDURE dbo.UpdateTicket
    @TicketID INT ,
    @Problem VARCHAR(50) ,
    @CausedBy VARCHAR(50) ,
    @ProposedSolution VARCHAR(50) ,
    @AssignedTo VARCHAR(50) ,
    @Status VARCHAR(50) ,
    @version ROWVERSION
AS
    BEGIN ;
        SET NOCOUNT ON ;
        SET XACT_ABORT ON ;
        SET TRANSACTION ISOLATION LEVEL READ COMMITTED ;
        BEGIN TRANSACTION ;
        UPDATE  dbo.Tickets
        SET     Problem = @Problem ,
                CausedBy = @CausedBy ,
                ProposedSolution = @ProposedSolution ,
                AssignedTo = @AssignedTo ,
                Status = @Status
        WHERE   TicketID = @TicketID
                AND CurrentVersion = @version ;

        IF @@ROWCOUNT = 0
            BEGIN ;
                ROLLBACK TRANSACTION ;
                RAISERROR('Ticket number %d not found
                  or modified after it was read',
                    16, 1, @TicketID) ;
            END ;
```

```
        ELSE
            BEGIN ;
                COMMIT TRANSACTION ;
            END ;
    END ;
```

Listing 10-11: The `UpdateTicket` **stored procedure saves changes only if the saved ROWVERSION matches the current ROWVERSION of the row being modified.**

Listing 10-12 shows how our new `UpdateTicket` stored procedure works in our bug tracking example.

```
DECLARE @version ROWVERSION ;

-- both Brian and Arnie retrieve the same version
SELECT  @version = CurrentVersion
FROM    dbo.Tickets
WHERE   TicketID = 123 ;

-- Arnie saves his changes
EXECUTE dbo.UpdateTicket @TicketID = 123,
  @Problem = 'TPS report for California not working',
  @CausedBy = 'The dbo.Customers table is empty',
  @ProposedSolution = 'Restore dbo.Customers table from
                       backup',
  @AssignedTo = 'DBA team',
  @Status = 'Opened',
  @version = @version ;

-- Brian tries to save his changes
EXECUTE dbo.UpdateTicket @TicketID = 123,
  @Problem = 'TPS report for California and Ohio not
              working',
  @CausedBy = NULL,
  @ProposedSolution = 'Expose yesterdays'' TPS report',
  @AssignedTo = 'TPS report team',
```

```
    @Status = 'Opened',
    @version = @version ;


-- Verify that Arnie's changes are intact
SELECT ProposedSolution
FROM   dbo.Tickets
WHERE  TicketID = 123;


Msg 50000, Level 16, State 1, Procedure UpdateTicket, Line 28
Ticket number 123 not found or modified after it was read
ProposedSolution
-----------------------------------------------------
Restore dbo.Customers table from backup
```

Listing 10-12: Detecting and preventing lost updates with ROWVERSION.

The stored procedure successfully saves Arnie's changes, because the row has not been changed between the time when he read the data into the bug tracker GUI and the time when he updated the ticket.

However, when we invoke the stored procedure to save Brian's changes, our UpdateTicket stored procedure detects that ticket 123 has been modified since Brian initially queried the data, as indicated by the fact that the value of the ROWVERSION column has changed, so the attempt to save Brian's changes fails, and a lost update is averted.

Up to now, all the cases we've discussed involved displaying information for the user and having the user perform some changes. Typically, in such cases, we do not keep the transaction open between the time we read a row and the time we modify it, so the only built-in mechanism to detect lost updates was the ROWVERSION.

If, however, the data is modified programmatically and quickly, then we can afford to keep the transaction open between the time we read a row and the time we modify it. In such cases, we can use snapshot isolation to detect and prevent lost updates.

Using snapshot isolation level

In the first example, we'll prevent a lost update using the **SNAPSHOT** isolation level. Before running the example, we need to establish some test data, as shown in Listing 10-13.

```
DELETE   FROM dbo.Tickets ;

INSERT   INTO dbo.Tickets
         ( TicketID ,
           Problem ,
           CausedBy ,
           ProposedSolution ,
           AssignedTo ,
           Status
         )
VALUES   ( 123 ,
           'TPS report for California not working' ,
           NULL ,
           'Restored Customers table from backup' ,
           'DBA team' ,
           'Closed'
         ) ;
```

Listing 10-13: Adding test data.

Suppose that we have a process that reads tickets one by one, determines if they are eligible for removal from the system, and deletes those that are. Listing 10-14 mimics the case where this automated process has opened a transaction and read ticket number 123.

```
SET TRANSACTION ISOLATION LEVEL SNAPSHOT ;
SET XACT_ABORT ON ;
BEGIN TRANSACTION ;

SELECT   TicketID ,
         Problem ,
         CausedBy ,
```

```
        ProposedSolution ,
        AssignedTo ,
        Status
FROM    dbo.Tickets
WHERE   TicketID = 123 ;

/*
DELETE dbo.Tickets
WHERE   TicketID = 123 ;
COMMIT TRANSACTION ;
*/
```

Listing 10-14: Opening transaction and reading ticket number 123.

At roughly the same time, another connection modifies the same ticket, as shown in Listing 10-15 (which should be run from a different tab).

```
SET NOCOUNT OFF ;
UPDATE  dbo.Tickets
SET     AssignedTo = 'ETL team' ,
        CausedBy = 'ETL truncates Customers table' ,
        Problem = 'TPS report for California not working' ,
        ProposedSolution = 'Fix ETL' ,
        Status = 'Opened'
WHERE   TicketID = 123 ;
```

Listing 10-15: Ticket number 123 is modified.

Clearly the situation has changed and the ticket should not be deleted. Highlight the commented DELETE statement in Listing 10-14 and execute it. Fortunately, under SNAPSHOT isolation, the potential lost update is detected and prevented, as shown in Listing 10-16.

```
Msg 3960, Level 16, State 2, Line 1
Snapshot isolation transaction aborted due to update
conflict. You cannot use snapshot isolation to access table
'dbo.Tickets' directly or indirectly in database 'Test4' to
update, delete, or insert the row that has been modified
or deleted by another transaction. Retry the transaction or
change the isolation level for the update/delete statement.
```

Listing 10-16: A lost update is prevented.

The initial transaction, to retrieve and then delete the ticket, fails. Note that when we started this transaction, we did nothing to prevent other connections from modifying the ticket. Instead, we chose to detect the potential problem and handle it. This is yet another typical example of optimistic concurrency control.

Note that the error message explicitly suggests that we should "Retry the transaction or change the isolation level for the update/delete statement." However, we must be very careful when we consider such recommendations. We need to determine, on a case-by-case basis, which action makes sense. Here, we do not want to change the isolation level because **SNAPSHOT** isolation did a very good job in detecting an error that we want to avoid. Should we retry the transaction? Maybe, but not automatically: we should consider retrying the transaction only after taking into account the new changes. In this particular case, the reopened ticket 123 should stay in the system.

As we have seen, **SNAPSHOT** isolation is very useful for detecting lost updates in this case. However, **SNAPSHOT** isolation detects lost updates only for the duration of the transaction, so using this approach will not help if the transactions do not overlap, as was the case in our first example in this chapter (Listings 10-1 to 10-5).

Before moving on, please make sure that snapshot isolation is disabled for your test database, as subsequent examples will run in normal, **READ COMMITTED** mode.

Pessimistic Concurrency Control to Prevent Lost Updates

Let's switch our attention now to ways in which we can implement pessimistic concurrency control, to prevent lost updates. This approach is appropriate when many short transactions are attempting to simultaneously modify the same rows. We'll discuss two approaches:

- using the UPDLOCK hint

- using sp_getapplock.

In these examples, the data is read and modified by a program, without any human interaction, and in a very short time. In such cases it is feasible to read and modify within the same transaction.

Again, these approaches only help us deal with concurrency for the duration of a transaction; they cannot prevent lost updates when transactions do not overlap. As such, they usually should not be used when users open screen forms to edit data and save their modifications at different times because, from the database's point of view, these modifications are not concurrent.

Serializing updates with UPDLOCK hint

We'll rerun the ticket deletion/archive example using UPDLOCK hint instead of SNAPSHOT isolation level. First, rerun the script from Listing 10-13 to restore the modified data to its original state. Next, in one SSMS tab, retrieve the ticket 123 in a transaction under READ COMMITTED isolation level and using the UPDLOCK hint, as shown in Listing 10-17.

```
SET TRANSACTION ISOLATION LEVEL READ COMMITTED ;
SET XACT_ABORT ON ;
BEGIN TRANSACTION ;

SELECT   TicketID ,
         Problem ,
         CausedBy ,
```

```
            ProposedSolution ,
            AssignedTo ,
            Status
FROM        dbo.Tickets WITH(UPDLOCK)
WHERE       TicketID = 123 ;

--DELETE dbo.Tickets
--WHERE    TicketID = 123 ;
--COMMIT TRANSACTION ;
```

Listing 10-17: Reading ticket 123 with UPDLOCK hint.

As in the previous example, modify the ticket being archived (deleted) in another tab, as per Listing 10-15.

Unlike in the previous example, this time the modification does not complete; it stays in lock-waiting state, as it is blocked by our outstanding transaction in the first tab. At the beginning of the transaction in the first tab, we selected data for ticket 123, and the UPDLOCK hint guarantees that this data cannot be modified by other connections for the life of the transaction, though it can still be read.

Return to the first tab and uncomment and run the DELETE statement, in order to delete ticket 123 and commit the transaction. The second tab will now finish too, but the row that was targeted by the UPDATE no longer exists, so it could not be updated.

As we have seen, UPDLOCK hint has prevented the second update from modifying ticket 123. This is typical of pessimistic concurrency control solutions.

The UPDLOCK hint is best suited to cases where our modifications are simple and short. In this example, we were dealing with a single row modification, and UPDLOCK hint works perfectly well. However, if we need to touch multiple rows, maybe in more than one table, and we hold locks for the duration of a long transaction, then our modifications are very prone to deadlocks (as demonstrated in Chapter 9).

The need to modify multiple rows in multiple tables in one transaction is very common. For example, saving a screen form with a customer's order may result in inserting or updating rows in the Orders, OrderItems, and OrderComments tables. In such cases, we can still use the locks that are implicitly acquired as the transaction progresses, and we can use UPDLOCK hints to get a better control over locking. This approach can work but is complex, as we often have to consider many possible combinations of different modifications, all occurring at the same time.

There is a simpler alternative in such cases: at the very beginning of our transaction, we can explicitly acquire one application lock for the whole Order object, which spans several rows in the involved tables, Orders, OrderItems, and OrderComments. Let's see how it works.

Using sp_getapplock to prevent collisions

In this example, our transactions will explicitly acquire an application lock, using sp_getapplock. This effectively serializes modifications, because only one connection can hold an exclusive application lock on the same resource. Other modifications to the same data will be forced to wait for that lock to be released, so there will be no collisions whatsoever. This is an example of pessimistic concurrency control, used to its fullest extent.

Note that application locks are different from other locks in that:

- the resource they lock is not a row or a page or a table, but a name, as will be demonstrated in the following example
- they are acquired explicitly, rather than implicitly.

Note that when transactions commit or roll back, all application locks are released, so they must be acquired in the context of an outstanding transaction, after we have explicitly started the transaction.

To demonstrate this approach, we first need to restore the modified data to its original state (Listing 10-13). Next, from one SSMS tab, begin a transaction, acquire an application lock, and start archiving ticket 123, as shown in Listing 10-18.

```
-- Run this script in the first tab
SET TRANSACTION ISOLATION LEVEL READ COMMITTED ;

BEGIN TRANSACTION ;

DECLARE @ret INT ;
SET @ret = NULL ;
EXEC @ret = sp_getapplock @Resource = 'TicketID = 123',
    @LockMode = 'Exclusive', @LockTimeout = 1000 ;

-- sp_getapplock return code values are:
-- >= 0 (success), or < 0 (failure)
IF @ret < 0
    BEGIN;
        RAISERROR('Failed to acquire lock', 16, 1) ;
        ROLLBACK ;
    END ;

--DELETE dbo.Tickets
--WHERE    TicketID = 123 ;
--COMMIT TRANSACTION ;
```

Listing 10-18: **Begin a transaction and acquire an application lock.**

After running the script, uncomment and highlight the DELETE and COMMIT commands at the bottom, but do not execute them just yet. In a second tab, we'll attempt to acquire an exclusive application lock and modify the same ticket, as shown in Listing 10-19.

```
-- Run this script in the second tab
SET TRANSACTION ISOLATION LEVEL READ COMMITTED ;

BEGIN TRANSACTION ;

DECLARE @ret INT ;
SET @ret = NULL ;
```

```
-- The @LockTimeout setting makes sp_getapplock
-- wait for 10 seconds for other connections
-- to release the lock on ticket number 123
EXEC @ret = sp_getapplock @Resource = 'TicketID = 123',
    @LockMode = 'Exclusive', @LockTimeout = 10000 ;


-- sp_getapplock return code values are:
-- >= 0 (success), or < 0 (failure)
IF @ret < 0
    BEGIN ;
        RAISERROR('Failed to acquire lock', 16, 1) ;
        ROLLBACK ;
    END ;
ELSE
    BEGIN ;

        UPDATE   dbo.Tickets
        SET      AssignedTo = 'TPS report team' ,
                 CausedBy = 'Bug in TPS report' ,
                 Problem = 'TPS report truncates
                            dbo.Customers' ,
                 ProposedSolution = 'Fix TPS report' ,
                 Status = 'Reopen'
        WHERE    TicketID = 123 ;

        IF @@ROWCOUNT = 0
            BEGIN ;
                RAISERROR('Ticket not found', 16, 1) ;
            END ;

        COMMIT ;

    END ;
```

Listing 10-19: Begin a transaction, attempt to acquire an application lock and modify the ticket being archived, if the application lock has been acquired.

Immediately return to the first tab and run the highlighted `DELETE` statement; this script will raise a `Ticket not found` error. If we wait longer than 10 seconds before trying to run this `DELETE`, then Listing 10-19 will raise a `Failed to acquire lock` error. Either way, lost updates have been prevented.

This proves that, if all modifications that wish to modify a ticket are programmed to acquire the corresponding application lock before touching it, then lost updates cannot occur. However, this approach *only* works if all modifications are programmed to acquire application locks. A failure to acquire an application lock, whether by accident or deliberately, bypasses our protection and, as such, may result in lost updates or other problems, such as deadlocks.

To demonstrate this, restore the original data, comment out the command that invokes `sp_getapplock`, in Listing 10-19, and then rerun the same example, as follows:

- in Listing 10-18, make sure that the `DELETE` and `COMMIT` commands are commented out

- run Listing 10-18

- in a second tab, run Listing 10-19

- return to Listing 10-19, uncomment the `DELETE` and `COMMIT` commands at the bottom, highlight them, and execute them.

When the `DELETE` completes, you'll find that ticket number 123 is gone, which means that we've suffered a lost update. In short, `sp_getapplock` is only useful when it is consistently used by all relevant modifications. If such consistency is not possible, we will need to use other methods.

T-SQL Patterns that Fail High Concurrency Stress Tests

In many cases, our T-SQL code works perfectly well when we execute it from one connection at a time, but intermittently fails when it runs in production systems, under high concurrency.

In this section, we'll examine the following two common T-SQL patterns and prove that they are generally unreliable under concurrent loads:

- `IF EXISTS(...) THEN`

- `UPDATE ... IF (@@ROWCOUNT = 0) BEGIN`

We'll then examine a third technique, **MERGE**, which is robust under concurrency.

The most important lesson to be learned is that, if our code is supposed to run under high concurrency, we need to stress test under such loads, and against realistic data volumes. If our production table has about 10 million rows, we should not run our tests against a tiny table of just 100 rows.

Important Note

If any of these scripts in this section run for too long on your server, and you cancel them, make sure to close the tabs or roll back the transactions. Otherwise, you could end up with an outstanding transaction holding locks, and subsequent examples may not work as expected.

Problems with IF EXISTS(...) THEN

The `IF EXISTS(...) THEN` pattern, as follows, is quite common and yet it frequently fails under high concurrency.

```
IF EXISTS(-- enter some condition here
) BEGIN ;
  -- perform some action here
END ;
```

Before we prove that the technique will cause our optimistic concurrency solution (using the `ROWVERSION` column) to fail under heavy concurrent loads, let's first examine a much simpler example, which demonstrates the general problem with this pattern.

May cause data integrity issues under concurrent access

To keep the example as simple and short as possible, we'll use a table with just four columns, as shown in Listing 10-20.

```
CREATE TABLE dbo.WebPageStats
    (
        WebPageID INT NOT NULL PRIMARY KEY,
        NumVisits INT NOT NULL ,
        NumAdClicks INT NOT NULL ,
        version ROWVERSION NOT NULL
    ) ;
GO

SET NOCOUNT ON ;
INSERT  INTO dbo.WebPageStats
        ( WebPageID, NumVisits, NumAdClicks )
VALUES  ( 0, 0, 0 ) ;

DECLARE @i INT ;
SET @i = 1 ;
WHILE @i < 1000000
    BEGIN ;
        INSERT  INTO dbo.WebPageStats
                ( WebPageID ,
                  NumVisits ,
                  NumAdClicks
                )
                SELECT  WebPageID + @i ,
                        NumVisits ,
                        NumAdClicks
                FROM    dbo.WebPageStats ;
        SET @i = @i * 2 ;
    END ;
GO
```

Listing 10-20: Create and populate the WebPageStats table.

We'll INSERT or UPDATE rows in a loop using the following simple logic, as expressed in Listing 10-21: if a row with given ID exists, update it; otherwise insert a new one. Cut and paste this code into two tabs, switch each tab into text mode, and run the code simultaneously in each tab.

```
-- Hit Ctrl+T to execute in text mode
SET NOCOUNT ON ;
DECLARE @WebPageID INT ,
    @MaxWebPageID INT ;
SET @WebPageID = 0 ;

SET @MaxWebPageID = ( SELECT    MAX(WebPageID)
                      FROM      dbo.WebPageStats
                    ) + 100000 ;

WHILE @WebPageID < @MaxWebPageID
    BEGIN ;
        SET @WebPageID = ( SELECT    MAX(WebPageID)
                           FROM      dbo.WebPageStats
                         ) + 1 ;
        BEGIN TRY ;
            BEGIN TRANSACTION ;
            IF EXISTS ( SELECT    *
                        FROM
                        dbo.WebPageStats --WITH(UPDLOCK)
                        WHERE   WebPageID = @WebPageID )
                BEGIN ;
                    UPDATE  dbo.WebPageStats
                    SET     NumVisits = 1
                    WHERE   WebPageID = @WebPageID ;
                END ;
            ELSE
                BEGIN ;
                    INSERT  INTO dbo.WebPageStats
                    ( WebPageID, NumVisits, NumAdClicks )
                    VALUES  ( @WebPageID, 0, 0 ) ;
                END ;
```

```
            COMMIT TRANSACTION ;
        END TRY
        BEGIN CATCH ;
            SELECT  ERROR_MESSAGE() ;
            ROLLBACK TRANSACTION ;
        END CATCH ;
    END ;
```

Listing 10-21: Inserting or updating rows in a loop.

You should see PRIMARY KEY violations. You may be wondering if our pessimistic technique, using UPDLOCK, would help us out here: unfortunately it won't. To try this out, uncomment the hint, comment out all BEGIN/COMMIT/ROLLBACK TRANSACTION commands, and rerun the test. You will still see PK violations. The UPDLOCK does not help, as there is no row to be locked if the NOT EXISTS is true. So, if both connections simultaneously check for existence of the same row, both will find it does not exist (so they won't acquire a U lock), and both will try to INSERT the row, leading to the violation.

The most important point to remember is that code that performs perfectly in single-user test cases may behave very differently when multiple processes are attempting to access and modify the same data. The defensive programmer must test on a case-by-case basis, and test as many different scenarios as possible. With that in mind, I encourage you to play with this simple example a little bit, exploring how small changes affect the behavior of our code under high concurrency.

For example:

- increase the isolation level in one or both tabs, and see how that affects the behavior

- run different scripts in the tabs, such as with commented hints in one tab and uncommented in another, and see what happens.

May break optimistic concurrency solutions

Having demonstrated how unreliable the IF EXISTS pattern may be when it executes under high concurrency, let's now prove that it will cause our optimistic concurrency solution to fail, under similarly high concurrency.

We'll develop a stored procedure to update the WebPageStats table and then execute it in rapid succession, from two connections. Of course, we could do the same thing with UpdateTickets procedure, but these examples involving loops are quite large, so I decided to use a narrower WebPageStats table, just to keep the examples shorter.

Listing 10-22 shows the UpdateWebPageStats stored procedure, which will detect any version mismatches when it saves changes.

```
CREATE PROCEDURE dbo.UpdateWebPageStats
    @WebPageID INT ,
    @NumVisits INT ,
    @NumAdClicks INT ,
    @version ROWVERSION
AS
    BEGIN ;
        SET NOCOUNT ON ;
        SET TRANSACTION ISOLATION LEVEL READ COMMITTED ;
        SET XACT_ABORT ON ;
        DECLARE @ret INT ;
        BEGIN TRANSACTION ;
        IF EXISTS ( SELECT   *
                    FROM     dbo.WebPageStats
                    WHERE    WebPageID = @WebPageID
                             AND version = @version )
            BEGIN ;
                UPDATE  dbo.WebPageStats
                SET     NumVisits = @NumVisits ,
                        NumAdClicks = @NumAdClicks
                WHERE   WebPageID = @WebPageID ;

                SET @ret = 0 ;
            END ;
```

```
    ELSE
        BEGIN ;
            SET @ret = 1 ;
        END ;
    COMMIT ;
    RETURN @ret ;
END ;
```

Listing 10-22: Create the dbo.UpdateWebPageStats stored procedure.

Of course, before testing how the stored procedure works under concurrency, we should make sure that it works without it. Testing the stored procedure without concurrency is left as an exercise for the reader.

The following two scripts will invoke the WebPageStats stored procedure multiple times in loops. Running these two scripts simultaneously from two connections will expose WebPageStats to high concurrency, and we shall see how it holds up.

The first script, in Listing 10-23, increments the column NumVisits for a single row, and does so 100,000 times, in a loop. Cut and paste this code into a tab, but do not run it yet.

```
DECLARE @NumVisits INT ,
    @NumAdClicks INT ,
    @version ROWVERSION ,
    @count INT ,
    @ret INT ;
SET @count = 0 ;
WHILE @count < 10000
    BEGIN ;
        SELECT  @NumVisits = NumVisits + 1 ,
                @NumAdClicks = NumAdClicks ,
                @version = version
        FROM    dbo.WebPageStats
        WHERE   WebPageID = 5 ;
        EXEC @ret = dbo.UpdateWebPageStats 5,
                @NumVisits, @NumAdClicks, @version ;
```

```
        IF @ret = 0
            SET @count = @count + 1 ;
    END ;
```

Listing 10-23: A loop that invokes `UpdateWebPageStats` to increment NumVisits for one and the same row 10,000 times.

Our second script, in Listing 10-24, increments another column, `NumAdClicks`, also 10,000 times in a loop. Cut and paste it into a second tab and run both scripts simultaneously.

```
DECLARE @NumVisits INT ,
    @NumAdClicks INT ,
    @version ROWVERSION ,
    @count INT ,
    @ret INT ;
SET @count = 0 ;
WHILE @count < 10000
    BEGIN ;
        SELECT  @NumVisits = NumVisits ,
                @NumAdClicks = NumAdClicks + 1 ,
                @version = version
        FROM    dbo.WebPageStats
        WHERE   WebPageID = 5 ;
        EXEC @ret = dbo.UpdateWebPageStats 5,
                @NumVisits, @NumAdClicks, @version ;
        IF @ret = 0
            SET @count = @count + 1 ;
    END ;
```

Listing 10-24: A loop that invokes `UpdateWebPageStats` to increment `NumAdClicks` for the same row 10,000 times.

These scripts may take some time to complete. When both scripts finish, we would expect both `NumVisits` and `NumAdClicks` to have the same value of 10,000. However, this is not the case, as Listing 10-25 demonstrates.

Each time we run these two scripts, we will get different numbers but, every time, neither column will have the expected value of 10,000.

```
SELECT   NumVisits ,
         NumAdClicks
FROM     dbo.WebPageStats
WHERE    WebPageID = 5 ;


NumVisits    NumAdClicks
-----------  -----------
9999         1056
```

Listing 10-25: NumVisits **and** NumAdClicks **should both be 10,000, but they do not have the expected values.**

As we can see, NumVisits and NumAdClicks do not have the expected value of 10,000. This means that many updates were lost. How could that happen? Suppose that both connections retrieve the version at approximately the same time, and then invoke the same stored procedure at approximately the same time. Clearly, in both executions the condition in the IF statement evaluates as TRUE. As a result, both executions will enter the branch with the UPDATE command.

UPDATE commands will execute one after another, and the second one will overwrite the changes of the first one, because the ROWVERSION value is not tested again in the actual UPDATE statement. Adding this test to the UPDATE will not help, though. If we do that, then the first one will increment the ROWVERSION value, and the second one will not update the row at all, because the condition (version = @version) in the WHERE clause will return FALSE, but the procedure will still return 0 to indicate success to the caller even though the requested update was not made, and the caller will not try the update again.

UPDATE ... IF (@@ROWCOUNT = 0) BEGIN

Another common approach is to attempt, first, to UPDATE an existing row that matches the search criteria and, if there is no matching row, then INSERT a new row. This is also unreliable.

In order to demonstrate this, we need to modify our loop from Listing 10-21 so that it uses the UPDATE ...IF (@@ROWCOUNT = 0) BEGIN pattern, as shown in Listing 10-26.

```
-- Hit Ctrl+T to execute in text mode
SET NOCOUNT ON ;
DECLARE @WebPageID INT ,
    @MaxWebPageID INT ;
SET @WebPageID = 0 ;

SET @MaxWebPageID = ( SELECT     MAX(WebPageID)
                      FROM       dbo.WebPageStats
                    ) + 100000 ;

WHILE @WebPageID < @MaxWebPageID
    BEGIN ;
        SET @WebPageID = ( SELECT     MAX(WebPageID)
                           FROM       dbo.WebPageStats
                         ) + 1 ;
        BEGIN TRY ;
            BEGIN TRANSACTION ;
            UPDATE  dbo.WebPageStats
            SET     NumVisits = 1
            WHERE   WebPageID = @WebPageID ;

            IF ( @@ROWCOUNT = 0 )
                BEGIN ;
                    INSERT  INTO dbo.WebPageStats
                    ( WebPageID, NumVisits, NumAdClicks )
                    VALUES ( @WebPageID, 0, 0 ) ;
                END ;
            COMMIT TRANSACTION ;
```

```
        END TRY
        BEGIN CATCH ;
            SELECT  ERROR_MESSAGE() ;
            ROLLBACK TRANSACTION ;
        END CATCH ;
    END ;
```

Listing 10-26: A loop that uses the UPDATE ... IF (@@ROWCOUNT = 0) pattern.

When we run script 10-26 simultaneously from two tabs, we get PRIMARY KEY violations, just as when we ran script 10-21 in our previous example.

In short, the UPDATE...IF (@@ROWCOUNT = 0) pattern is also unreliable under high concurrency. As before, we can (and should!) try out different isolation levels and hints. For example, I encourage you to add WITH(SERIALIZABLE) hint to the UPDATE command and see what happens. This is left as an advanced exercise for the reader.

Stress Testing the MERGE Command

If we are running SQL Server 2008, we can use the MERGE command to implement the same logic, i.e. UPDATE rows if they exist, otherwise INSERT. In the context of our loop, MERGE may also intermittently fail but, with the help of a hint, it always completes without a single error. Let's modify the script of Listing 10-26 to use MERGE command, as shown in Listing 10-27.

```
-- Hit Ctrl+T to execute in text mode
SET NOCOUNT ON ;
DECLARE @WebPageID INT ,
    @MaxWebPageID INT ;
SET @WebPageID = 0 ;

SET @MaxWebPageID = ( SELECT    MAX(WebPageID)
                      FROM      dbo.WebPageStats
                    ) + 100000 ;
```

```
WHILE @WebPageID < @MaxWebPageID
    BEGIN ;
        SET @WebPageID = ( SELECT   MAX(WebPageID)
                           FROM     dbo.WebPageStats
                         ) + 1 ;
        BEGIN TRY ;
            BEGIN TRANSACTION ;

                MERGE dbo.WebPageStats --WITH (HOLDLOCK)
                    AS target
                    USING
                        ( SELECT   @WebPageID
                        ) AS source ( WebPageID )
                    ON (target.WebPageID = source.WebPageID)
                    WHEN MATCHED
                        THEN
                            UPDATE SET NumVisits = 1
                    WHEN NOT MATCHED
                        THEN
                            INSERT( WebPageID, NumVisits,
                                NumAdClicks )
                                VALUES
                                ( @WebPageID ,
                                    0 ,
                                    0
                                ) ;
            COMMIT TRANSACTION ;
        END TRY
        BEGIN CATCH ;
            SELECT  ERROR_MESSAGE() ;
            ROLLBACK TRANSACTION ;
        END CATCH ;
    END ;
```

Listing 10-27: Implement our loop using the MERGE command.

When we run this script in two tabs at the same time, we should get PRIMARY KEY violations. As usual, if we cancel a query, we must make sure to commit or roll back the outstanding transaction in that tab.

Next, uncomment the hint in both tabs and rerun the scripts; in this particular case, with the help of the HOLDLOCK hint, MERGE holds up under high concurrency perfectly well. Of course, this does not mean that we can always use this new command without stress testing. However, it means that we should at least consider using it whenever we INSERT or UPDATE under high concurrency.

For example, we can consider rewriting our UpdateWebPageStats stored procedure using the MERGE command, as well as exposing this new version of the procedure to the same thorough testing. This is left as an advanced exercise.

One final comment: in the examples in this chapter, we only stress test how one stored procedure runs from multiple connections. In real life, this might not be good enough. If we have two different stored procedures modifying the same table, and if it is possible that these different modules will try to modify the same data concurrently, then we need to include such cases in our stress testing.

Creating New Objects May Hurt Concurrency

In some cases, when we create an index, an indexed view, or a trigger, we may introduce serious issues, such as blocking or deadlocks. Let me provide an example of how creating an indexed view increases the probability of blocking and deadlocks. Consider the table, ChildTable, shown in Listing 10-28.

```
CREATE TABLE dbo.ChildTable
    (
        ChildID INT NOT NULL ,
        ParentID INT NOT NULL ,
        Amount INT NOT NULL ,
        CONSTRAINT PK_ChildTable PRIMARY KEY ( ChildID )
    ) ;
```

Listing 10-28: Creating the ChildTable table.

Let's subject our table to concurrent modification. In one tab, run the script in Listing 10-29, and in the second tab, run the script in Listing 10-30.

```
BEGIN TRAN ;
INSERT  INTO dbo.ChildTable
        ( ChildID, ParentID, Amount )
VALUES  ( 1, 1, 1 ) ;
-- ROLLBACK TRAN ;
```

Listing 10-29: The modification to run in the first tab.

```
BEGIN TRAN ;
INSERT  INTO dbo.ChildTable
        ( ChildID, ParentID, Amount )
VALUES  ( 2, 1, 1 ) ;
ROLLBACK TRAN ;
```

Listing 10-30: The modification to run in the second tab.

The second modification completes right away. Return to the first tab and roll back the transaction. As we have seen, these two modifications do not block each other. However, what happens if we create an indexed view, based on our table, as shown in Listing 10-31?

```
CREATE VIEW dbo.ChildTableTotals WITH SCHEMABINDING
AS
SELECT ParentID,
COUNT_BIG(*) AS ChildRowsPerParent,
SUM(Amount) AS SumAmount
FROM dbo.ChildTable
GROUP BY ParentID ;
GO

CREATE UNIQUE CLUSTERED INDEX ChildTableTotals_CI
ON dbo.ChildTableTotals(ParentID) ;
```

Listing 10-31: Create the indexed view.

373

Rerun the script of Listing 10-29 followed by 10-30. This time, script 10-30 will not complete; it will be blocked by script 10-29, because both modifications also need to modify the same row in the indexed view, and so script 10-30 is waiting for an exclusive lock on the view. Return to the first tab and roll back or commit the transaction to release the locks, and script 10-35 will complete right away.

Similarly, creating new indexes or triggers may affect concurrent modifications. This means that if we stress test modules to determine how they handle concurrency, we may need to repeat stress testing when we add new indexes, indexed views, or triggers.

Of course, not all indexed views, indexes and so on will cause such blocking, and there are no general rules, which is why I stress the need to test on a case-by-case basis.

Conclusion

We have seen that, when modifications run concurrently from multiple connections, we may end up with inconsistent results or errors. We also investigated two T-SQL patterns that are in common use, and yet can fail under high concurrency, resulting either in lost updates or in blocking or deadlocks.

We have investigated several approaches, both pessimistic and optimistic, for avoiding lost updates and, for SQL Server 2008 users, demonstrated how MERGE can improve the robustness of our code.

The most important point of this chapter is that our modules need to be concurrency-proof. We need to expose our modules to concurrency during stress testing, expose vulnerabilities in our code and proactively fix them.

I hope that this chapter, like the entire book, has served, not only to provide several techniques that will make your code more robust, but also as an eye-opener as to just what situations your database code has to contend with, when deployed on a live production system.

I haven't covered every conceivable case of what can go wrong; that would be impossible. Hopefully, however, the common cases that have been covered will prove useful in making your code more robust; when a defensive programmer becomes aware of a frailty in one case, he or she knows that very careful testing will be needed in other, similar, cases.

More generally, however, I hope I've convinced you that we, as SQL Server programmers, need to be proactive and creative in our testing. After all, *"a hard drill makes an easy battle."*

Index

A

Application layer
enforcing data integrity in,. *See* Data
integrity: in the application layer
Application lock
using to avoid collisions 357–360
Avoiding ambiguous updates. *See* **Data
modification errors: ambiguous updates**

C

Changes in SQL Server settings 33–47
SET LANGUAGE 42–47
SET ROWCOUNT and triggers 34–41
Changes to database objects 81–107
changes in nullability 99–104
changes to columns 95–96
changes to data types and sizes
104–107
changes to the primary or unique keys
82–92
changes to the signature of a stored
procedure 92–95
Common misconceptions 61–79
conditions in a WHERE clause 61–68
data order and ORDER BY 76–79
Concurrency
control logic 343–344
damaged by new objects 372–374
high concurrency stress tests
T-SQL patterns which fail 360–370
surviving 337–375
**Concurrent Queries and Transaction
Isolation Levels** 297–336
incorrect results returned 304–319
isolation levels 297–304
querying multiple tables that are being
simultaneously modified 319–332

Constraints. *See* **Reusing T-SQL code:
reusing business logic**
advanced use of, 213–258
and rock-solid inventory systems.
See Inventory systems and constraints
disabled 179–181
enabled 181–182
enforcing business rules 215–225
enforcing data integrity in,. *See* Data
integrity: in constraints
trusted 182–184
UDFs wrapped in CHECK constraints
184–212
Copy-and-paste, dangers of. *See* **Reusing
T-SQL code**

D

Data integrity 167–212
common problems with, 167–212
enforcing with triggers 196–211
in constraints 170–196
disabled, enabled, and trusted
constraints 177–184
foreign key constraints and NULLs
175–177
nulls in CHECK constraints
172–174
in the application layer 167–170
Data modification errors 47–59
ambiguous updates 49–52
avoiding ambiguous updates 53–60
ANSI-standard method 54–55
improving UPDATE...FROM
57–60
inline view updates 55–57
using MERGE to detect ambiguity
53–54

updating more rows than intended 47–49

using UPDATE...FROM 51

Deadlocks 271

minimizing 332–335

DRY (Don't Repeat Yourself) principle 140

E

Error handling 259–295

client-side error handling 289–294

using transactions and XACT_ ABORT 266–270

using transactions for data modifications 261–266

using TRY...CATCH blocks 270–277

TRY...CATCH gotchas. *See* TRY... CATCH gotchas

F

False negatives 189–192

False positives 192–194

H

Helper tables 62

I

IF EXISTS(...) THEN

problems with 361–368

breaking optimistic concurrency solutions 364–368

data integrity issues under concurrent access 362–364

Inline UDFs 151–155

Inventory systems and constraints 231–257

adding new rows 241–249

adding rows out of date order 253–257

updating existing rows 249–252

Isolation levels. *See* **Concurrent Queries and Transaction Isolation Levels**

choosing the right isolation level 318–319

READ COMMITTED 299–301, 304–312

Behavior in 321–328

Mode 117–121

REPEATABLE READ 302–303, 312–316

SERIALIZABLE 303–304, 316

SNAPSHOT 317–318

Mode 122–125

Mode, behavior in 328–330

Versus READ_COMMITTED_ SNAPSHOT 330–332

snapshot isolation 110–114, 352–354

breaking code 114–127

M

MERGE Command

stress testing 370–372

MERGE statement 127–129

and @@ROWCOUNT 129–133

Modes. *See* **Isolation levels**

Modifications

lost 338–339

optimistic approach 338, 344–355

pessimistic approach 338, 355–360

non-overlapping 339–354

Multi-row modifications 196–204

N

NOT IN vulnerability 99–104

O

OLE DB 267

P

Performance hit
ON UPDATE CASCADE 225–231

Q

Qualify column names 95–99

R

READ COMMITTED. *See* Isolation levels
Reducing code vulnerability 24–25
REPEATABLE READ. *See* Isolation levels
Reusing T-SQL code 135–165
    copy-and-paste, dangers of 136–140
    multi-statement table-valued UDFs
    155
    reusing business logic 156–164
        stored procedures and constraints
        156–158
        triggers 158–163
        unique filtered indexes 164–165
    reusing parameterized queries
    145–150
    scalar UDFs and performance 151–155
    to improve robustness 141–145
    wrapping SELECTs in views 145
ROWVERSION 348

S

Scalar UDFs. *See* Reusing T-SQL code
SERIALIZABLE. *See* Isolation levels
SET, SELECT, and variables values
68–76
SNAPSHOT. *See* Isolation levels
sp_getapplock 357–360
Stored Procedures. *See* Reusing T-SQL
code: reusing business logic
    versus Inline UDFs. *See* Reusing
    T-SQL code: reusing parameterized
    queries

T

Transaction Isolation Levels. *See* Concurrent Queries and Transaction Isolation Levels
Trigger behavior. *See* Reusing T-SQL
code: reusing business logic
    building more robust triggers
    126–134
    in READ COMMITTED mode
    117–121
    in SNAPSHOT mode 122–125
    overriding changes made by other
    triggers 209–211
    @@ROWCOUNT and MERGE
    129–133
    triggers do not fire 208–209
    under snapshot isolation levels 211
TRY...CATCH gotchas 277–289
    not catching all errors 282–295
        doomed transactions 285
        killed connections and timeouts
        282
        problems with scope 283
        re-throwing errors 277–281

U

UDFs

    multi-statement table-valued 155

    scalar and inline 151–155

Unintended use of code 26–33

    handling special characters 28–34

        special characters assumption 31

Unique filtered indexes 194–196. *See also* **Reusing T-SQL code: reusing business logic**

UPDATE ...IF (@@ROWCOUNT = 0) BEGIN 369–370

Updates. *See* **Modifications**

    affecting the primary key 204–208

    serializing with UPDLOCK hint 355–357

Updating changed columns 342–343

UPDLOCK 355

Upgrading, problems caused by 109–134

    MERGE statement 127–134

Using @@ROWCOUNT 89–90

Using SET instead of SELECT 90–95

Using unit tests 86–88

W

Wrapping SELECTs in Views. *See* **Reusing T-SQL code**

SQL Server, .NET
and Exchange Tools
from Red Gate Software

SQL Backup Pro $795

Compress, encrypt, and strengthen SQL Server backups

- ↗ Compress database backups by up to 95% for faster backups and restores

- ↗ Protect your data with up to 256-bit AES encryption

- ↗ Strengthen your backups with network resilience to enable the fault-tolerant transfer of backups across flaky networks

- ↗ Save time and space with the SQL Object Level Recovery Pro feature, so you can recover individual database objects instead of full database backups

> "SQL Backup has always been a great product – giving significant savings in HDD space and time over native backup and many other third-party products. With version 6 introducing a fourth level of compression and network resilience, it will be a REAL boost to any DBA."
>
> **Jonathan Allen** Senior Database Administrator

SQL Monitor

Proactive SQL Server performance monitoring and alerting

- ↗ Intuitive overviews at global, machine, SQL Server and database levels for up-to-the minute performance data

- ↗ SQL Monitor's web UI means you can check your server health and performance on the go with many mobile devices, including tablets

- ↗ Intelligent SQL Server alerts via email and an alert inbox in the UI, so you know about problems first

- ↗ Comprehensive historical data, so you can go back in time to identify the source of a problem fast

- ↗ Generate reports via the UI and with SQL Server Reporting Services

- ↗ Investigate long-running queries, SQL deadlocks, blocked processes, and more, to resolve problems sooner

- ↗ Fast, simple installation and administration

Due for release Q4 2010

Visit **www.red-gate.com** for a 14-day, free trial

SQL Compare Pro®

Compare and synchronize SQL Server database schemas

- ↗ Automate database comparisons, and synchronize your databases
- ↗ Simple, easy to use, 100% accurate
- ↗ Save hours of tedious work, and eliminate manual scripting errors
- ↗ Work with live databases, snapshots, script files, or backups

> "SQL Compare and SQL Data Compare are the best purchases we've made in the .NET/ SQL environment. They've saved us hours of development time, and the fast, easy-to-use database comparison gives us maximum confidence that our migration scripts are correct. We rely on these products for every deployment."
>
> **Paul Tebbutt** Technical Lead, Universal Music Group

SQL Data Compare Pro™

Compare and synchronize SQL Server database contents

- ↗ Compare your database contents
- ↗ Automatically synchronize your data
- ↗ Row-level data restore
- ↗ Compare to scripts, backups, or live databases

> "We use SQL Data Compare daily and it has become an indispensable part of delivering our service to our customers. It has also streamlined our daily update process and cut back literally a good solid hour per day."
>
> **George Pantela** GPAnalysis.com

Visit **www.red-gate.com** for a 14-day, free trial

SQL Toolbelt   **$1,995**

The essential SQL Server tools for
database professionals

You can buy our acclaimed SQL Server tools individually or bundled. Our most popular deal is the SQL Toolbelt: all thirteen of our SQL Server tools in a single installer, with **a combined value of $5,635 but an actual price of $1,995**, a saving of 65%.

Fully compatible with SQL Server 2000, 2005, and 2008.

SQL Toolbelt contains:

- ↗ **SQL Compare Pro**
- ↗ **SQL Data Compare Pro**
- ↗ **SQL Backup Pro**
- ↗ **SQL Response**
- ↗ **SQL Prompt Pro**
- ↗ **SQL Data Generator**
- ↗ **SQL Doc**

- ↗ **SQL Dependency Tracker**
- ↗ **SQL Packager**
- ↗ **SQL Multi Script Unlimited**
- ↗ **SQL Refactor**
- ↗ **SQL Comparison SDK**
- ↗ **SQL Object Level Recovery Native**

Visit **www.red-gate.com** for a 14-day, free trial

.NET Reflector ®   **Free**

Explore, browse, and analyze .NET assemblies

- ↗ View, navigate, and search through the class hierarchies of .NET assemblies, even if you don't have the source code for them
- ↗ Decompile and analyze .NET assemblies in C#, Visual Basic and IL
- ↗ Understand the relationships between classes and methods
- ↗ Check that your code has been correctly obfuscated before release

.NET Reflector ® Pro   **$195**

Debug third-party code and assemblies

- ↗ Integrates the power of .NET Reflector into Visual Studio
- ↗ Decompile third-party assemblies from within VS
- ↗ Step through decompiled assemblies and use all the debugging techniques you would use on your own code

SmartAssembly™   from **$295**

Obfuscate .NET code and monitor the stability of your program

- ↗ Obfuscate and protect your .NET application
- ↗ Discover the volume of crashes your end-users experience with the automated error reporting mechanism
- ↗ Get a complete state of your program when it crashed, including the values of variables when the crash happened
- ↗ Optimize your .NET assemblies (remove non-useful code and metadata and perform other code optimization) and simplify the deployment of your application

Visit **www.red-gate.com** for a 14-day, free trial

Exchange Server Archiver

Email archiving software for Exchange

- ↗ Email archiving for Exchange Server

- ↗ Reduce size of information store – no more PSTs/mailbox quotas

- ↗ Archive only the mailboxes you want to

- ↗ Exchange, Outlook, and OWA 2003 and 2007 supported

- ↗ Transparent end-user experience – message preview, instant retrieval, and integrated search

> **"Exchange Server Archiver is almost 100% invisible to Outlook end-users. The tool is simple to install and manage. This combined with the ability to set up different rules depending on user mailbox, makes the system easy to configure for all types of situations. I'd recommend this product to anyone who needs to archive exchange email."**
> **Matthew Studer** Riverside Radiology Associates

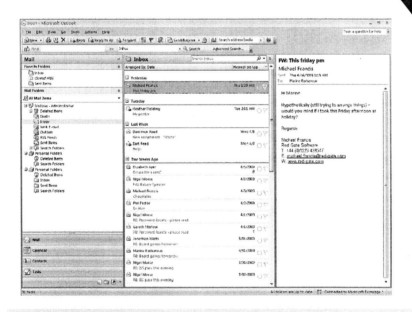

Visit **www.red-gate.com** for a 30-day, free trial

Protecting SQL Server Data
John Magnabosco

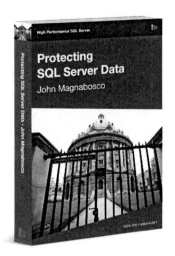

Protecting SQL Server Data holds the key to "encryption without fear." Data security expert, John Magnabosco sweeps away some of the misconceptions surrounding SQL Server's encryption technologies, and demonstrates that, when properly planned and implemented, they are an essential tool in the DBA's fight to safeguard sensitive data.

ISBN: 978-1-906434-27-4
Published: September 2009

SQL Server Tacklebox
Rodney Landrum

As a DBA, how well prepared are you to tackle "monsters" such as backup failure due to lack of disk space, or locking and blocking that is preventing critical business processes from running, or data corruption due to a power failure in the disk subsystem? If you have any hesitation in your answers to these questions, then Rodney Landrum's SQL Server Tacklebox is a must-read.

ISBN: 978-1-906434-25-0
Published: August 2009

ormation can be obtained at www.ICGtesting.com
ie USA
010130214
.V00003B/8/P